Karlsruher Beiträge zur wirtschaftspolitischen Forschung

Karlsruhe Papers in Economic Policy Research

edited by Prof. Dr. Jan Kowalski und Prof. Dr. Werner Rothengatter

Karlsruhe Institute of Technology

Institut für Volkswirtschaftslehre (ECON)

Band 33

Jeanette Stohr

Evolution of Technological Profiles in the European Life Sciences Industry

Nomos

Die Deutsche Nationalbibliothek lists this publication in the Deutsche Nationalbibliografie; detailed bibliographic data is available in the Internet at http://dnb.d-nb.de.

Zugl.: Karlsruhe, Karlsruher Institut für Technologie (KIT)., Diss., 2012

ISBN 978-3-8487-0998-4

1. Edition 2013

Foreword by the editor

Corporate innovative activities are not carried out in isolation. They are characterised by the companies' interactions with external actors, organisations and institutions. Against this background, in the 1990s the systems of innovation approach has been elaborated. Within this concept innovation systems have been defined at different aggregation levels, emphasising the impact of the technological, sectoral or national (or generally speaking: geographical) environment on innovation processes. However, the systems of innovation approach neglects the interactions which additionally take place between different innovation systems. It is therefore questionable whether the approach is suitable for capturing the innovative activities in dynamic knowledge-intensive industries in their entirety.

By taking into account that R&D-intensive companies today span their innovative activities over different technologies, sectors and nations the author assumes that the technological orientation of companies is influenced by its technological, sectoral and national environment. Furthermore, the author breaks away from the 'traditional' systems of innovation approach which considers innovative activities mostly from a single particular perspective. For this purpose, an integrated framework, taking into account different aggregation levels as well as the interactions between the respective levels, is applied. Moreover, in order to leave the quasi-static perspective of the 'traditional' approaches an observation period of 20 years is chosen.

This volume examines the evolution of technological profiles in the life sciences industry. Due to its R&D-intensity and due to the structural changes caused by the evolution of modern biotechnology this highly dynamic industry represents an intriguing field of research.

Based on a large patent data set, detailed technological profiles are produced for six European countries and 114 life science companies. Using a multivariate statistical method the similarity between the national technological profiles and the corporate technological profiles is examined.

The theoretical and empirical findings give evidence of the interactions between the technological, sectoral and national dimensions. It is hoped that these findings are taken into consideration for the formulation of modern innovation policies. This can be done by choosing appropriate instruments not only from a one-dimensional but from a multi-dimensional view.

Prof. Dr. Jan Kowalski

Foreword by the author

The present dissertation was created during my time as research associate at the Institute for Economic Policy Research (IWW) at the Karlsruhe Institute of Technology (KIT). I would like to thank all those who supported and inspired me during this time.

First and foremost, I would like to thank Prof. Dr. Hariolf Grupp (†) for giving me the opportunity to work at the chair of System Dynamics and Innovation and for supporting my research project. My special thanks go to Prof. Dr. Jan Kowalski for acting as my supervisor and for the good cooperation. Furthermore, I would like to thank Prof. Dr. Knut Koschatzky for acting as second reviewer and for providing valuable, constructive hints during the doctoral phase. Many thanks also to Dr. Rainer Frietsch for all the interesting technical discussions.

Finally, I want to express my gratitude to my family. Their support and the trust placed in me was a constant motivation. I thank my parents for supporting my academic education which laid the foundation for this dissertation. My sincere thanks go to my boyfriend Jochen who always believed in me. Thank you for your loving support!

Jeanette Stohr

Vorwort des Verfassers

Die vorliegende Arbeit entstand während meiner Zeit als akademische Mitarbeiterin am Institut für Wirtschaftspolitik und Wirtschaftsforschung (IWW) des Karlsruher Instituts für Technologie (KIT). Ich danke all denen, die mich auf diesem Weg begleitet und untersützt haben.

Insbesondere Prof. Dr. Hariolf Grupp (†) für die Möglichkeit am Lehrstuhl für Systemdynamik und Innovation zu arbeiten und für die Unterstützung in der Anfangsphase meines Forschungsvorhabens. Mein besonderer Dank richtet sich auch an meinen Doktorvater Prof. Dr. Jan Kowalski für die Bereitschaft zur Betreuung der Arbeit sowie für die stets gute Zusammenarbeit. Ebenso danke ich Prof. Dr. Knut Koschatzky für die Übernahme des Korreferats sowie für viele wertvolle, konstruktive Hinweise während meiner Promotionsphase. Weiterhin danke ich Dr. Rainer Frietsch für zahlreiche interessante Gespräche und Diskussionen.

Ein außerordentlich großer Dank gebührt meiner Familie. Der familiäre Rückhalt und das in mich gesetzte Vertrauen haben mich immer wieder von neuem motiviert. Meinen Eltern danke ich insbesondere für die Unterstützung während meiner akademischen Ausbildung, die den Grundstein für meine Promotion gelegt hat. Mein innigster Dank gilt meinem Lebensgefährten Jochen, der immer an mich geglaubt hat und mir stets mit viel Liebe zu Seite stand.

Jeanette Stohr

Contents

Figures

Tables

Abbreviations

BIS	Department of Business, Innovation & Skills
BMBS	Biomedicine and Molecular Biosciences
cf.	confer, conferatur (lat.)
CMST	Chemistry and Molecular Sciences and Technologies
COST	European Cooperation in Science and Technology
DNA	Desoxyribo-Nucleic Acid
DTI	Department of Trade and Industry of the British government
ed.	editor
EPO	European Patent Office
et al.	et alii (lat.)
FA	Food and Agriculture
HTS	High-throughput screening
ibid.	ibidem (lat.)
ICB	Industry Classification Benchmark
ICT	Information and Communication Technology
INPI	Institut National de la Propriété Industrielle
IPC	International Patent Classification
ISI	Fraunhofer-Institut für Systemtechnik und Innovationsforschung, Karlsruhe
MLP	Multi Level Perspective
MNC	Multi-National Corporation
MRI	Magnetic Resonance Imaging
MTC	Multi-Technology Corporation
NBF	New Biotechnology Firm
NCEs	New Chemical Entities
NIS	National Innovation Systems
NSSI	National Supersystem of Innovation
OECD	Organisation for Economic Co-operation and Development
OST	Observatoire des Sciences et des Techniques
PATSTAT	Worldwide Statistical Patent Database of the European Patent Office
R&D	Research and Development
RBV	Resource-based view
RTA	Revealed Technological Advantage
SI	System of Innovation
SIS	Sectoral Innovation Systems
SPSS	Statistical Program for Social Sciences
SSI	Sectoral Systems of Innovation
ST	Socio-technical

TIS	Technological Innovation System
TS	Technological System
WIPO	World Intellectual Property Organization

Country codes

CH	Switzerland
DE	Germany
FR	France
IT	Italy
NL	The Netherlands
UK	United Kingdom

Technological classes

BioMat	Analysis of biological materials
Biotech	Biotechnology
Chem	Basic materials chemistry
ChemEng	Chemical engineering
Env	Environmental technology
FineChem	Organic fine chemistry
Food	Food chemistry
Measure	Measurement
MedTech	Medical technology
Machines	Other special machines
Pharma	Pharmaceuticals

Variables

μ_{ij}	Expected number of patents attributed to technology class i and j
σ_{ij}	Variance in the number of patents attributed to technology class i and j
C_k	Co-occurrence matrix of country k
c_{ij}	Co-occurrences of technology i and j
CD_k	Cognitive distance of country k's knowledge base
Coh_k	Coherence of country k's knowledge base
d_{ij}	Distance between technology class i and j
$d_{ii'}$	Euclidean distance of the objects e_i and $e_{i'}$
DT_x	Prevalent diversification type of company x
p_i	Total number of patent application in technology class i
p_k	Total patent applications of country k
p_{total}	Total number of patent applications
p_x	Total patent applications of company x
$\overrightarrow{P_{i,k}}$	Technology vector of country k
$\overrightarrow{P_{i,x}}$	Technology vector of company x
P_{ik}	Share of country k's patent applications in technology class i
p_{ik}	Number of patents country k holds in technology class i
P_{ix}	Share of company x's patent applications in technology class i
p_{ik}	Number of patents company x holds in technology class i
$p_{new,tx^{[t-1]}}$	Number of company x's patent applications in new technological classes during period *t* in comparison with the patent stock in *t-1*
p_{tx}	Total number of company x's patent applications in period t
P_{ijk}	Share of country k's patent applications in technology class i in total patent applications in technology field j
P_{ijx}	Share of company x's patent applications in technology class i in total patent applications in technology field j
P_{jk}	Share of country k's patent applications in technology field j
P_{jx}	Share of company x's patent applications in technology field j
PS_{tx}	Patent scope of company x in period t
r_{ij}	Relatedness between technology class i and j
RD_k	Related diversification of country k
RD_x	Related diversification of company x
RTA_{ik}	Revealed technological advantage of country k in technology class i
RTA_{ix}	Revealed technological advantage of company x in technology class i
$RTA_{h_{ik}}$	Hyperbolic tangent of the RTA_{ik}
$RTA_{h_{ix}}$	Hyperbolic tangent of the RTA_{ix}
s_{ij}	Similarity between technology class i and j

$T_{country}$	Technological profile of country k
$T_{company}$	Technological profile of company x
TD_k	Total diversification of country k
TD_x	Total diversification of company x
TD_{jk}	Total diversification of country k in technology field j
TD_{jx}	Total diversification of company x in technology field j
UD_k	Unrelated diversification of country k
WAD_i^k	Weighted average distance of country k's technological activities in technology class i related to all other technological classes i´
WAR_i^k	Weighted average relatedness of country k's technological activities in technology class i related to all other technological classes i´
x_i	Attribute i
x_{ij}	Characteristic of object e_i concerning the variable j
Z_i	Cluster center of cluster i

Chapter 1 Introduction

In the 1980s researchers observed the increasing technological diversification of large companies. The pioneering works of Kodama (1986), Pavitt/Robson/Townsend (1989) and Granstrand/Sjölander (1990) showed that firms have continuously expanded the range of their technological activities. These observations gave rise to a number of contributions dealing with the topic of technological diversification. In this context, the importance of so called 'platform technologies', facilitating the entrance into new technological areas, has been emphasised (Kim/Kogut, 1996). However, the question of the main factors influencing the rates and directions of technological diversification remained open. Most empirical studies contended themselves with analysing the increasing corporate technological diversification at the national or sectoral level.

At the same time the systems of innovation approach, dealing with impact of firm-external factors on the innovation process, has attracted the attention of scholars. They recognised that the innovative activities are shaped by various interactions between firms, other organisations and institutions. Within this framework different kinds of innovation systems have been defined. While the national innovation systems take the innovative activities within national borders as point of departure, sectoral or technological systems focus on innovative activities within specific sectors or technologies (Fischer, 2001). However, it has to be noted that innovation has nowadays become a global, cross-sectoral and multi-technological process. As a consequence, one-sided views from single perspectives should be avoided. In order to understand the complex nature of technological innovation a multi-level framework, taking into account the different innovation systems and their interactions, is needed. Additionally, it is necessary to provide an understanding of the linkages between the national, sectoral and technological level and the micro level of the firm (Archibugi/Howells/Michie, 1999).

In this context, the life sciences seem to be a quite intriguing object of research because this sector is strongly science-based and has faced some remarkable changes during the last years due to the evolution of modern biotechnology (see among others Malerba/Orsenigo, 2002, p. 668 f.). The life science revolution had an impact on different industry sectors: pharmaceuticals, chemicals, agriculture, food production, laboratory equipment and environmental technologies (Russel, 1999, p. 236 f.; Menrad, 2005, p. 35 f.). Thus, modern biotechnology represents a platform technology with cross-sectoral effects.

Furthermore, it is assumed that the biotechnology revolution favours the convergence of different industrial sectors, i.e. the boundaries between the different sectors will blur (Enriquez/Goldberg, 2000, p. 96 ff.).

I.1 Phenomenon of technological diversification

> 'The evidence about technological diversification shows that firms large and small, single-product or multi-product tend to increase the diversity of their technological capabilities over time […].' (Torrisi/Granstrand, 2004, p. 30)

During the last decades the technological diversification of firms has continuously increased due to the growing technological complexity of products and processes as well as due to the fusion of formerly independent technologies. Most firms are now operating in more than one technological class (Kodama, 1986; Kodama, 1992; Breschi/Lissoni/Malerba, 2004; Torrisi/Granstand, 2004).

And although the diversity of products, markets and business areas has been intensively discussed in academic research, until the 1980s little attention has been paid to the diversification of the technological capabilities (Stephan, 2003, p. 125). In their pioneering works Kodama (1986), Pavitt/Robson/Townsend (1989) and Granstrand/Sjölander (1990) describe the increasing technological diversification of firms in the Triads (Japan, Europe, United States) since the beginning of the 1980s. The notation of *technological diversification* refers to the spread of technological capabilities across technological classes, i.e. the number of technological classes where innovative activities take place (Leten, 2008, p. 1).

Firms are nowadays operating in a wider range of sectors and accumulate technological competencies outside their core business. The degree of technological diversification often exceeds the degree of product diversification. A considerable amount of firms' technologies lie outside the fields of excellence (Pavitt/Robson/Townsend, 1989, p. 88 ff.; Kodama, 1986, p. 291 ff.). Moreover, empirical studies show that some technological classes (e.g. biotechnology, information technology) are becoming essential for a wider range of sectors. These so called 'platform technologies' can be applied to different products and sectors (see among others Gambardella/Torrisi, 1998, p. 446; Cesaroni, 2004, p. 177). Furthermore, Kim/Kogut (1996) argue that competences in platform technologies facilitate the entrance into new technological fields. Conversely, competences in declining technologies may lead to competence traps and lock-in effects.

Concerning the direction of technological diversification it has been shown that new technological competences mainly arise in the neighbourhood of the existing technological capabilities (Malerba, 1992, p. 847 f.). Furthermore, technological profiles tend to remain quite persistent over time, i.e. original technological core competences are maintained. Companies lean to diversify in those fields which are of prior importance for the prevailing technological paradigm. When new paradigms evolve, the companies appear to maintain their technological core competences and begin to experiment with the emerging technologies (Cantwell/Fai, 1999, p. 341 f.). However, the links between the changes in the technological structure at the industrial or national level and the technological diversity of firms have been less studied so far. The literature on technological diversification has its primary focus on the evolution of the technological knowledge base. Scholars have paid particular attention to the direction of technological diversification by taking into account the overlaps between the established technological competences and the new pieces of technological knowledge. Another strand of literature deals with the firm specific determinants of technological diversification (e.g. the development of new business areas). Thus, previous contributions to technological diversification mainly discuss company-internal factors shaping the rates and directions of technological diversification. They pay little attention to external factors influencing the technological focus of companies. Little is known about the impact of country-, sector- and technology-specific circumstances on the rates and directions of technological diversification.

Kim/Kogut (1996) argue that there must be an analogy between the diversification patterns of firms and the underlying technological trajectories in the respective industries. Firms with competences in platform technologies are more likely to diversify into related subfields and to imitate the branching process of the underlying technological trajectories. However, until recently there is little empirical evidence about these relationships. Furthermore, the framework provided by Kim/Kogut (1996) does not explicitly take into account the main characteristics of knowledge processes. The emergence of new technologies and the development of industry-specific technological trajectories are driven by two important factors: path dependence and the national environment. The former refers to the fact that the technology bases of industries seem to be rather stable over time and that changes are gradual. The latter refers to the fact that nations differ in their technological trajectories due to country specific innovation systems (Ramani/de Looze, 2002). In 1999, de Looze/Ramani show that Europe's biotechnology industry is characterised by distinct national technological trajectories. Furthermore, Castellacci (2009) emphasises that technological developments are shaped by sectoral as well as national factors.

> '[…] the characteristics and dynamics of sectoral technological trajectories are affected by a great variety of factors related to the national system of innovation, such as the patterns of technological, scientific and economic specialization, […], and other country-specific factors of social, institutional and cultural nature.' (ibid., 2009, p. 322)

From this point of view it can be argued that a detailed analysis of the technology profiles in science-based industries has to pay attention to the above mentioned characteristic of the underlying knowledge processes.

Empirical evidence shows that the national environment has an impact on the technology portfolios of companies. This means that firms' technological decisions are driven by the national innovation system of their home country (Tidd/Bessant/Pavitt, 2005, p. 131 ff.). Additionally, firms are also affected by the technological developments which take place in their sectors of main economic activity. The product segment constrains the directions of technological search. There is empirical evidence that firms within the same sectors or firms located in the same country are more similar concerning their technological profile than firms from different sectors and nations (Patel/Pavitt, 1997). However, recent contributions are limited to the mapping of sectoral *or* national patterns of technological diversification. Moreover, they focus on the impact of sectoral and national factors, but they do not take into account the interactions between the two perspectives of consideration. Thus, the strength of influence of sectoral and national factors, i.e. the degree of similarity between sectoral, national and corporate technological profiles, is neglected.

I.2 Systems of innovation

During the last decades the systems of innovation approach, emphasising the impact of external environmental factors on the innovation process, has attracted the attention of scholars. They recognised that innovative activities are not carried out in isolation, but through interactions among various actors (Lundvall, 1992; Freeman, 1995; Fischer, 2001). In this context, the systems of innovation concept stresses that the economic and technological performance of sectors and nations hardly depends on the various interactions between firms, public and private research institutes and universities. They define the system of innovation

> '[…] as a set of actors or entities such as firms, other organisations and institutions that interact in the generation, use and diffusion of new – and economically useful – knowledge in the production process.' (Fischer, 2001, p. 207)

Within the systems of innovation approach different innovation systems with varying borders have been defined. The national system of innovation (NIS) concept going back to List (1841) builds the origin of the systems of innovation approach. In the 1990s the approach has been put forward by Lundvall (1992), Nelson (1993), Freeman (1995) and others. The NIS concept emphasises the impact of national specificities on the technological and economic development of nations. However, scholars recognised that technological activities have not necessarily a national perspective, but can be related to global, regional, sectoral or technological areas (Fischer, 2001, p. 211). In this context, the concept of regional, sectoral and technological innovation systems evolved. The sectoral innovation systems (SIS) approach elaborated by Breschi/Malerba (1997) is a firm-centric concept with transcend boundaries that takes into account the selection and competition processes among firms shaping the dynamics of SIS. While the NIS approach encompasses various sectors, the SIS concept focuses on single value chains. The borders of the system are determined by the specific technological knowledge involved in the innovation processes of the respective sector.

> '[…], the boundaries of the SIS are endogenous: they emerge from the specific conditions of each sector. As a matter of fact, different industries may have different competitive, interactive and organizational boundaries which are not necessarily national.' (Breschi/Malerba, 1997, p. 131)

Carlsson/Stankiewicz (1991) applied the innovation systems approach to the technological perspective. Technological systems (TS) focus on the forces fostering and hampering the utilisation, generation and diffusion of new technological knowledge in particular technological fields. Similar to the SIS approach the TS concept has a firm-centric perspective and is characterised by cross-national and cross-sectoral borders. Scholars argue that the technological knowledge of specific technologies is often dispersed across different sectors and nations (Hekkert et al., 2007, p. 416 f.).

The different systems of innovation approaches have specific characteristics and borders. However, they should not be seen as exclusive concepts (Christ, 2007, p. 1). Although firms within the same industrial sector may be mainly affected by the sectoral environment, their innovative performance is also determined by national and technological forces. On the one hand the innovative activities are influenced by national institutions, on the other hand the technological breakthroughs in new promising technologies (e.g. biotechnology) can have cross-sectoral and cross-national impacts (Malerba, 2004, p. 17 ff.; Hekkert et al., 2007, p. 416 f.). As a consequence, particular emphasis should be put on the interactions between the various systems of innovation (Archibugi/Howells/Michie, 1999, p. 528; Castellacci, 2009, p. 321 ff.).

I.3 Objective of the thesis

> 'Perhaps the biggest task that remains in the development of the systems of innovation approach remains in providing better linkage between the more aggregate, macro level studies and the micro analysis of firm relationships and behaviour.' (Archibugi/Howells/Michie, 1999, p. 533)

While previous research has considered the technological diversification of companies and the impact of innovation systems on firms' technology decisions in isolation, this thesis aims to combine the different research strands. The challenge of this doctoral thesis is to link the technological diversification patterns of companies with the technological, sectoral and national innovation processes.

Recent contributions indicate that factors internal *and* external to the firm affect the direction of technological competence accumulation. Large companies are mastering a variety of different technologies and operate in several sectors and nations. Consequently, this raises the question how far the technological, sectoral and national environment affects the technological scope decisions of companies. This dissertation aims to answer this question by analysing the impact of technological, sectoral and national innovation processes on the technological profiles of companies. For this purpose, the narrow perspective of the 'traditional' approaches to the systems of innovation, which take a one-side view of the innovative activities from the technological, sectoral *or* national perspective, is left. This dissertation uses an integrated framework that takes into account all three levels of consideration as well as their interactions. While recent studies are limited to the mapping of sectoral or national patterns of technological diversification, this thesis aims to investigate the linkages between the developments that take place at the firm level, on the one hand, and the evolutions at the technological, sectoral and national level, on the other hand. Furthermore, this thesis looks beyond the quasi-static perspective of the systems of innovation approach. It investigates the evolution of the technological profiles in the life sciences industry during an observation period of 20 years.

Based on the theoretical framework of this dissertation, research theses about the rates and directions of technological change are developed. They draw on theoretical contributions dealing with technological diversification as well as economic theories focusing on systems of innovation. The research theses are tested empirically on a large patent dataset, containing the patent profiles of 114 life sciences companies and six European nations. First, this thesis analyses the evolution of new technological paradigms and trajectories in the European life sciences industry. Second, the technological diversification patterns of selected life sciences companies are investigated. The challenge of the analyses is to find the analogies between the firm specific technological scope decisions and the technological changes which take place at the level of nations, sectors and technologies.

The remainder of this thesis consists of four chapters and is structured as follows (Figure 1):

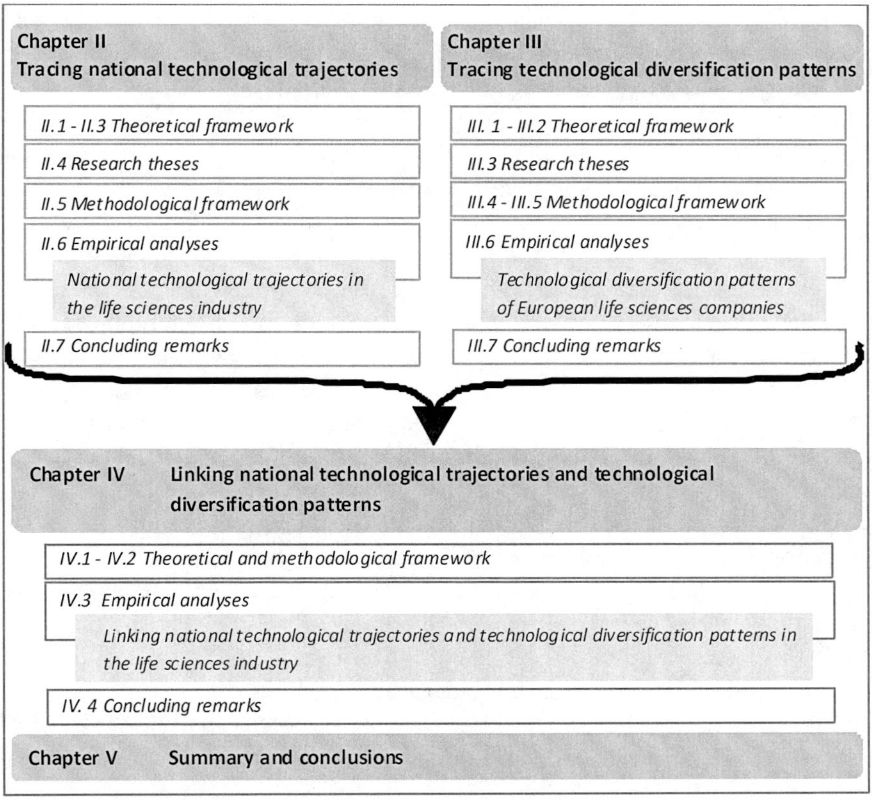

Figure 1: Structure of the thesis
Source: own illustration

Chapter II aims to trace the national technological trajectories in the European life sciences industry. After introducing the theoretical and methodological framework the empirical analyses of the technological trajectories are presented. The *theoretical framework* begins by providing some basic definitions of the term 'technology' and the general principles of technological knowledge. Next, the process of technological change is investigated. The contributions of evolutionary scholars are used to put forward an understanding of the process of technological change. The systems of innovation concept provides an understanding of the factors influencing the development, diffusion and application of new technologies. The multi-level perspective (MLP) is introduced in order to illustrate the interactions between the various innovation systems. Concluding, based on these theoretical contributions, the research theses can be formulated. These theses serve as guideline for the empirical analyses. The *methodological framework* discusses common used indicators of technological activities. It introduces patents as indicator of technological change. Furthermore, a technology classification scheme is provided. Using different knowledge base indicators the *empirical analyses* trace the national technological trajectories in the life sciences during the period 1986-2005.

Chapter III analyses the technological diversification patterns of R&D-intensive companies operating in the life sciences. First, the *theoretical framework* introduces the phenomenon of technological diversification. It discusses the main determinants of technological diversification. Furthermore, the advantages arising from a diversified technological portfolio are pointed out. Next, the process of technological change is discussed from the firm perspective. Based on the theoretical contributions, additional research theses are formulated. The *empirical analyses* provide a detailed overview of the breadth and depth of the knowledge bases for a sample of European life sciences companies. In order to determine the factors influencing the technological decisions of firms, the patterns of technological diversification are assessed at the national and sectoral level.

Chapter IV draws on the findings elaborated in *Chapter II* and *Chapter III*. A cluster approach is used in order to specify the mechanisms underpinning technological decisions at the company level. By linking the national technological trajectories with the technological profiles of the life sciences companies the main factors influencing the technology decisions of firms are determined.

Chapter V summarises the main findings and draws the conclusions.

Chapter II Tracing national technological trajectories

In this chapter the evolution of the national technological trajectories in the life sciences industry is investigated. The theoretical framework provides some basic definitions and explains the mechanisms shaping technological change. The systems of innovation approach serves as a 'toolkit' to describe the different factors affecting the development, diffusion and application of new technological knowledge and innovations. The methodological framework introduces patents as indicators of technological change. Using different knowledge base indicators the empirical analyses investigate the technological changes in the European life sciences industry.

II.1 Technology – a conceptualisation

A key step towards the understanding of the patterns of technological change is the conceptualisation of technology. Aim of this section is to provide a definition of technology and its general principles.

Different scientific fields have used various definitions (see among others Sahal, 1981; Olsen/Engen, 2007, p. 457 f.). Following Dosi (1982) technology can be defined as

> '[…] a set of pieces of knowledge, both directly "practical" (related to concret problems and devices) and "theoretical" (but practically applicable although not necessarily already applied), know-how, methods, procedures, experience of successes and failures and also, of course, physical devices and equipment.' (Dosi, 1982, p. 151 f.)

In this definition technology refers to tangible and intangible assets as well. First, the term is associated with the *stock of technological knowledge* including theoretical expert knowledge as well as the application of the technological knowledge (see also Granstrand/Sjölander, 1990, p. 59; Nieto, 2004, p. 315). Technology in this conception is codified but disembodied and exists in form of patents, licences etc. Second, technological knowledge also refers to *technological capabilities and experiences* which are required to apply and integrate technological information. This kind of non-codified and disembodied technological knowledge is mostly acquired via personal communication (Howells, 1996, p. 91 ff.; Stephan, 2003, p. 136). Organisational routines often represent successful solutions to complex technological problems. They represent the joint contributions and interactions of several persons (Teece et al., 1994, p. 15; Nelson/Winter, 1982, p. 96 ff.). Third, technological knowledge is also associated with complex *technological artefacts* which manifest themselves in physical objects (Stephan, 2003, p. 136) and production processes. The artefacts and production processes represent the physical design and the performance parameters of the respective technology (Granstrand, 1998, p. 480). As a consequence, these artefacts represent the codified and embodied part of technological knowledge (Howells, 1996, p. 91 ff.). Summarising technological knowledge can be defined as a cookbook recipe:

> '[…] a physical artifact together with a set of procedures for achieving it. The recipe specifies a set of actions that need to be taken to achieve the desired outcome and identifies, if sometimes implicitly, the inputs that are to be acted on and any required equipment.' (Dosi/Grazzi, 2010, p. 173)

The different components of the corporate technology base are illustrated in Figure 2.

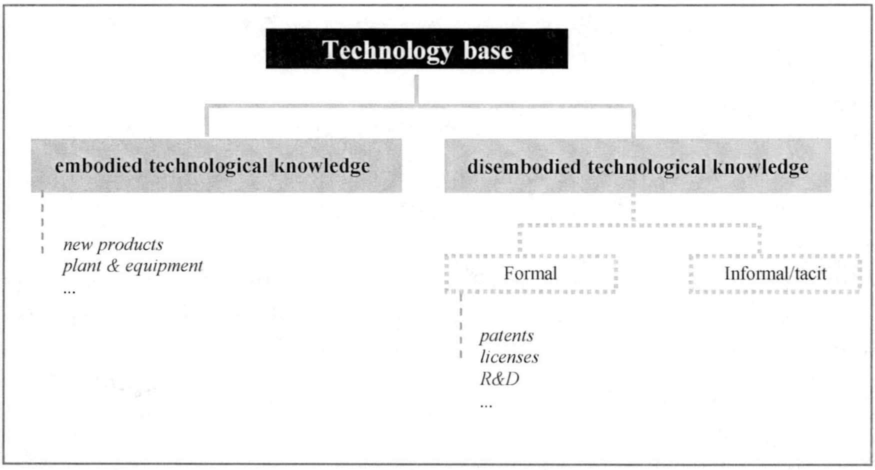

Figure 2: Components of the technology base
Source: cf. Howells, 1996, p. 92, own illustration

In the following the general principles of technological knowledge are introduced. This may be useful to understand the process of technological change at the level of firms and industries. Three general principles are highlighted here:

- *Uncertainty:* The development of new technological knowledge is a highly uncertain and complex process. Thus, in the early development stages the future usefulness of new technologies cannot be appreciated. For instance, after the development of new visualisation technology – like magnetic resonance imaging (MRI) – its potential for medical diagnostics has for a long time not been recognised. Especially radical technological developments have long gestation periods before their future application areas are exploited (Rosenberg, 1996, p. 97 ff.; Granstrand/Patel/Pavitt, 1997, p. 13).

- *Complementarity and cumulativeness:* The technological developments in a particular technological area often depend upon the developments in complementary technology fields. As a consequence, the search for new technological solutions often takes place in the neighbourhood of the existing competences. Technological improvements in one area favour the research in related technological areas. Furthermore, simultaneous improvements in a number of cumulative technological fields often lead to radical technological innovations, while improvements in single technologies frequently result in incremental innovations (Nelson/Winter, 1982, p. 255 ff.; Rosenberg, 1996, p. 97 ff.; Breschi/Lissoni/Malerba, 1998, p. 3).
- *Codification vs. tacitness:* Technologies are characterised by links to science and high degrees of codifiability. The codification results, for instance, from the use of patent documents or publications in scientific journals. They enable the generation, diffusion and accumulation of technological knowledge. However, technological knowledge does also have a tacit nature. This involves, for instance, the firm-specific knowledge how to generate new technological knowledge. As such, it is mostly transmitted via personal communication (Granstrand, 1998, p. 479; Mandeville, 1998, p. 357 ff.).

Summarising it can be noted that the development of new technological knowledge is a highly uncertain and cumulative process that often draws upon tacit knowledge. In the following the process of technological change is described from an evolutionary perspective.

II.2 Technological change as an evolutionary process

The distribution of economic activities and the process of technological change are discussed in a wide range of literature. There are different research strands which investigate the patterns of innovation at different aggregation levels (for a detailed overview see Hullmann, 2001, p. 61).

Traditional theories of technological change can be classified into *'demand-pull'* and *'technology-push'* theories. In the demand-pull theories the market forces, i.e. the demand for particular technologies, are the main drivers of technological change. The technology-push theory is based on the assumption that technological change is driven by technological opportunities. However, both theories have their shortcomings and cannot serve as theoretical framework for the process of technological change. The demand-pull approach draws on the assumption that the technological needs are known a-priory (Dosi, 1982, p. 148 f.). This is in contrast to the highly uncertain nature of technological change. Furthermore, as argued by Rosenberg (1996) the future development potentials of emerging technologies cannot be predicted in advance. There was also criticism of the technology-push theory for not taking into account the uncertain nature of technological activity. Furthermore, additional economic factors which might also affect the direction of technological change are not taken into consideration. Thus, both approaches neglect that technological change is a complex inter-active process (Dosi, 1982, p. 148 ff.).

From an evolutionary perspective technological change is a gradual and non-linear process. The process involves the development of new technological knowledge leading to an increasing range of alternatives, i.e. increasing variety. The development of the new technologies is shaped by the boundaries of existing routines. This is due to the fact that the search for new technological opportunities is an uncertain process. Furthermore, information on new technologies is only rarely available (*'idiosyncratic nature of technologies'*). Hence, decisions are affected by uncertainty and bounded rationality. As a consequence, the search for new technologies is locally constraint and takes place in the neighborhood of existing technological competences (*'path dependence'*; cf. *Chapter II.2.3*). The search for new technological solutions proceeds along defined development paths – so called *'technological trajectories'* (cf. *Chapter II.2.1*) – which limit the range of alternative solutions and shape the direction of technological change (McKelvey, 1997; Lambooy/ Boschma, 2001, p. 115 ff.; Dominguez Lacasa, 2005, p. 19 ff.).

II.2.1 Technological trajectories and paradigms – the search for technological solutions

During the last decades a number of concepts (like technological regimes, technological trajectories and paradigms, dominant design), which try to explain the direction of technological change and the underlying procedures, have emerged (Dosi/Labini, 2007, p. 332). This thesis will mainly focus on the notations *'technological paradigms'* and *'technological trajectories'*.

Dosi's definition of the term technology introduced in *Chapter II.1* assumes that the number of possible technological solutions and the number of potential development paths is limited (Dosi, 1982, p. 152). To explain the patterns of technological change Dosi (1982) developed the concept of technological paradigms and trajectories.[1]

A *technological paradigm* can be defined as: *'[...] an "outlook", a set of procedures, a definition of the "relevant" problems and of the specific knowledge related to their solution'* (Dosi, 1982, p. 148). Thus, a technological paradigm can be seen as a problem-solving activity. It contains not yet exploited technological solutions as well as constraints. The paradigm shapes the direction of technological change in determining which technological solutions should be pursued or neglected. It defines the constraints and frontiers, but also the technological trajectories to these frontiers (Nelson/Winter, 1977, p. 56 f.; Dosi, 1982, p. 152).

The three core ideas in the notation of technological paradigms are the following (Cimoli/Dosi, 1995, p. 245 f.):

- They capture problem-solving activities which may partly consist of tacit knowledge embodied in individuals or organisational procedures.
- They include specific heuristics and visions which describe how things should be done and how they can be improved.
- They entail basic models of artefacts and systems, i.e. they include information about some fundamental technological and economic characteristics.

A *technological trajectory* is defined as: *'[...] the direction of advance within a technological paradigm'* (Dosi, 1982, p. 148). Thus, the trajectories can be seen as a bundle of possible technological solutions which are constrained by the paradigm. Although technological trajectories comprise a bundle of possible technological solutions, not all directions of technological opportunities can be followed, as the technological change is rooted into certain development paths. The rates and directions of technological changes are shaped by the technological paradigms. Thus, technological trajectories are characterised by continuous and incremental changes, while technological paradigms lead to more radical changes. Different markets and radical changes in the technological paradigms may lead to irregularities and invariances in the pattern of technological change (Cimoli/Dosi, 1995, p. 246; Andersen, 2001, pp. 35-39; Russel, 1999, p. 237).

Following Nelson/Winter (1977) technological trajectories can have different scopes. While some trajectories are associated with one specific technology or

1 This concept builds on Kuhn's (1962) notation of the scientific paradigms.

industry, there are also trajectories which can affect several technologies or industries ('general natural trajectories').[2]

The relationship between technological paradigms and trajectories is illustrated in Figure 3. A technological paradigm consists of several different trajectories. Within a technological trajectory, a specific technological solution path – the so-called *dominant design* – may establish dominance among competing technological solution paths. A dominant design is shaped by the available technology as well as by the evolution of customer preferences (Utterback/Suárez, 1993; Suárez/Utterback, 1995).

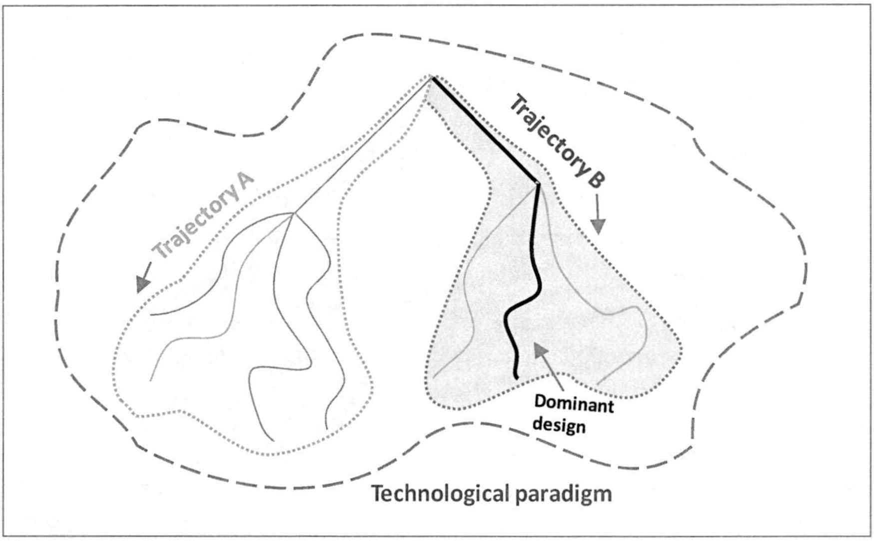

Figure 3: Technological paradigms and trajectories

Source: cf. Utterback/Suárez, 1993, p. 6; Suárez/Utterback, 1995, p. 416, own illustration

Following Teece (2008) the concept of technological paradigms helps to explain how incremental technological innovations take place. Radical or breakthrough innovations are more likely to occur outside the paradigm. Thus, sometimes it is necessary to break away from established paradigms in order to identify new promising technological opportunities. Hence, in order to sustain their competitive position firms should not solely rely on the technological solutions within the paradigm, but also search outside these frontiers for new technological opportunities (ibid., p. 509 f.).

2 Corresponding to the concept of 'general natural trajectories' Freeman/Perez (1988) refer to the concept of the meta-paradigms. These paradigms are highly pervasive and can affect the whole economy (ibid., p. 47).

The evolutions described by Dosi's concept can manifest themselves at the technology level as well as at the industry and corporate level. While some trajectories are associated with specific technologies, industries or companies, there are also trajectories which are of general importance (Nelson/Winter, 1977, p. 58; Andersen, 1998, p. 12 f.; Teece, 2008, p. 510).

II.2.2 Technology life cycles – the evolution of new technologies

Dosi's concept of the technological trajectories provides an understanding of the factors that shape the evolution of new technological knowledge. Long-term cycles of technology do further take into account its development over time (see for example Freeman/Perez, 1988).[3] However, these theories explain the evolution of technologies at the macro-level. This means that the development of technologies is described at high aggregation levels. As a consequence, these theories are not useful for tracing the evolution of specific industries (meso-level). At the meso-level the development of new technologies can be described using the six phases model ('6-Phasen-Modell') of Meyer-Krahmer/Dreher (2004) (Dreher et al., 2006, p. 280 ff.; Schmoch, 2007, p. 1002).

Following this concept, the development of new technologies is characterised by two phases of boom ('double-boom cycle', see also Grupp, 1997, p. 31 ff.; Schmoch, 2007). After the 'discovery' of new technological opportunities *(Phase 1)*, the potential application areas are explored and tested. In the 'euphoria' phase *(Phase 2)* the breadth of new technological insights increases. New technological competences are combined with existing technological solutions and pave the way for transdisciplinary research areas. Over time it becomes obvious which technological solutions are feasible and which ones should be limited or ceased. As a consequence, the breadth of application areas decreases and the research efforts are rooted towards promising possibilities of use (*Phase 3*). The 'disillusionment' of this phase results in a phase of 'reorientation' which is characterised by radical new inventions (*Phase 4*). Those technological solutions that penetrate the market cause the imitation by competitors and lead to the development of a dominant design (*Phase 5*). In the following the 'diffusion' of the new technologies takes place (*Phase 6*). The greater availability of the new technology as well as falling production costs due to economies of scale lead to numerous application areas (Dreher et al., 2006, pp. 280-284). The six phases model is illustrated in Figure 4.

3 One of the most famous approaches in this context is the technology cycle theory of Kondratieff (1926).

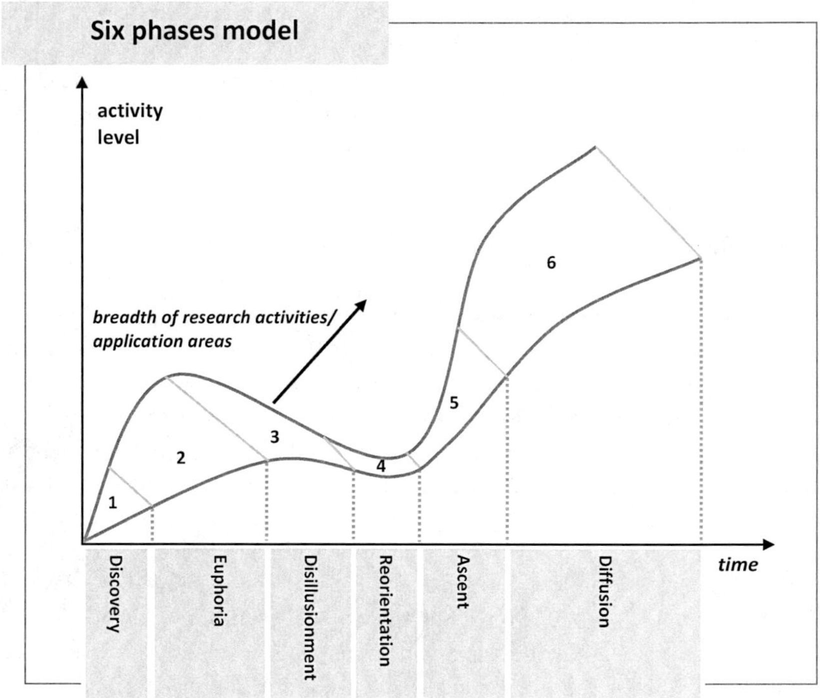

Figure 4: Six phases model
Source: cf. Dreher et al., 2006, p. 281, own illustration

II.2.3 Technological change as a path dependent process

Empirical evidence shows, that innovative activities tend to be rather path dependent. I.e. the evolution of technologies is affected by the technological paths which have been developed in the past (see among others Cantwell, 2004, p. 289 f.). Path dependence in technologies means that the future distribution of technological competences (in time $t + 1$) depends more upon the historically developed competences than upon the current profile of the technology base (at time t) (Liebowitz/Margolis, 2000, p. 981 f.). However, path dependence differs from past dependence (Figure 5). Past dependence is a fully non-ergodic process. This means that the evolution of technologies is completely determined by historical conditions. In contrast to this, the outcomes of an ergodic process are not affected by its initial conditions. Path dependent processes are influenced by historical as well as other factors (Antonelli, 2006, p. 51 ff.). '*In so doing path dependence can be considered at the border between fully ergodic processes and fully non-ergodic ones*' (ibid., p. 54).

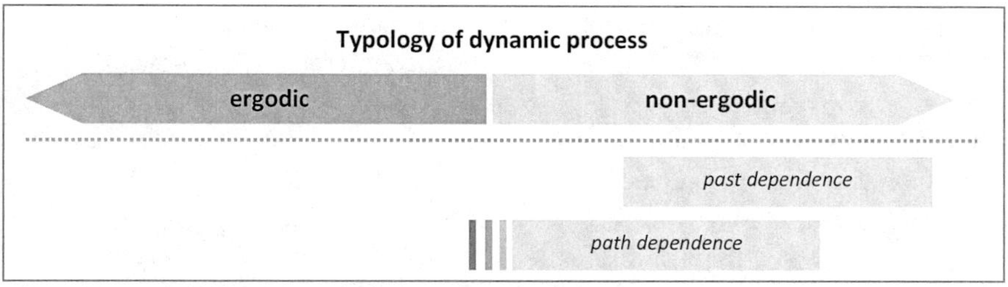

Figure 5: Path dependence vs. past dependence
Source: cf. Antonelli, 2006, p. 53, own illustration

As argued by Arthur (1989) the path dependence of processes or technologies can lead to 'lock-in by historical events'. Lock-in in this context means that the outcome of the technological path is not satisfactory because superior alternatives exist (Liebowitz/Margolis, 1995, p. 206 f.).[4] However, it has to be noted that the path dependence of technologies does not automatically lead to a lock-in in inferior outcomes. There are three different kinds of path dependence which have to be distinguished (Liebowitz/Margolis, 1995, p. 206 f.; Liebowitz/Margolis, 2000, p. 985 f.):

- *First degree path dependence*: The chosen path is persistent and switching to other paths entails some costs, but the path is not inefficient.
- *Second degree path dependence*: Superior paths exist but are not known at the time of the decision. Also in this case the path is not inefficient, although the outcomes are regrettable and switching to the superior path entails some costs.
- *Third degree path dependence:* The superior paths are known at the time the choice is made. It is therefore possible to improve the paths and to receive superior outcomes. As a consequence, this form of path dependence is said to be inefficient.

Technological profiles of firms, sectors and nations are very persistent over time. This means that historically developed strengths – and also weaknesses – are still present in the technological profiles of subsequent periods. Although technological trajectories may change over time, it can be assumed that most of these

4 There are two prominent examples. First, the introduction of the videocassette recorder with the two competing formats: *VHS* and *Beta*. The VHS format began to dominate the market, although the Beta format was the superior technology. Second, the *'QWERTY'* arrangement of the typewriter keyboard which is said to be inferior to the *Dvorak* arrangement (David, 1985; Arthur, 1990, p. 92 f.; Liebowitz/Margolis, 1995, p. 208 f.).

changes will occur slowly according to the characteristics of the underlying learning processes. Two dimensions of knowledge are relevant here: '*locality*' and '*cumulativeness*'. 'Locality' or 'knowledge proximity' means that the exploration and development of new technologies will occur close to the existing technologies. 'Cumulativeness' refers to the fact that the existing knowledge base builds the origin for further developments and that learning processes are incremental (Dosi/Labini, 2007, p. 333; Breschi/Lissoni/Malerba, 1998, p. 3).[5] The technological profiles of firms and nations seem to remain quite stable over time. Thus, the core competences which large companies or nations have historically developed can be identified in their subsequent trajectories. This means that technological trajectories tend to be highly path dependent. Drifts away from the initial technology bases are gradual (see among others Cantwell/ Fai, 1999; Cantwell, 2004, p. 289). The path dependence of technological trajectories can therefore lead to a lock-in situation in inferior technological paths. However, it should be noted, that there may also be several ways in which nations and firms may escape from path dependence. One possible way is the diversification into related industries (Lester, 2005, p. 18 f.; Martin/Sunley, 2006, p. 414 ff.).

II.3 Multi-dimensionality of innovative activities and the innovation system approach

Innovative activities can nowadays be characterised as a multi-national, multi-technological and multi-sectoral process. The *multi-national dimension* refers to the following fact: Large corporations span their technological activities over different countries and are often labelled as multi-national corporations (MNCs). Following Cantwell/Odile (2000) MNCs tend to establish abroad research facilities in order to gain access to complementary sources of technological knowledge (ibid., p. 245).

Furthermore, large companies are characterised by increasing technological diversification (see among others Granstrand/Patel/Pavitt, 1997). In this context, Granstrand/Sjölander (1990) introduced the concept of the multi-technology corporation (MTC) which spans its technological activities over three or more technologies. The concept therefore refers to the *multi-technological dimension* of corporate R&D activities. Moreover, there is also a *multi-sectoral dimension* of R&D activities. This refers among other things to the increasing importance of

5 Cumulativeness means that *'[...] firms which have innovated at time t have –* ***ceteris paribus*** *[emphasis in original] – a higher probability of innovation at time t + 1 [...]'* (Malerba/Orsenigo, 1996, p. 55).

so called 'platform technologies', which can be applied in a wide range of products and sectors (Torrisi/Granstrand, 2004, p. 53; Cesaroni, 2004, p. 177).

As a consequence, technological activities of firms are complex processes, affected by numerous agents and institutions as well as by the collaborative interactions between the various actors. In this context, the systems of innovation approach attempts to shed light on the complex nature of technological change. The concept tries to explain the development, diffusion and application of new technological knowledge and innovations (see among others OECD, 1997, p. 12; Fischer, 2001, p. 207).

> 'In the centre of this system are the firms, the way they organise production and innovation and the channels by which they gain access to external sources of knowledge. These sources might be other firms, public and private research institutes, universities or transfer institutions – either regional, national or international.' (OECD, 1997, p. 12)

The systems of innovation concept has been elaborated at different aggregation levels. A first group of contributions has introduced the 'national systems of innovation' approach. Later the 'sectoral innovation systems' as well as the 'technological innovation systems' focusing on innovative activities within specific sectors or in particular technological areas have been brought forward (Carlsson, 2006, p. 57 f.).

II.3.1 National systems of innovation

Recent studies show that countries with similar resource profiles are characterised by distinct technological specialisation patterns. There is empirical evidence that the technological profiles of leading companies reflect the technological strengths and weaknesses of their home country. The creation of new knowledge seems to be affected by the national environment ranging from the state policy to the organisation of the public research system. Thus, the national characteristics have an influence on the direction of technological innovation (Ramani/de Looze, 2002, p. 458; Tidd/Bessant/Pavitt, 2005, p. 131 f.).

> '[…], each country has its own institutional profile depending on the governance regime for enterprises, the organisation of the university sector and the level and orientation of government-funded research. There are marked differences in the relative roles and weight of different institutions in national innovation systems [...].' (OECD, 1997, p. 12)

These country-specific factors have an influence on the technological trajectories. De Looze/Ramani (1999) show that Europe's leading countries in the biotechnology sector are characterised by distinct evolutionary trajectories. Thus, the patterns in new technology investment are influenced by the national environment. These observations led to the elaboration of the *National Systems of Innovation (NIS)* approach.[6] List's (1841) concept of '*The National System of Political Economy'* builds the origin of this approach. He stresses that the historically developed knowledge of a nation as well as the links to sciences are important for the innovativeness of industries (Freeman, 1995, p. 5).

Although there have been numerous contributions, which discuss the concept of national innovation systems, a general definition of the NIS does not exist. The main ideas of the national innovation system approach are reflected in the pioneering works of Lundvall (1992), Nelson (1993) and Patel/Pavitt (1994a). These contributions define the national innovation systems as follows:

> '[…] the wide range of factors, organizations, and policies influencing the capabilities of a nation's firms to innovate […].' (Nelson/Rosenberg, 1993, p. 18)

> '[…] a system of innovation is constituted by the elements and relationships which interact in the production, diffusion and use of new, and economically useful, knowledge […] a national system encompasses elements and relationships, either located within or rooted inside the borders of a nation state.' (Lundvall, 1992, p. 2)

> '[…] the national institutions, their incentive structures and their competencies, that determine the rate and direction of technological learning […] in a country.' (Patel/Pavitt, 1994a, p. 79)

These approaches emphasise the interactions between distinct institutions which favour the development and diffusion of new technological knowledge. Within the framework of the NIS the national policies can support the innovation process (Metcalfe, 1995, p. 38). Following these definitions the notation of NIS can be seen as an attempt to explain the uneven development of technological and competitive performance of companies and countries (Patel/Pavitt, 1994a, p. 78). However, it should be noted that differences in countries' technological performance can be only partly explained by the NIS approach. Although, national characteristics have an influence on the technological profiles of firms, they do not determine their technological strategies (Tidd/Bessant/Pavitt, 2005, p. 163). Thus, there are also other factors, like the sectoral environment, which determine the rates and directions of technological change.

The NIS approach focuses on all industries and technologies which are present in the respective country. I.e. the concept is not industry or technology specific (Breschi/Malerba, 1997, p. 130). By taking into account that the scope of innovative activities may not coincide with national borders scholars developed the concepts of technological, sectoral and regional innovation systems (Carlsson, 2006, p. 58). In the following the sectoral and technological

6 There are numerous contributions which discuss the impact of national innovation systems. For a detailed overview see among others Lundvall (1992) and Nelson (1993).

systems of innovation are introduced. The concept of regional systems of innovation will not be discussed in this thesis.[7]

II.3.2 Sectoral and technological systems of innovation

Empirical evidence shows that different industries or sectors are characterised by distinct innovation environments. These observations led to the framework of the *Sectoral Innovation System (SIS).* It provides an understanding of the specific learning processes and actors within sectors and examines the characteristics and frontiers of the sectors (Malerba, 2005, p. 63 ff.). The sectoral system of innovation can be defined as follows as:

> ‚Sectoral systems of innovation have a knowledge base, technologies, inputs and a (potential or existing) demand. They are composed of a set of agents carrying out market and non-market interactions for the creation, development and diffusion of new sectoral products. […] They interact through processes of communication, exchange, cooperation, competition and command. Their interaction is shaped by institutions.' (ibid., p. 65 f.)
>
> '[…] a set of new and established products for specific uses, and a set of agents carrying out activities and market and non-market interactions for the creation, production and sale of those products.' (Malerba, 2004, p. 16)
>
> '[…] that system (group) of firms active in developing and making a sector's products and in generating and utilizing a sector's technologies […].' (Breschi/Malerba, 1997, p. 131)

The sectoral innovation systems consist of the three main components 'knowledge and technology, actors and networks, institutions' which can be described as follows (Malerba, 2004, p. 17 ff.; Malerba, 2005, p. 66 f.):

- *Knowledge and technology:* This point refers to the fact that different sectors are characterised by distinct knowledge bases.
- *Actors and networks:* The sectoral innovation system encompasses various actors (organisations, individuals) which are interacting through processes of communication, competition etc. *'Firms are the key actors in a sectoral system. They are involved in the innovation, production and sale of sectoral products, and in the generation, adaption and use of new technologies'* (Malerba, 2004, p. 24).
- *Institutions:* The interactions within the sectoral innovation systems are shaped by the rules, routines etc. of the different institutions.

7 For an overview of the concept see for example Cooke (2001) and Doloreux (2002).

It is argued that each sector has its specific knowledge base and distinct technological capabilities. Interactions among heterogeneous agents, which include the generation and the exchange of technological knowledge, are the main sources for innovation. The sectoral systems are shaped by specific institutions. Some of these institutions are national ones (e.g. the patent system) while others are sector specific (e.g. regulation in pharmaceuticals). Thus, the boundaries between the national and sectoral level are not always clear-cut (Malerba, 2005, p. 66 f.). Furthermore, the impact of the national institutions is not the same in all sectors. For instance, the effects of the patent system play a decisive role in those sectors, which rely heavily on patent protection (e.g. the pharmaceutical industry), while other sectors may be affected only slightly. Moreover, national institutions of different countries often show varying characteristics. As a consequence, the same sectors may face unequal conditions in different countries (e.g. the first-to-invent versus first-to-file rules of the patent systems in the United States or Japan). Conversely, some sectoral institutions may also be crucial for the national economy in terms of employment or competitiveness. This implies, though, that national and sectoral systems are intertwined. Furthermore, there is empirical evidence that the same sectors show rather similar development patterns in different countries. Thus, on the one hand the national innovation system seems to affect the innovative performance of sectors, on the other hand sectoral patterns of innovation can become predominant at the country level (Levin et al., 1987; Malerba, 2002, p. 257 ff.; Malerba, 2004, p. 33 ff.; Malerba, 2005, p. 66 f.).

At the beginning of the 1990s Swedish scholars introduced the concept of *Technological Systems (TS)* (Carlsson, 2006, p. 58). They define technological systems as a:

> '[…] network of agents interacting in a specific *economic/industrial area* [emphasis in original] under a particular *institutional infrastructure* [emphasis in original] or set of infrastructures and involved in the generation, diffusion, and utilization of technology. Technological systems are defined in terms of knowledge/competence flows rather than flows of ordinary goods and services.' (Carlsson/Stankiewicz, 1991, p. 111)

Following this definition the main objective of the technological systems (also referred to as Technological Innovation System (TIS)) is the generation, diffusion and utilisation of technological knowledge. The technological system and the government policy should favour the diffusion of new knowledge in order to facilitate the identification and utilisation of the new technology. As a result, the local industry can invest earlier in the new technology than their international competitors and may therefore have a competitive advantage (Carlsson/Jacobsson, 1994, p. 236).

The building blocks of the technological system ('economic competence, networks and institutions') are presented in the following:

- *Economic competence* refers to the firm's ability to identify and adapt emerging technological opportunities in order to avoid lock-in situations in declining technologies. This can be achieved through changes in organisational routines and the corporate technology base (Carlsson/ Jacobsson, 1997, p. 269 f.; Jacobsson, 1997, p. 330 f.).
- *Networks: '[...] a well-functioning technological system rests on strongly positive and reciprocal external economies [...] which tie together users, suppliers and competitors'* (Carlsson/Jacobsson, 1997, p. 270). Indeed, the linkages between buyers, sellers and bridging institutions such as universities or industries are important for the process of technological change within technological systems (ibid., p. 270 f.).
- *Institutions* play a major role for the exchange of information within the networks of the technological systems. Although firms are the key actors within the system, the importance of other institutions (especially of the educational system) is emphasised (Carlsson/Jacobsson, 1997, p. 271).

Compared to the national innovation system approach, the concept of technological systems is not restricted to a fixed geographical area. While some technology systems have a regional dimension (e.g. Silicon Valley) others have an international or global context. Furthermore, there is not just a single technological system but different technological systems among various technologies like biotechnology or new materials. Those technological systems which are bounded to the national level have much in common with the national innovation systems approach. But there are also some differences to the NIS approach: While the technological system focuses on one specific technology, the national innovation system refers to all technological areas. Furthermore, the NIS emphasises the generation and distribution of knowledge, whereas the technological system approach focuses on the adaption and utilisation of new technologies (Carlsson/ Stankiewicz, 1991, p. 111 ff.; Carlsson/Jacobsson, 1994, p. 236).

Furthermore, the technological innovation system can include transcend sectoral boundaries. This refers to the fact that some technologies may span over different sectors. Biotechnology, for example, is applied in various industrial sectors like Pharmaceuticals, Food, etc. (Coenen/Díaz López, 2010, p. 1152 ff.).

II.3.3 Comparison of the innovation system approaches

During the last two decades the systems of innovation concept has attracted numerous researchers. The different strands of research focus on specific dimensions of the innovation process. While some contributions investigate the country-specific nature of technological activities, others refer to the sectoral or technological dimension of the innovation process. National systems of innovation are an important framework for technology policy. However, with regard to the evolution of new technologies it is questionable if the national boundaries are an adequate approach. On the one hand the R&D activities of multi-national companies may span over different countries, on the other hand dynamics of new technology evolution are complex and may be difficult to understand in the broad national context (Metcalfe, 1995, p. 41). However, the both approaches should be seen as complementary rather than conflicting concepts. While technology-specific evolutions affect the structure of industries, the national system of innovation influences the innovation process (Archibugi/Michie, 1997, p. 130). It shows that the different research fields are in some aspects related to another. However, we know little about the interactions between the different systems of innovation. Previous contributions mainly focus on the commonalities and differences of various concepts. Castellacci (2009) emphasises that *'[...] there does not exist any body of literature that systematically and explicitly investigates the mechanism that link the meso and macro level in innovation systems'* (ibid., p. 322).

In his empirical study Castellacci (2009) investigates the relationships between the national and sectoral patterns of innovation. He identified eight sector- and country-specific technological trajectories in European manufacturing industries. Moreover, he shows that the sectoral systems interact with their respective national systems. The forces of the national environment may put pressure on the sectoral trajectories and stabilise or destabilise the sectoral innovation system. Conversely, the sectoral patterns of innovation can also affect the development of the national technological trajectories (ibid., p. 342 f.). Koschatzky et al. (2009) investigate the overlaps between sectoral and geographical innovation systems. They show that the developments in the Information and Communication Technology (ICT) sector are affected by sectoral and geographical factors.

This thesis goes a step further by linking the micro-, meso- and macro-level. It is argued that companies are nowadays embedded in different innovation systems (Figure 6).

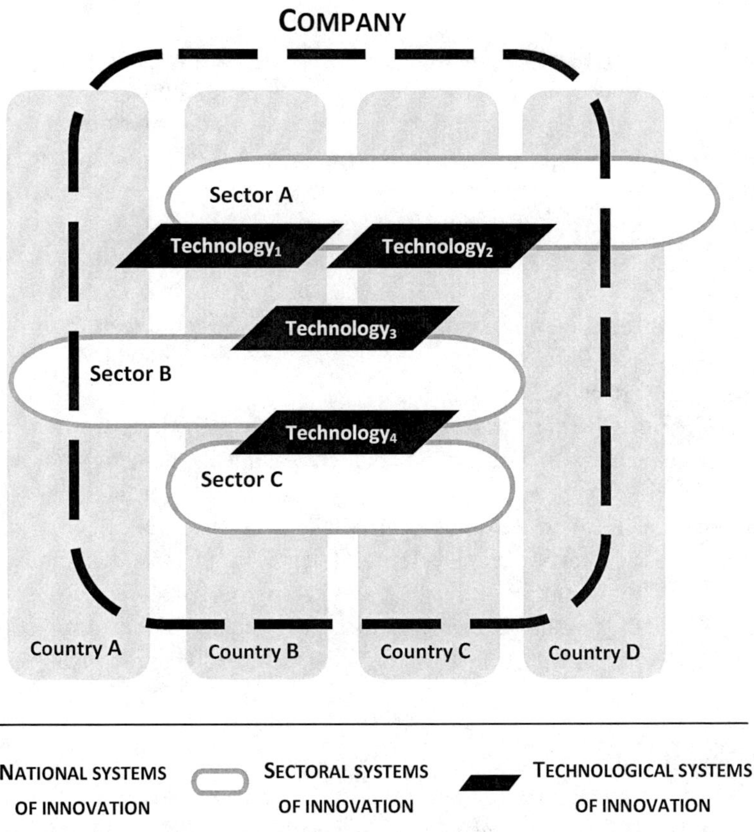

Figure 6: Multi-dimensional level of innovative activities
Source: cf. Hekkert et al. (2007), p. 417, own illustration

Starting from the perspective of multi-national, multi-sectoral and multi-technological companies, spanning their innovative activities over different technologies, sectors and nations, this contribution aims to determine the mechanisms that shape the technology base of companies.

Particular emphasis will be placed on the interactions between the national, sectoral and technological environment and the firm specific development patterns in the life sciences technologies.

II.3.4 Dynamics of innovation systems: The multi-level perspective

The recent remarks show that the innovation system approaches do neglect the interactions between the various innovation systems. Furthermore, the concepts have been criticised for not taking into account the dynamic perspective of technological change. Innovation systems are mostly regarded as quasi-static process. Therefore, these approaches fail to explain the mechanisms shaping long-term technological change (Hekkert et al., 2007, p. 414 f.). The multi-level perspective attempts to map technological change in so called *socio-technical systems* over time (Genus/Coles, 2008, p. 1437).[8] The transition process is analysed at the three different aggregation levels: the micro-level of niches, the meso-level of socio-technical regimes and the macro-level of the landscape (Geels, 2002; Geels, 2004; Geels, 2006).

The *landscape* refers to the macro-level and is characterised by heterogeneous factors that are shaping innovation and technological change processes. It entails processes like 'economic growth' or 'oil prices'. Accordingly, the landscape includes the technological trajectories and wider technology-external factors. These landscape level factors have an influence on the innovation and production process without being affected by the outcome of these processes in the short-run. As such, the landscape refers to deep structural trends and changes only slowly (Geels, 2002, p. 1260 ff.; Markard/Truffer, 2008, p. 603 ff.).

The meso-level, the so called *socio-technical regime*, is an extension of Nelson/Winter's concept of 'technological regime'. While the 'technological regime' focuses on cognitive routines embodied in the engineers practices, the socio-technical regimes refer to a wider range of rules. As a consequence, the socio-technical regime takes into account more social groups. Thus, the technological trajectories are affected by a wider range of actors as, for example, policy makers and scientists (Geels, 2002, p. 1259 f.; Geels, 2006, p. 169 ff.). A re-definition of the concept 'technological regime' is given by Rip/Kemp (1998):

> 'A technological regime is the rule-set or grammar embedded in a complex of engineering practices, production process technologies, product characteristics, skills and procedures, ways of handling relevant artifacts and persons, ways of defining problems – all of them embedded in institutions and infrastructures.' (ibid., p. 338)

Taken together the technical regime *'[...] represents the selection environment for technological development in a certain field or sector [...]'* (Markard/Truffer, 2008, p. 603). It is the rule-set or grammar that is embedded, for instance, in the

8 For a detailed discussion of the concept see among others Kemp (1994) and Kemp/Schot/Hoogma (1998). This thesis focuses on the key characteristics of the concept and draws mainly on the elaborations of Geels (2002, 2004, 2006) and Markard/Truffer (2008).

knowledge bases or engineer practices. As such, the regime is characterised by 'dynamic stability' and refers to incumbent technologies. Innovation still takes place (dynamic perspective), but has an incremental nature (static perspective) (Hekkert et al. 2007, p. 415; Geels, 2006, p. 169 ff.).

At the micro-level the *niches* provide protected and isolated spaces for the development and use of new technologies ('incubation rooms'). Compared to the regimes they have less clear-cut rules. As a consequence, the search space is not restricted to certain directions. Thus, niches enable the generation and development of radical innovations separated from the pressure of the regime (Kemp/Schot/Hoogma, 1998, p. 185 ff.; Geels, 2002, p. 1260 ff.; Geels, 2004, p. 912 f.; Markard/Truffer, 2008, p. 603 ff.).

At the niche level the emergence of new technological innovations is highly affected by the existing regime. However, inside the protected spaces of the niches learning processes favour the specialisation in certain areas as well as the exploration of new functionalities. As a result, the rules of the niches are becoming more stable and enable the development of a dominant design. The diffusion of the new technology may lead to a competitive relationship with the existing regime. Moreover, the further adaption of the new technology may modify or replace the existing regime (Geels, 2006, pp. 172-177). The interplay of the different levels is illustrated in Figure 7.

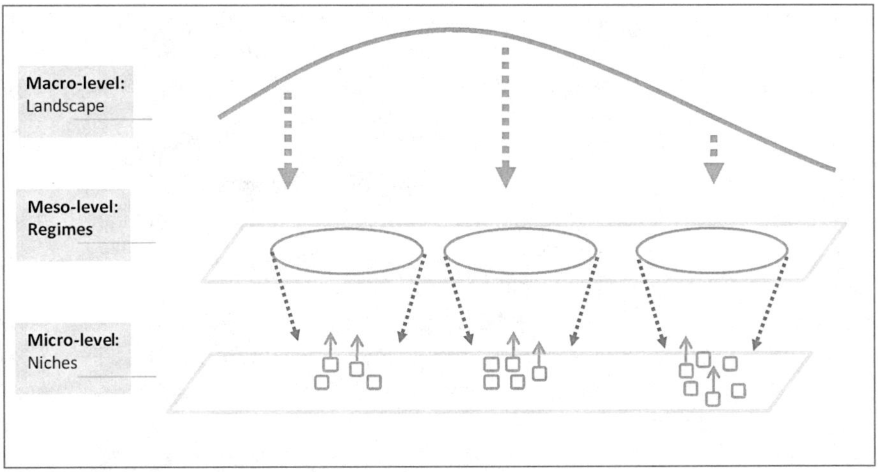

Figure 7: Multi-level framework
Source: cf. Geels, 2002, p. 1261, own illustration/extensions

The framework represents a nested hierarchy: The niches are embedded within regimes. Equally, the regimes are part of the landscape. As a consequence, the developments in the niches are shaped by the regimes and the landscape.

Changes at the landscape level can put pressure on the existing regimes. The landscape forces may weaken the structure of the regime by destroying the coherence of the existing knowledge base. Depending on the stability of the technological regime, radical innovations will slowly (strong regime) or rapidly (weak regime) diffuse beyond the niche level (Geels, 2002, p. 1257 ff.; Geels, 2006, p. 170 ff.).

II.3.5 Combining the multi-level framework and the systems of innovation approach

Recent contributions show that the systems of innovation approach (especially sectoral and technological innovation systems) and the socio-technical system are partly based on similar concepts. Coenen/Díaz López (2010) provide a systematic comparison of the different approaches. The key facts are presented in the following: With regard to the *system boundaries*, the comparison shows that the Sectoral Innovation System (SIS) and the Technological System (TS) have transcend geographical boundaries and involve multiple technologies (→SIS) or sectors (→TS). In contrast to this, the socio-technical (ST) concept is mainly restricted to national boundaries and encompasses multiple technologies and sectors. Turning the analysis to the *actors* the firm-centric perspective of the SIS and TS is emphasised. Non-firm organisations such as universities or local authorities play a minor role. Contrary, the ST-system consists of heterogeneous actors, conceptualised as social groups and focuses on the interactions within and between these social groups. There are also differences concerning the way *institutions* are treated in the systems of innovation approach and in the ST-system. While the SIS and TS comprise mainly a narrow set of regulative and cognitive institutions, the ST-regimes additionally take into account normative institutions. With regard to the *innovation process* and the *dynamics* of the concepts it has to be noted that the SIS, TS and ST-system show striking differences (ibid., pp. 1149-1158). The systems of innovation approach has been criticised for not taking into account the dynamics of technological change (Hekkert et al., 2007, p. 414). Technological change in sectoral innovation systems is mainly driven by the evolutionary processes of variety creation and selection. The emergence of new agents or technologies contributes to changes in the product and knowledge base of the sector. Thus, technological change is often path dependent and incremental (Malerba, 2005, p. 76 f.). The TS takes a more dynamic perspective by focusing on the generation, diffusion and utilisation of technologies (Carlsson/Stankiewicz, 1991, p. 111). The ST-system aims to explain technological transitions which take place through the interaction of the different system components: niche, regime, landscape (Coenen/Díaz López, 2010, p. 1154 ff.)

The previous contributions show that the different concepts show some similarities but also some differences. Furthermore, the innovation system approaches seem to correspond with specific components of the multi-level concept (Figure 8). These linkages are elaborated by Markard/Truffer (2008). They compare technological and sectoral innovation systems with the ST-concept by taking into account the different levels – niche, regime, landscape – of the framework. With regard to the *level of aggregation* they argue that sectoral innovation systems and regimes are defined at similar observation perspectives: they focus on the level of industries or sectors. However, Markard/Truffer (2008) stress that a SIS (which they label as Sectoral System of Innovation (SSI)) may encompass several regimes. Technological systems can be defined at different aggregation levels depending on the maturity of the technology. While mature technological systems may affect sectors and industries, emerging technological systems refer to different application contexts of the new technology. In contrast to this, the influence of niches is mostly restricted to one specific application context. Thus, technological systems may comprise more than one niche (ibid., p. 608 f.).

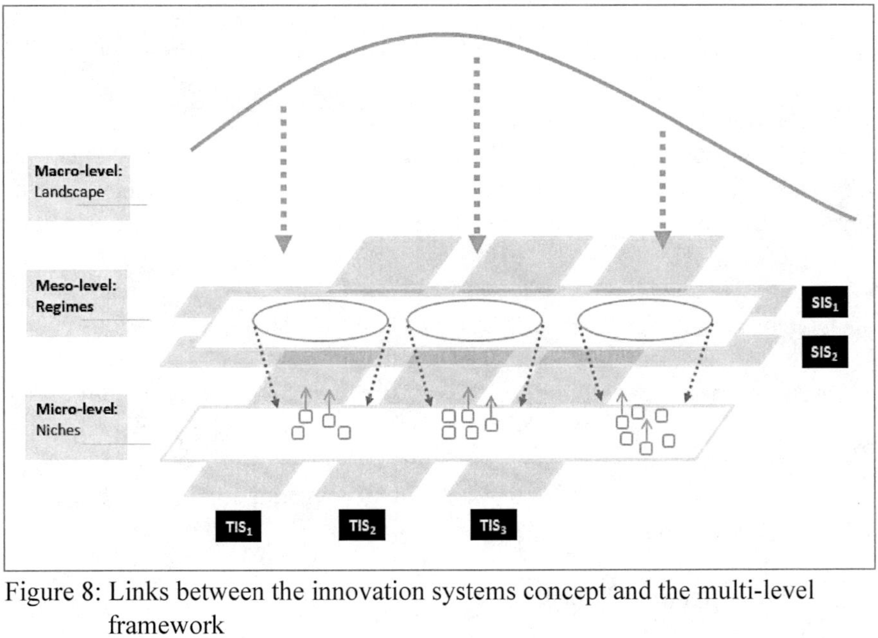

Figure 8: Links between the innovation systems concept and the multi-level framework

Source: cf. Markard/Truffer, p. 609 (adapted from Geels, 2002, p. 1261), own illustration/extensions

With regard to the *role for the innovation process*, the links are also less clear-cut. It is argued that the sectoral innovation system primarily focuses on incremental innovations, while the technological innovation systems include incremental as well as radical innovations (Markard/Truffer, 2008, p. 608 f.). However, it has to be noted that both concepts have an innovation part (focusing on the generation of new technologies) and a production part (referring to the use and diffusion of established technologies) (ibid., p. 599). By focusing on the innovation part the TS is rather similar to niches, providing protected spaces for the generation of new technologies (ibid., 2008, p. 608 f.).

The integrated framework of Markard/Truffer (2008) includes a particular notation of technological systems and includes niches, regimes and the landscapes as further factors in order to link the multi-level framework and the innovation system approach. The technological system is defined as:

> '[…] a set of networks of actors and institutions that jointly interact in a specific technological field and contribute to the generation, diffusion and utilization of variants of a new technology and/or a new product.' (Markard/Truffer, 2008, p. 611 f.)

This thesis adapts the framework of Markard/Truffer (2008) by putting the main emphasis on the different innovation systems and their interactions. The preceding theoretical contributions showed that the different aggregation levels cannot be regarded separated from each other. The developments that take place on the national level affect the technological activities in the sectoral and technological systems as well as specific application contexts of the technologies (niches). Conversely, it can be argued that radical technological developments in niches may shape the innovative activities of the technological and sectoral innovations systems. Such breakthrough innovations have the potential to change existing technological trajectories and paradigms. Moreover, they may have an impact upon the whole economy and therefore also affect the national innovation systems.

This thesis aims at bridging the different innovation systems by applying the integrated framework of Markard/Truffer (2008). Although the previous contributions pointed out that the links between the different systems are not always clear-cut, the multi-level framework seems to be appropriate in order to illustrate the interactions between the various systems of innovation. By combining the elements of the systems of innovation approach and the multi-level perspective, the strengths of both concepts are exploited. The integrated framework consists of the following building blocks:

- Niches or application contexts,
- socio-technical regimes,
- technological innovation systems and
- a landscape.

As noted earlier, the landscape at the macro-level refers to deep structural trends and entails the technological trajectories. The macro-level factors shape the technological developments of the regimes and the technological innovation systems, but are the other way round not affected by the technological changes which take place at lower hierarchy levels (Markard/Truffer, 2008, p. 613). In this context the landscape may refer to the national innovation system. The national technological trajectories can be seen as external factors shaping the technological developments of regimes and niches. For instance, new national policies concerning the patentability of medical procedures can affect the innovative activities in sectors (e.g. life sciences) and technologies (e.g. biotechnology).

Additionally, the cross-national and global dimension of technological activities pursued by R&D-intensive companies has to be taken into account. Although technological activities are less internationalised than, for instance, international trade activities, the national innovation systems are becoming global. Foreign R&D activities of large MNCs favour the production and diffusion of technology regardless of national borders (Niosi/Bellon, 1994, p. 176 f.; Carlsson, 2006). Thus, with regard to the international dimension of R&D activities, the landscape may also refer to the supra-national level of the European Community. It can be argued that European funding actions like COST (European Cooperation in Science and Technology)[9] have an impact on the technological activities within sectors and technological systems. Thus, in the context of this thesis the landscape is considered as a macro-level concept that detaches itself from the rigid borders of one particular innovation system. This offers the possibility to take into account structural effects which emerge at the national, supra-national or global level.[10]

Concerning the socio-technical regimes Markard/Truffer (2008) argue that the regimes definition of the MLP-framework is ambiguous. The concepts delineation is not clear-cut. Regimes can be defined at the level of sectors, sub-sectors and technologies. Thus, the regime level may refer to sectoral or technological innovation systems. As a consequence, the selection of the particular aggregation level should be oriented towards the research question (ibid., p. 606 f.). Within

9 The COST program was launched 1971 in order to strengthen the scientific and technical research collaborations in Europe. The project aims at coordination nationally funded research activities and, therefore, represents a building block of the European Research Area. For further information see Cost (2011) and www.cost.eu.

10 The impact of the supra-national or international environment has also been conceptualised as 'supra-national innovation system' or 'National Supersystem of Innovation (NSSI)'. For an overview of this topic see Niosi/Bellon (1994), Carlsson (2006) and Fromhold-Eisebith (2007).

the integrated framework the socio-technical regimes represent dominant production structures (ibid., p. 613).

The technological innovation system interacts with the socio-technological regimes as well as with other competing or complementary technological innovation systems. Technological developments in the technological innovation systems encompassing different application contexts of technologies ('niches') may influence the structures of the socio-technical regimes (Markard/Truffer, 2008, pp. 610-613). Especially radical breakthroughs in new emerging technologies (e.g. biotechnology) may have cross-sectoral impacts. The interactions of the various levels are illustrated in Figure 9.

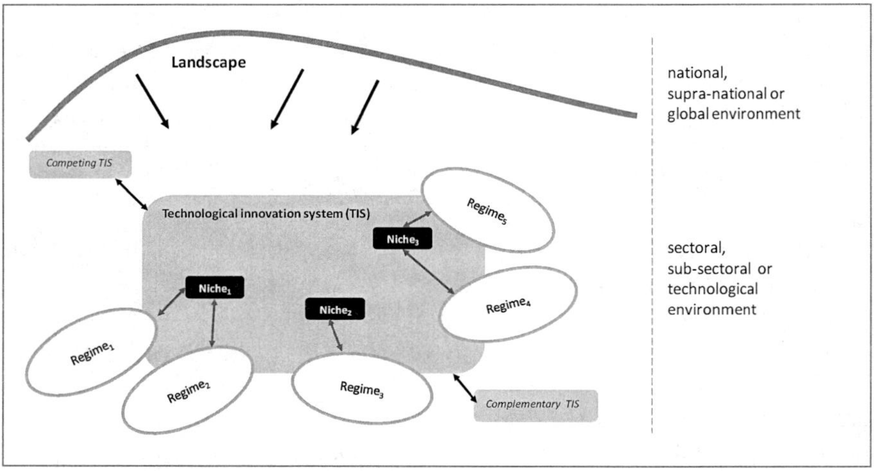

Figure 9: Multi-level dimension of the innovation systems approach
Source: cf. Markard/Truffer, 2008, p. 612, own illustration/extensions

In the light of the above mentioned, it shows that compared to the 'traditional' systems of innovation approaches, the multi-level perspective is more suitable to capture the dynamics of technological change. The framework makes it possible to take into account technological, sectoral and national innovation activities in their entirety and addresses explicitly the interactions between the various aggregation levels. Furthermore, the combined framework of Markard/Truffer (2008), which encompasses elements of the multi-level perspective and the innovation systems approach, allows departing from the rigid borders of recent concepts.

In the context of this thesis the integrated framework is adapted in order to provide a dynamic view of the technological change in the life sciences industry. While the innovation systems approach takes a quasi-static perspective which might neglect the dynamic nature of technological change, this dissertation investigates the evolution of technological profiles in the life sciences industry from a multi-level perspective. Aim is to take into account the dynamic interactions between the technological, sectoral and national environment.

II.4 Research theses

Based on the preceding theoretical contributions of *Chapter II*, the research theses can be formulated. These theses may serve as guidelines for the empirical analyses.

Thesis 1: **The evolution of technological profiles is a path dependent process.**
Changes in the technological profiles are supposed to be incremental and cumulative.

Chapter II + III

Thesis 1 argues that the technology portfolio of firms and nations will evolve in a technologically coherent way. New technologies will build upon the existing technological competences and the 'historically' developed core competences will be maintained.

Thesis 2: **Different innovation systems have an impact on the evolution of technological profiles.**

Thesis 2a: The national innovation system has an impact on the evolution of the national technological trajectories. Thus, the technological profiles of different countries are characterised by distinct technological specialisation patterns.

Chapter II

Thesis 2b: Large R&D-intensive companies are embedded in different innovation environments. Hence, it can be assumed that the technological profiles of these companies are shaped by national, sectoral and technological innovation systems.

Chapter III + IV

Thesis 2a argues that the technological developments at the country level are shaped by the national environment. By turning the focus on the firm level *Thesis 2b* assumes that large MTCs span their innovative activities over different countries, sectors and technologies. As a consequence, different innovation systems may have an influence on the development of the corporate technological competences.

The evolution of the national technological trajectories in the life sciences is explored in *Chapter II.6.* Aim is to show the path dependent development of the technological competences. Furthermore, the thesis attempts to identify the similarities and dissimilarities in the technology portfolios of different countries. In advance, the used methodological framework is introduced in *Chapter II.5*.

II.5 Methodological framework

> 'Patent statistics have one compelling advantage over alternative indexes of technological activity: availability in great abundance. Yearly counts are readily obtained for a span of more than a century, either in aggregated form or broken down by class of invention or sponsoring firm.' (Comanor/Scherer, 1969, p. 392)

In order to identify the technological portfolios of countries or companies as well as their evolution over time an adequate indicator that allows tracing the technological competence portfolios has to be determined (see among others Fai, 2003, p. 29; Stephan, 2003, pp. 174-189; Stohr, 2007). This section discusses three different indicators that can be used as proxy for technological innovation. Furthermore, a technological classification system that enables the allocation of technological activities to technological classes is introduced.

II.5.1 Indicators of technological innovation

A general variable which captures innovative activities does not exist. Thus, to measure the technological activities of countries or companies adequate indicators have to be determined. In general, two levels of consideration are distinguished: the input and the output level (see Figure 10).[11]

The input level covers resources which can contribute to the development of the technology base. In contrast to this, the output level considers the results of technological activities. R&D expenditures and educational statistics are the most important input indicators. Common used output indicators to measure technological activities are patent documents (see among others Grupp, 1997,

11 For a detailed overview see Grupp (1997), p. 143 ff.

p. 143 ff.; Stephan, 2003, p. 174 ff.; Fai, 2003, p. 29 ff.). Furthermore, a number of studies draw on the patent stocks of companies in order to assess their technological diversification (Archibugi, 1992, p. 362).

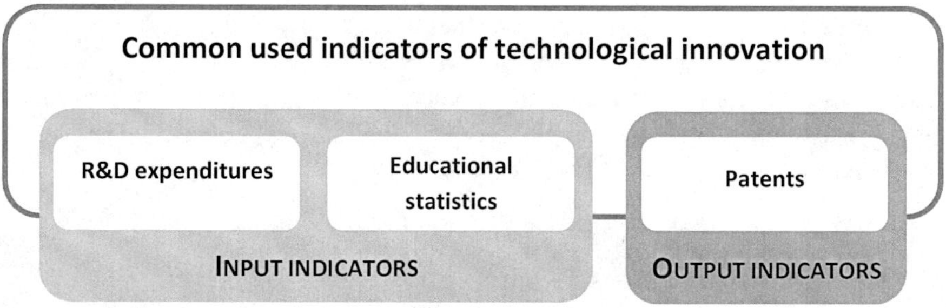

Figure 10: Indicators of technological innovation
Source: own illustration

II.5.1.1 R&D expenditures

R&D expenditures are one of the most common used input indicators of technological innovation. They represent financial investments which are spent on the development of technological competences. If published at the technology or industry level they can be used to assess the breadth of the technological competences of countries, industries or companies (Jacobsson/Oskarsson/Philipson, 1996, p. 574; Stephan, 2003, p. 175).

Kodama (1986) introduces R&D expenditures as indicator of technological diversification. Based on the Japanese 'Survey of Research and Development', which disaggregates R&D expenditures into 31 product fields, he studies the technology diversification of the Japanese industry.[12]

However, as any other indicator of technological change, R&D surveys have also some shortcomings. Normally, R&D data represent only those expenses which are directly linked to R&D departments. Thus, these data neglect expenses which are not classified as formal R&D (Pavitt, 1982, p. 35). Patel/Pavitt (1994b) also note that R&D expenditures are often only reported for the company's or industry's main product areas.

> '[...] they neglect both the range and specific mix of technologies necessary to develop and make any particular class of product.' (Patel/Pavitt, 1994b, p. 543)

12 The survey reports the R&D expenses of Japanese companies with a capital of at least 100 million yen.

Furthermore, in practice, R&D statistics are only rarely available. Until the 1990s most of the European countries were not forced to publish data about R&D expenditures. Hence, it is not possible to trace long time developments of technological change (Stephan, 2003, p. 175 f.). Additionally, R&D data neglect a large part of the technological activities undertaken by small- and medium-sized companies.[13] However, the main disadvantage of R&D data is that they are often only available at the aggregated company level and not at the technology level. Thus, they are not suitable for studying the technological profiles of companies (Breschi/Lissoni/Malerba, 2004, p. 72).

II.5.1.2 Educational statistics

Jacobsson/Oskarsson (1995) introduced educational statistics as indicators of technological activities under the assumption that staff with higher education in engineering and science is the main carrier of technological knowledge. By using different educational categories the educational counts are employed to measure the breadth of the technology base.

Following Jacobsson/Oskarsson (1995) educational statistics have the following advantages: Compared to other indicators, educational statistics take into account the technological activities which cannot directly be linked to formal R&D. Furthermore, they also reflect the tacit knowledge embodied in the staff, which cannot or only partly be captured by patent applications and scientific publications (ibid., p. 129).

However, educational statistics do also have the following weaknesses: It is assumed that the substitutability of engineers and scientists from different areas is limited. This assumption neglects that the employees are characterised by different kinds of educational knowledge. While some engineers (i.e. engineering physicists) may have a broad education and can be employed in different areas, others may possess specialised knowledge in certain technologies. Additionally, it has to be mentioned that engineers can enhance their technological competences and work in tasks which are not directly linked with their original education. Thus, the deviation between the original education and the actual tasks increases over time (Granstrand/Oskarsson, 1994, p. 357; Jacobsson/Oskarsson, 1995, p. 128 f.).

Another weakness of engineer counts is their limited availability. Educational statistics are not collected for all countries and companies. Furthermore, these data are usually provided at the very aggregated level. Jacobsson/Oskarsson

13 Following Patel/Pavitt (1994b) R&D statistics neglect up to 40% of the technological efforts made by small firms or firms acting outside science-based industries.

(1995), for instance, distinguish only between nine different educational classes. Thus, based on educational counts, it is not possible to assess the breadth of the technology base in detail (Fai, 2003, p. 32; Stephan, 2003, p. 177 f.).

II.5.1.3 Patent data

Most of the existing studies attempt to capture the technological activities of firms and nations by using patent data. Patents are one of the most comprehensive data sources on technological activities. They reflect the technological competencies which have been established in specific technological classes.

> '[…] as long as a company applies for a patent to protect the output of its own research efforts, this means that such a company is very close to the technological frontier of the chosen field.' (Breschi/Lissoni/Malerba, 2004, p. 72)

Compared to other indicators patents have numerous advantages (see among others Pavitt, 1985; Basberg, 1987; Griliches, 1990; Stephan, 2003; Breschi/ Lissoni/Malerba, 2004):

Patent applications are published 18 months after the application or priority date.[14] This means that patent data provide actual information about the technological inventions of companies (Schmoch, 1990, p. 12). Furthermore, patent data are available in large numbers and for quite long time periods. I.e. they can be used to capture the temporal changes in the technology profiles of firms, industries and nations (Archibugi 1992, p. 358; Fai, 2003, p. 34).

Compared to other indicators, like R&D surveys, patent data provide information on innovative activities at a much more disaggregated, technical level due to the detailed classification scheme of the International Patent Classification (IPC). Thus, the technology base of firms and nations can be illustrated at different levels of aggregation. This is particularly important when the technological strengths of specialised companies should be described in detail (Schmoch, 1990, p. 161). Patent data also offer information on the geography of R&D activities. Each patent document contains the names and addresses of the applicants and inventors. Based on this geographical information the technological profiles of different nations can be compared (Archibugi, 1992, p. 358; Zander, 1997, p. 211).

Like any indicator patents have also some shortcomings (see among others: Basberg, 1987; Narin/Noma/Perry, 1987; Argyres, 1996; Grupp, 1997, p. 158 f.; Stephan, 2003, p. 174 ff.; Cantwell, 2004). Patents cover only certain innovations and therefore cannot depict the whole technology base of firms or nations.

14 The priority date is the date of the first application (Schmoch, 1999, p. 120).

Some inventions – like medical therapeutic methods or software - are not patentable, because they are not directly linked to technological processes and products (Schmoch, 1990, p. 16; Archibugi, 1992, p. 358; Grupp, 1997, p. 161).

Additionally, inventors are faced with the choice of either applying for a patent or keeping their invention secret.[15] Furthermore, they can protect their inventions by other methods such as trade secrets, so that not all discoveries are patented.[16] As a consequence, the propensity to patent, i.e. the use of patents to protect against imitation, differs across industries, firms and technologies (Basberg, 1987, p. 133 f.; Comanor/Scherer, 1969, p. 393). The pharmaceutical industry, for instance, is characterised by a high propensity to patent, while electrical engineering firms tend to patent fewer (Argyres, 1996, p. 402). Thus, at the industry level, this problem can be tackled by analysing industries with a high propensity to patent. At the firm level a different attitude towards patenting is more significant, when firms from different industries are compared. It can be assumed that firms of the same industry have a similar propensity to patent. However, it has to be mentioned that a company's propensity to patent also varies with regard to different technological fields. To face this problem at the industry level an indicator of relative specialisation can be used (Cantwell, 2004, p. 272).

Patents do also differ in their economic value (see among others Comanor/ Scherer, 1969, p. 393). While some inventions are close to the technological frontier and have a high economic and commercial value, others only reflect incremental improvements of existing technologies. To deal with this problem it is common to consider patent applications at international patent offices (e.g. European Patent Office (EPO), World Intellectual Property Organization (WIPO)). Applications at these offices provide patent protection for several countries and are therefore associated with high costs. Hence, it can be assumed that only inventions with a certain economic value are applied for at these offices (Basberg, 1987, p. 135 ff.; Schmoch et al. 1988, p. 30 f.). Additionally, it has to be stated that the economic value of a patent is not that relevant if the breadth of a technology portfolio is assessed. Furthermore, irrespective of the 'patent quality' shifts in the distribution of patent activities across different technologies can provide important information about changes in the technological trajectories. In this context, it can be assumed that the economic significance of a

15 One example is the recipe of 'Coca-Cola' which has been secrecy for many years (Archibugi, 1992, p. 359).

16 There are also other factors which might affect the choice between patenting or secrecy: the expected life of the invention or its economic value (for a detailed discussion see Basberg, 1987, p. 133 f.).

patent plays a minor role by assessing technological specialisation and diversification patterns (Cantwell, 2004, p. 272).

Previous remarks show that patent data have their strengths and weaknesses. However, compared to other technological indicators they have one main advantage: their availability in great abundance (Comanor/Scherer, 1969, p. 392).

> 'In spite of all the difficulties, patents statistics remain a unique source for the analysis of the process of technical change. Nothing else even comes close in the quantity of available data, accessibility, and the potential industrial, organizational, and technological detail.' (Griliches, 1990, p. 1702)

II.5.2 Technology classification scheme

Patents were categorised based on the International Patent Classification (IPC). The IPC is a hierarchical classification scheme (see Figure 11) distinguishing eight sections on the highest level of aggregation which can be further divided into classes, sub-classes, groups and sub-groups (Schmoch, 1990, p. 42 f.).

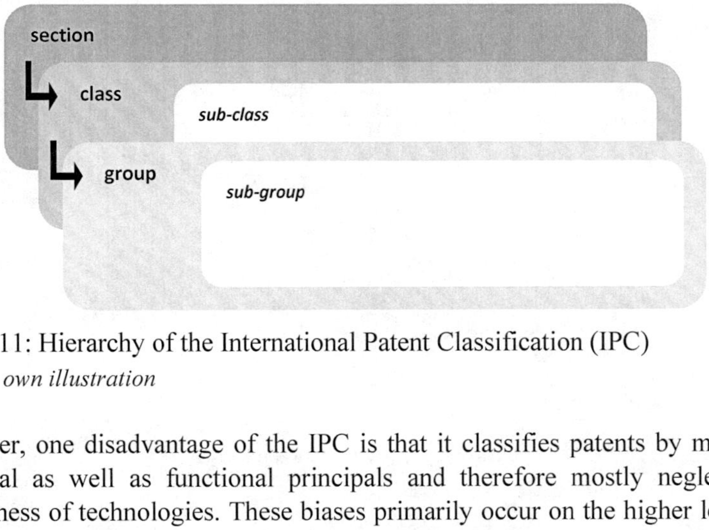

Figure 11: Hierarchy of the International Patent Classification (IPC)
Source: own illustration

However, one disadvantage of the IPC is that it classifies patents by means of technical as well as functional principals and therefore mostly neglects the relatedness of technologies. These biases primarily occur on the higher levels of aggregation, while the classification at the finer levels seems to be more homogenous. Thus, the IPC can be used to determine the breadth of a knowledge base but not their relatedness (Stephan, 2003, p. 188 f.).

For this purpose, a technology-oriented classification scheme based on the IPC codes, the so called *OST/INPI/ISI concordance,* can be used. The original version of the classification scheme was jointly elaborated by experts of the

Observatoire des Sciences et des Techniques (OST), the Institut National de la Propriété Industrielle (INPI) and the Fraunhofer-ISI in 1997.[17] In 2006, the IPC has faced substantial changes in its 8th edition. These changes concerned also the introduction of new IPC codes which were not included in the original *OST/INPI/ISI concordance*. Hence, this thesis uses a revised version of the classification scheme: the *WIPO IPC Technology Concordance Table.*[18] The current version of the technology classification distinguishes 35 technological classes and five technological fields (Figure 12).

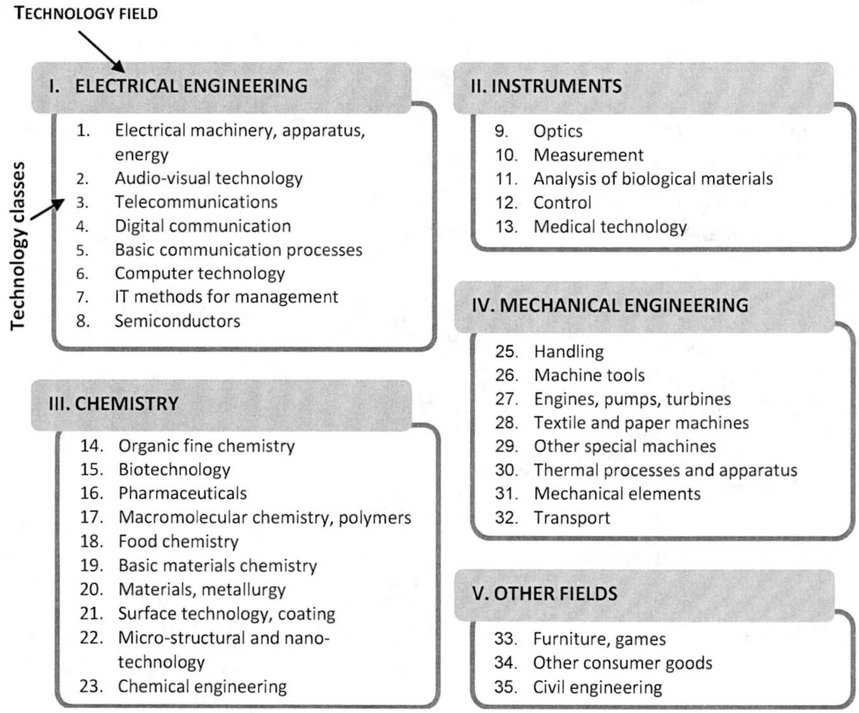

Figure 12: WIPO IPC Technology Concordance Table
Source: own illustration

Technological classes of the same technological field are more related than technological classes belonging to different technological fields. Thus, this classification scheme makes it possible to take into account the technological relatedness of patents (Stephan, 2003, p. 189).

17 For more details see Hinze/Reiss/Schmoch (1997).
18 For more details see Schmoch (2008) and *Annex I.*

II.6 National technological trajectories in the life sciences

> 'Life sciences encompass different scientific fields such as biology, chemistry, physics, medical technology, pharmaceutics, information technology, nutritional service, environmental technology. Life sciences advances, for example in the field of biotechnology, resulted in new disciplines such as genetic engineering, and promise innovative solutions to fundamental challenges related to medicine, food, agriculture and environment.' (WIPO, 2011)

During the last years the life sciences have faced some remarkable changes due to the evolution of biotechnology. Innovation economists describe biotechnology as one of the most innovatory technologies which have evolved at the end of the 20th century. They define biotechnology as a new technological paradigm encompassing a variety of new technological trajectories. As a consequence, the evolution of biotechnology has affected the knowledge bases of several sectors (Russel 1999, p. 236 f.). Most prominent are the changes which have taken place in pharmaceutical R&D (Malerba/Orsenigo, 2002, p. 668; Schweizer, 2002, p. 41 f.). Modern biotechnology became the dominant technology in pharmaceuticals in the 1970s and led to dramatically changes in the drug discovery process. As biotechnology covers a wide range of applications, the benefits resulting from this technology are widespread and affect different areas like pharmaceuticals, fine chemicals and agriculture (Russel, 1999, p. 236 ff.). In addition, the advances in modern biotechnology have an influence on food producers and manufacturers of laboratory equipment as well as on environmental technology (Menrad, 2005, p. 35 f.). In this sense, biotechnology embodies the characteristics of a platform or key technology with cross-sectoral impacts (Russel, 1999, p. 236). Furthermore, Enriquez/Goldberg (2000) assume that the boundaries between the different sectors will blur. This development trend has already taken place in the agricultural seed business. At the beginning the seed companies sold genetically modified seeds, which promised to be resistant to common varmints, to agricultural companies. These genetically designed plants suddenly represented a threat to the pesticide and herbicide business of the chemical industry. As a consequence, the chemical companies reacted promptly with investments into the seed business and a scientific shift towards biotechnology. By recognising that the genetic engineering can also design crops with higher nutritional or medicinal value pharmaceutical companies perceived genetically modified seeds as a threat. Not surprisingly, also large pharmaceutical players like Novartis began to invest in the agricultural seeds business. This example shows that the advantages in modern biotechnology led to the convergence of the pharmaceutical, agriculture and chemical industry. Furthermore, it can be assumed that the breakthroughs in genetic engineering do also affect other industries like food processing and environmental mining (ibid., p. 96 ff.).

The main characteristics of the life sciences industry are the following:

a) *Structural changes in the life sciences:*
The scientific breakthroughs in modern biotechnology affected numerous industries. Especially, for the pharmaceutical industry the new technology opened enormous opportunities. The advent of biotechnology has modified the industry structure by pushing new agents (new biotechnology firms (NBFs)) onto the market. These companies often represented university spin-offs or collaborations between scientists, characterised by specific knowledge in the new scientific disciplines. One major problem for these companies, however, was the lack of competencies in the marketing and approval of new drugs. The market entry of these firms was purely science driven, i.e. most of these NBFs are specialised in specific research niches and lack the resources to market new products. In contrast to this, large established pharmaceutical companies are fully integrated, i.e. they are able to manage all stages in the innovation process (from drug discovery to marketing).[19] However, the adoption of the new technologies was a slow and difficult process requiring shifts in the established knowledge base. As a result, numerous collaborations between NBFs and established pharmaceutical companies evolved (Grabwoski/Vernon, 1994; McKelvey/Orsenigo, 2001, pp. 27-31; Cockburn, 2004, pp. 13-16; Mckelvey/Orsenigo/Pammolli, 2004, pp. 92-95). Thus, on the one hand the advent of biotechnology brought forward specialised biotechnology firms, on the other hand pharmaceutical MTCs were forced to extend their knowledge bases.

b) *Changes in the drug discovery process:*
Through the revolution in the life sciences the development of new drugs became more science intensive. The nature of the research activities changed completely from 'random screening' to 'rational drug design'. Traditionally, the biological causes of specific diseases were often unknown. As a consequence, chemical derived compounds had to be screened for potential therapeutic activities. During this research area the introduction and discovery of new chemical entities (NCEs) was a time-consuming, expensive and serendipitous process. To protect new and promising 'blockbuster' drugs the pharmaceutical companies relied heavily on patent rights. Nowadays, modern biotechnology enables a more structured, science-guided rational drug design. The revolution in the life sciences brought forward new research techniques like high-throughput screening (HTS) and combinatorial

19 Most of these are long-lived and their origins go back to the chemical industry in the 19th century (Cockburn, 2004, p. 14).

chemistry as well as bioinformatics.[20] These research techniques make it possible to screen thousands of components with high speed (McKelvey/ Orsenigo/Pammolli, 2004, pp. 78-91; Schweizer, 2002, pp. 42-45).

c) *Patent protection:*
The life sciences industry is one of the most research-intensive and innovative sectors. Especially, the pharmaceutical industry spends large amounts for the research and development of new drugs. Furthermore, as stated by Cockburn (2004), investments in R&D have continuously increased during the last decades. The development of new drugs has become more expensive. In order to protect the expensive inventions, the industry relies heavily on patent protection. As reported by Mansfield (1986), 60% of the pharmaceutical inventions would not have been developed in the absence of the patent protection. His contribution shows that the pharmaceutical as well as the chemical industry have a high propensity to patent. In these industries more than 80% of the patentable inventions were patented (Mansfield, 1986; Scherer, 2000, p. 1316-1318; Cockburn, 2004).

Concluding it can be said that that the life sciences industry is for several reasons an interesting object for studying the evolution of technological profiles.

First, the life sciences industry is a highly R&D- and knowledge-intensive industry. It is therefore possible to trace the technological developments of this industry using patent data (Malerba/Orsenigo, 2002, p. 668; Krafft/Quatraro/ Saviotti, 2009, p. 3).

Second, the life sciences industry has faced remarkable changes due to the evolution of modern biotechnology. Previous considerations have stressed that modern biotechnology acts as platform technology which affects the innovative activities of different sectors. Thus, modern biotechnology represents a new technological system influencing the technological development patterns in related industries.

Third, the life sciences industry is affected by a variety of institutional factors. This entails, for instance, different forms of regulation as well as the organisation of the public research systems (Malerba/Orsenigo, 2002, p. 668). As a consequence, the life sciences industry is especially suitable for studying the influence

20 The high-throughput screening (HTS) methods enable the vast automatic screening of compounds. Combinatorial chemistry is used to test chemical variations from molecular entities in order to identify potential lead compounds. Bioinformatics enable the screening of DNA (desoxyribo-nucleic acid) sequences (McKelvey/Orsenigo/Pammolli, 2004, p. 90 f.; Schweizer, 2002, p. 43).

of technological, sectoral and national innovation systems on the technological diversification patterns of firms.

II.6.1 Database and sample

The technological paradigms and trajectories in the life sciences will be determined by using patent data. The starting point for the analysis is therefore the definition of life sciences patents. I.e. the subset of relevant technological classes or IPC classes that define the life sciences has to be determined. Following Hinze/Gaisser (2003) the life sciences comprise seven technological classes of the *OST/INPI/ISI concordance* (cf. *Chapter II.5.2*): *Biotechnology; Environmental technology*; *Pharmaceuticals, cosmetics; Medical technology*; *Agriculture, food chemistry*; *Agricultural and food machinery apparatus* as well as parts of the technology class *Chemical industry and petrol industry, basic materials chemistry* (ibid., p. 6 f.).

Using the *WIPO IPC Technology Concordance*, the revised version of the *OST/INPI/ISI concordance* table, I received an update version of this initial set of technological classes (Figure 13). The life sciences then contain the classes: *Medical technology; Biotechnology; Pharmaceuticals; Food chemistry; Environmental technology; Other special machines* and parts of *Basic materials chemistry*.[21]

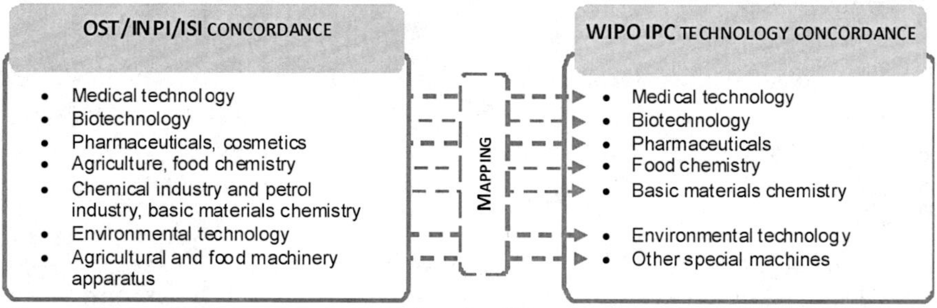

Figure 13: Technology classes defining the life sciences industry
Source: own illustration

21 Some IPCs of the former technology class *Agricultural and food machinery and apparatus* are now listed in the class *Other special machines*.

Building on these technological classes the set of relevant IPC classes can be defined.[22] These queries were used in order to extract the relevant set of patents from the EPO Worldwide Statistical Patent Database (PATSTAT October 2007). The initial data set includes EU and worldwide applications at the EPO and WIPO and covers the period from 1986 to 2005. The delimitations of the time periods were done by using the priority date of the patent. This approach has the advantage that the data are closely related to the R&D investments and the invention (Schmoch, 1999, p. 120). To control for cyclical fluctuations the whole period is divided into four sub-periods (1986/1990, 1991/1995, 1996/2000, 2001/2005). Patents were assigned to the countries in which the inventor has his residence. If a patent has more than one inventor, a proportional fraction of the patent is assigned to each inventor's country of residence.

II.6.2 Technological performance in the life sciences

In the following the evolution of the technological profiles in the life sciences industry is investigated. For this purpose, a large patent data set, comprising the worldwide patent applications in the life sciences as well as the patent applications of single European countries, has been compiled. The aim of this subsection is to provide a general overview of the technological activities in the life sciences industry during the period 1986-2005.

Figure 14 illustrates the trends in the worldwide patent applications in comparison to the patent output of Europe's leading countries. The sample of European countries is restricted to the six countries which have accounted for the largest amount of patents during the period 1986-2005: Germany, France, Italy, the Netherlands, Switzerland and the United Kingdom.

Worldwide a total of 414,787 patents have been generated. Furthermore, over the time horizon considered, the worldwide amount of patents has continuously increased, ranging from 10,000 patents per year in 1986 to about 35,000 patents in 2005 (Figure 14, primary axis, black line). Analogous to the worldwide pattern the European countries (secondary axis, coloured lines) have continuously expanded their technological activities in the life sciences. Especially Germany is characterised by high growth rates and clearly dominates the technological activities in Europe.

22 The complete list of all IPCs defining the life sciences is reported in *Annex II*.

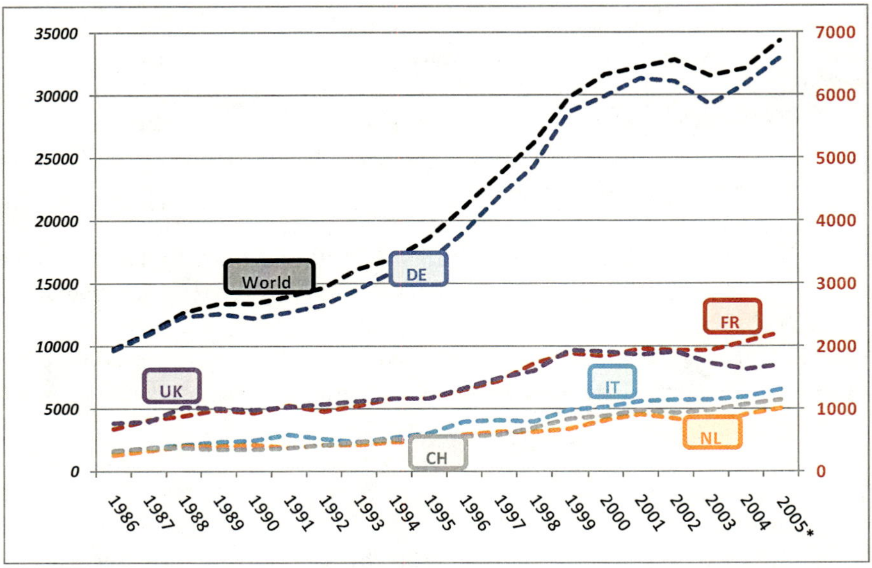

Figure 14: Development of patent output in the life sciences industry

Source: PATSTAT October 2007, own computations

* Estimated value, calculated on average growth rates between 1986-2004

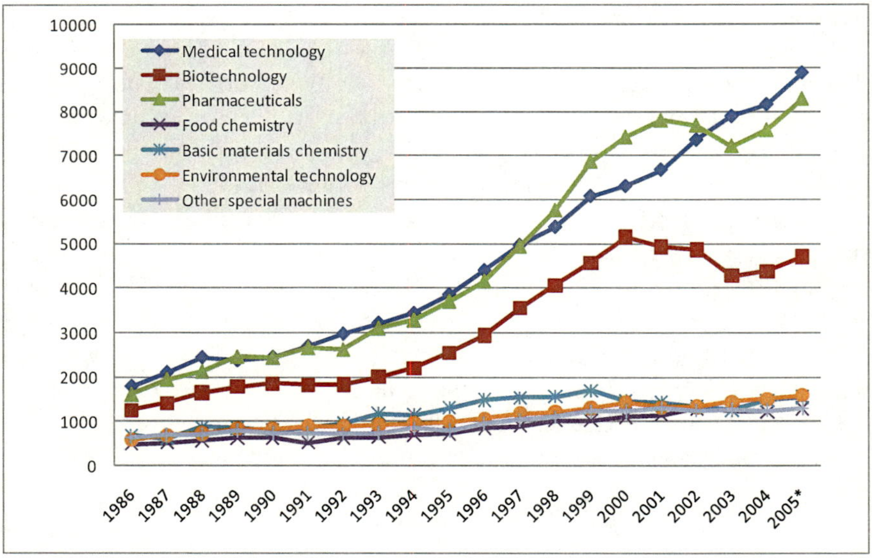

Figure 15: Development of patent output in specific life sciences technologies

Source: PATSTAT October 2007, own computations

* Estimated value, calculated on average growth rates between 1986-2004

Figure 15 illustrates the evolution of the patent activities in specific life sciences technologies. The classes *Medical technology, Pharmaceuticals* and *Biotechnology* dominate the technological activities of the six sample countries with average annual growth rates between 8% and 9%. The remaining technologies *(Food chemistry, Basic materials chemistry, Environmental technology* and *Other special machines)* also show a slight increase in the patent output and account for growth rates between 4% and 6%.

In the following the developments in the sample countries are investigated. Figure 16 reports for each technology the share in worldwide patent applications at the country level during the period 1986-2005.

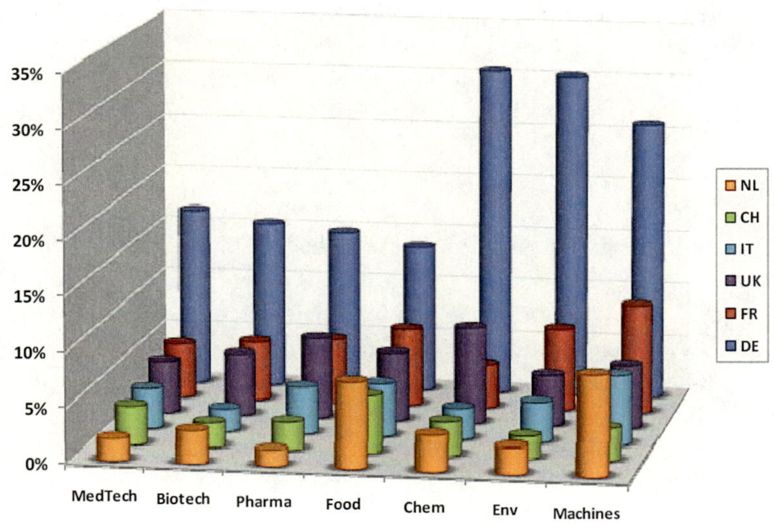

MedTech	Medical technology	**Chem**	Basic materials chemistry
Pharma	Pharmaceuticals	**Env**	Environmental technology
Biotech	Biotechnology	**Machines**	Other special machines
Food	Food chemistry		

Figure 16: Patent output in specific life sciences technologies during the period 1986-2005 (country level)

Source: PATSTAT October 2007, own computations

Germany dominates the patent output in all technological classes. The highest patent shares (ranging from 26% to 31% of the worldwide patent output) are achieved in the classes *Basic materials chemistry, Environmental technology* and *Other special machines*. The patent output in the remaining classes ranges between 14% and 15%. France and the United Kingdom follow in terms of technological performance although their patent output in the different life sciences technologies is comparatively low ranging from 4% to 10% of the total patent output. Italy, Switzerland and the Netherlands show the lowest patent shares in all technological classes. There is one exception: The Netherlands are doing comparatively well in the classes *Food chemistry* and *Other special machines* (8% to 9% of the worldwide patent output).

II.6.3 Tracing technological trajectories using knowledge base indicators

In this section the evolution of the knowledge base in the life sciences is investigated. *Chapter II.6.3.1* presents the dynamics of the technological classes in the six sample countries. The structural changes in the knowledge bases are analysed in *Chapter II.6.3.2.* For this purpose, three different knowledge base indicators which proxy the characteristics of the knowledge base were introduced.

II.6.3.1 Evolution of the knowledge base in the life sciences

As already pointed out in *Chapter II.5.2*, all patent applications are classified by IPC codes. Additionally this study uses the *WIPO IPC Technology Concordance Table* to assign each IPC code to one of the 35 different technological classes. Because all patent applications are classified by one or more IPC codes, they can be assigned to one or more technology classes (see Figure 17).

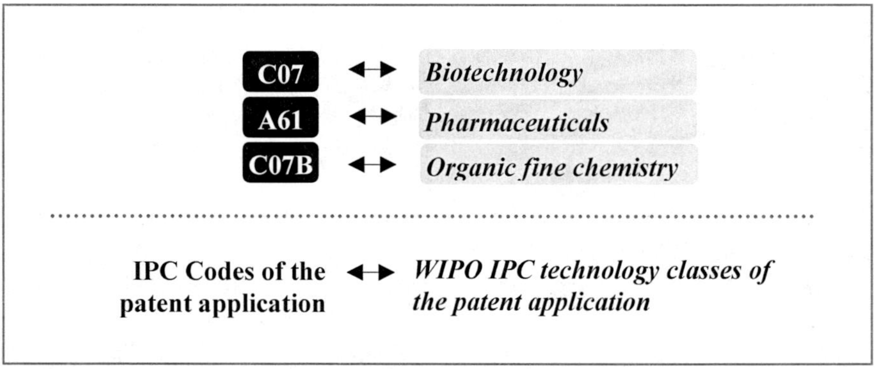

Figure 17: Assigning IPC codes to technological classes
Source: own illustration

The joint occurrence of different technology codes (IPC codes or WIPO IPC technology classes respectively) in the same patent application indicates that these technologies are related. It can be assumed that the more two technologies co-occur, the lower is the technological distance between the respective technologies (Breschi/Lissoni/Malerba, 2003, p. 77). The co-occurrence[23] of IPCs can be used to describe the evolution of the knowledge base (Krafft/Quatraro/Saviotti, 2009).

The knowledge base matrix C of country k is then defined as:

$$C_k = \begin{bmatrix} c_{11} & \cdots & c_{1n} \\ c_{12} & \cdots & c_{2n} \\ \vdots & \ddots & \vdots \\ c_{1n} & \cdots & c_{nn} \end{bmatrix} \qquad \text{(II.1)}$$

where c_{ij} is the number of patents which are affiliated to technology i and j. Thus, the non-diagonal terms represent the number of co-occurrences of technology i and j.

Worldwide patterns

Figure 18 illustrates the worldwide technology co-occurrences in the life sciences industry. The whole time period (1986-2005) is divided into four sub-periods in order to show how the relationships among the different technology classes have evolved over time. Each period represents the accumulated number of co-occurrences during the respective time frame.

23 In the following the term co-occurrence refers to the pairwise occurrence of two technologies.

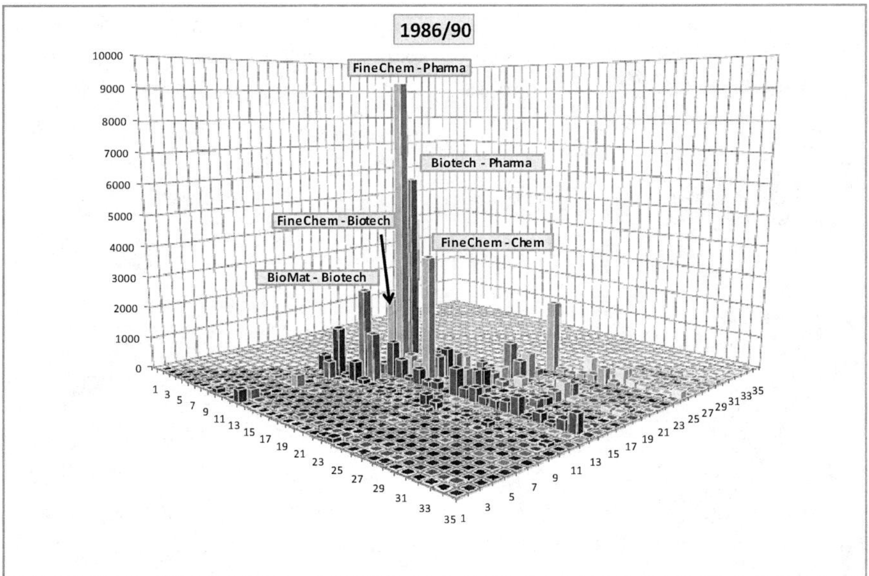

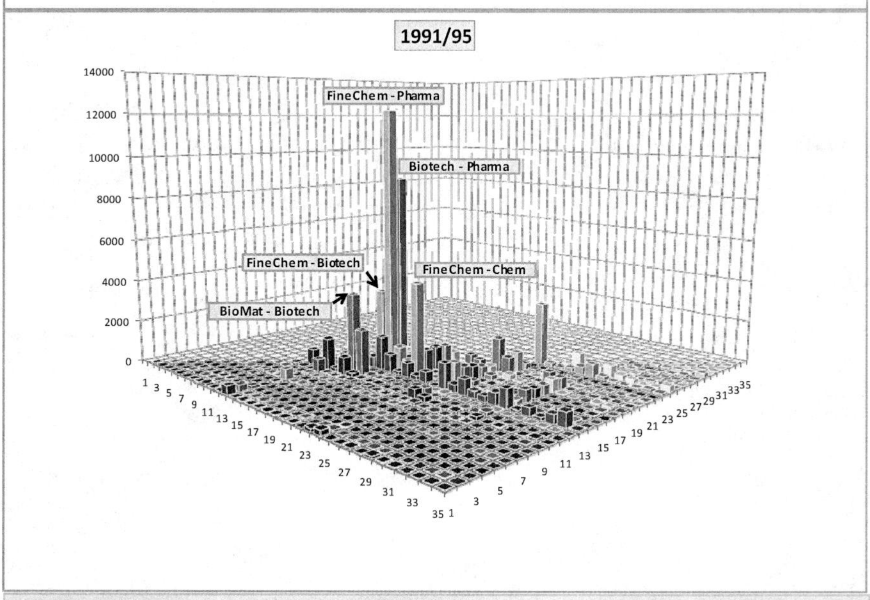

Legend:

BioMat	Analysis of biological materials	**Chem**	Basic materials chemistry
Biotech	Biotechnology	**FineChem**	Organic fine chemistry
Pharma	Pharmaceuticals		

Figure 18: Matrices of technology co-occurrences

Source: PATSTAT October 2007, own computations

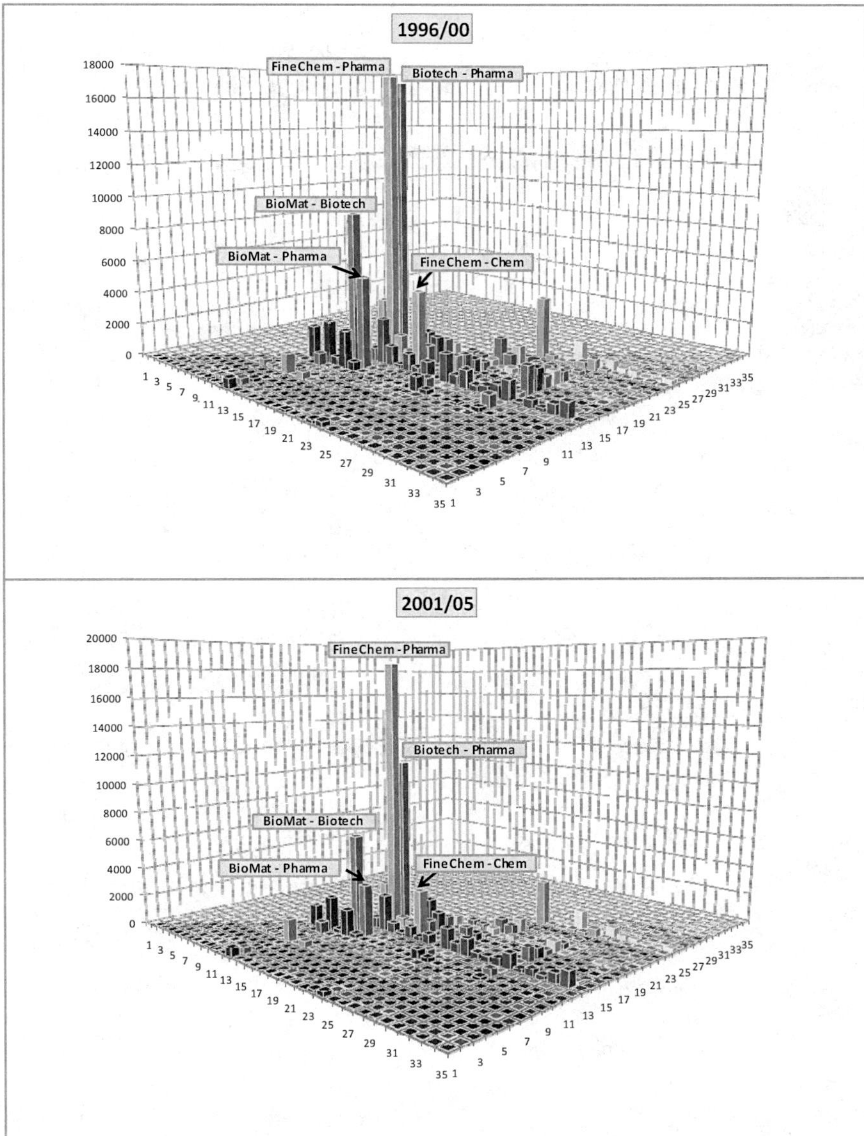

Legend:

BioMat	Analysis of biological materials	**Chem**	Basic materials chemistry
Biotech	Biotechnology	**FineChem**	Organic fine chemistry
Pharma	Pharmaceuticals		

Figure 18: Matrices of technology co-occurrences (continued)

Source: PATSTAT October 2007, own computations

The five most frequent technology co-occurrences of the four time periods are reported in Table 1.

Table 1: Dominant technology combinations in worldwide patent applications
Source: PATSTAT October 2007, own computations

	1.	2.	3.	4.	5.
1986/90	FineChem - Pharma	Biotech - Pharma	FineChem - Chem	BioMat - Biotech	FineChem - Biotech
1991/95	FineChem - Pharma	Biotech - Pharma	FineChem - Chem	BioMat - Biotech	FineChem - Biotech
1996/00	FineChem - Pharma	Biotech - Pharma	**BioMat - Biotech** ↑	**BioMat - Pharma** ↑	**FineChem - Chem** ↓
2001/05	FineChem - Pharma	Biotech - Pharma	BioMat - Biotech	BioMat - Pharma	FineChem - Chem

Legend:

BioMat	Analysis of biological materials	**Chem**	Basic materials chemistry
Biotech	Biotechnology	**MedTech**	Medical technology
FineChem	Organic fine chemistry	**Pharma**	Pharmaceuticals

Between 1986 and 2005 the knowledge base in the life sciences is dominated by two technology combinations: *Organic fine Chemistry - Pharmaceuticals* as well as *Biotechnology - Pharmaceuticals*. Thus, there seems to be a high persistence in the technology portfolio.

However, as reported in Table 1, the knowledge base has faced some incremental changes. On the one hand the combination *Organic fine chemistry - Basic materials chemistry*, which is the third most technology co-occurrence between 1986 and 1995, loses its position in the following periods. The same holds for the co-occurrence of *Organic fine chemistry - Biotechnology* which ranks fifth during Period 1 and 2. On the other hand the combination *Analysis of biological materials - Biotechnology* as well as the combination *Analysis of biological materials - Pharmaceuticals* seem to become more important.

Thus, there has been a change in the technological paradigm of the life sciences. The knowledge base has faced a shift from 'chemical' dominated technology combinations to 'biological' oriented ones. *Biotechnology* and the *Analysis of biological materials* are becoming more important, while knowledge in *Organic fine chemistry* and *Basic materials chemistry* seems to be of minor importance since the mid of the 1990s. The dominating chemical paradigm is now replaced by a biotechnology paradigm (see also Hinze et al., 2001, p. 5).

Country specific patterns

The technology co-occurrence matrices for all sample countries are illustrated in *Annex III, Annex IV, Annex V, Annex VI, Annex VII* and *Annex VIII.* To compare the worldwide patterns with the country specific evolutions Table 2 reports for each country the five most frequent technology co-occurrences.

Table 2: Dominant technology combinations (country level)

Source: PATSTAT October 2007, own computations

	1.	2.	3.	4.	5.
CH					
1986/90	FineChem - Chem	FineChem - Pharma	Biotech - Pharma	FineChem - Biotech	ChemEng - Env
1991/95	**FineChem - Pharma** ↑	**Biotech - Pharma** ↑	**FineChem - Chem** ↓	FineChem - Biotech	**BioMat - Biotech** ↑
1996/00	FineChem - Pharma	Biotech - Pharma	FineChem - Chem	**BioMat - Biotech** ↑	**Pharma - Chem** ↑
2001/05	FineChem - Pharma	Biotech - Pharma	FineChem - Chem	BioMat – Biotech	Pharma - Chem
DE					
1986/90	FineChem - Pharma	FineChem - Chem	Biotech - Pharma	ChemEng - Env	Chem - ChemEng
1991/95	FineChem - Pharma	FineChem - Chem	Biotech - Pharma	ChemEng- Env	Chem - ChemEng
1996/00	FineChem - Pharma	**Biotech - Pharma** ↑	**FineChem - Chem** ↓	**BioMat - Biotech** ↑	**ChemEng - Env** ↓
2001/05	FineChem - Pharma	Biotech - Pharma	**BioMat - Biotech** ↑	**FineChem - Chem** ↓	ChemEng - Env
FR					
1986/90	FineChem - Pharma	Biotech - Pharma	FineChem - Chem	BioMat - Biotech	ChemEng- Env
1991/95	FineChem - Pharma	Biotech - Pharma	FineChem - Chem	**FineChem - Biotech** ↑	ChemEng- Env
1996/00	FineChem - Pharma	Biotech - Pharma	**BioMat - Biotech** ↑	**FineChem - Chem** ↓	**FineChem - MacroChem** ↑
2001/05	FineChem - Pharma	Biotech - Pharma	BioMat - Biotech	FineChem - Chem	**BioMat - Pharma** ↑
IT					
1986/90	FineChem - Pharma	Biotech - Pharma	FineChem - Chem	FineChem - Biotech	ChemEng- Env
1991/95	FineChem - Pharma	Biotech - Pharma	**FineChem - Biotech** ↑	BioMat - Biotech	ChemEng - Env
1996/00	FineChem - Pharma	Biotech - Pharma	**BioMat - Biotech** ↑	**BioMat- Pharma** ↑	**MedTech - Pharma** ↑
2001/05	FineChem - Pharma	Biotech - Pharma	BioMat – Biotech	**ChemEng- Env** ↑	**Pharma - Food** ↑

Table 2: Dominant technology combinations (country level) (continued)
Source: PATSTAT October 2007, own computations

NL	1.	2.	3.	4.	5.
1986/90	FineChem - Pharma	Biotech - Pharma	Measure - MedTech	Biotech - Food	FineChem - Chem
1991/95	**Biotech - Pharma** ↑	**Biotech - Food** ↑	**FineChem - Pharma** ↓	**BioMat - Biotech** ↑	**Food - Chem** ↑
1996/00	Biotech - Pharma	**FineChem - Pharma** ↑	**Biotech - Food** ↓	BioMat - Biotech	**BioMat - Pharma** ↑
2001/05	Biotech - Pharma	FineChem - Pharma	**BioMat - Biotech** ↑	**Measure - MedTech** ↑	**Pharma - Food** ↑

UK	1.	2.	3.	4.	5.
1986/90	FineChem - Pharma	Biotech - Pharma	FineChem - Chem	BioMat - Biotech	FineChem - Biotech
1991/95	FineChem - Pharma	Biotech - Pharma	FineChem - Chem	**FineChem - Biotech** ↑	**BioMat - Biotech** ↓
1996/00	FineChem - Pharma	Biotech - Pharma	**BioMat - Biotech** ↑	**BioMat - Pharma** ↑	**FineChem - Chem** ↓
2001/05	FineChem - Pharma	Biotech - Pharma	BioMat - Biotech	BioMat - Pharma	**FineChem - Biotech** ↑

Legend:

Biotech	Biotechnology	**FineChem**	Organic fine chemistry
BioMat	Analysis of biological materials	**Food**	Food chemistry
Chem	Basic materials chemistry	**Measure**	Measurement
ChemEng	Chemical engineering	**MedTech**	Medical technology
Env	Environmental technology	**Pharma**	Pharmaceuticals

It shows that the developments in the sample countries are similar to those observed in the worldwide view. During the whole period of investigation *Organic fine chemistry - Pharmaceuticals* and *Biotechnology - Pharmaceuticals* are the dominant technology combinations in all sample countries. At the same time the knowledge bases have faced some incremental changes. In most of the countries the co-occurrences of *Organic fine chemistry - Basic materials chemistry* are becoming less frequent. Despite this, the competences from the classes *Biotechnology* and *Analysis of biological materials* are now combined more often.

The developments in the Netherlands are different to the ones in the other countries. Here the co-occurrences of *Biotechnology - Pharmaceuticals* dominate since the beginning of the 1990s. Furthermore, *Biotechnology - Food chemistry* is one of the dominant technology combinations what cannot be observed in any of the other countries.

The findings support *Thesis 1* predicting the path dependent evolution of technological profiles. The analyses clearly show that the technological changes in the life sciences have an incremental nature. The dominating chemical paradigm is gradually replaced by the biotechnology paradigm. At the same time the co-occurrences of *Organic fine chemistry - Pharmaceuticals* and *Biotechnology - Pharmaceuticals* dominate the knowledge base of the life sciences during the whole period of investigation. Furthermore, the increasing importance of *Biotechnology* and *Analysis of biological materials* can be observed while the more chemical oriented combinations decrease. The same holds for the co-occurrences of *Chemical engineering* and *Environmental technology.*

II.6.3.2 Measurement of the knowledge base characteristics

In the following the evolution of the knowledge base is analysed with regard to structural changes in the accumulation of technological knowledge. Particular emphasis is thereby placed on the factors: technological diversification, technological relatedness and cognitive distance.

a) Technological diversification:

Technological diversification or variety is defined as the spread of the patent portfolio over the 35 technological classes of the *WIPO IPC Technology Concordance.* Thus, the term refers to the breadth of the knowledge base. The entropy measure is used to investigate the technological variety. The index has the advantage that it takes into account the number of technology classes as well as their relative importance (Stephan, 2003, p. 190). The *technological diversification (TD)* is defined as:

$$TD_k = \sum_{i=1}^{N} P_{ik} log\left(\frac{1}{P_{ik}}\right) \qquad \text{(II.2)}$$

where P_{ik} is country k's share of patent applications in technology class i (i = 1, …, N; N ≤ 35). The index takes values between zero and log N. If the technology base covers only one technology class the value is zero – 'complete specialisation'. Otherwise if the patent applications are distributed over all N technological classes the index takes the maximum value of log N – 'complete diversification'. Higher values of the measure therefore indicate higher technological diversification (Jacquemin, 1975, p. 835 f.; Stephan, 2003, p. 190 f.).

One of the main advantages of the entropy measure is its additivity; i.e. the index has the advantage that it can be decomposed into a 'within' and 'between' part. While the 'between' part measures the technological activities across technological fields (*unrelated diversification*), the 'within' part takes into account the distribution of patent activities among the technological classes inside a technological field (*related diversification*). Thus, the entropy measure makes it possible to capture also the diversification type, i.e. the degree of relatedness in the technology portfolio. To determine the diversification type the different aggregation levels of the *WIPO IPC Technology Concordance* have to be distinguished. The N technological classes can be aggregated to M technological fields, where M ≤ N (i = 1, …, N; j = 1, …, M; M ≤ 5). It can be assumed that technological classes within the same technology field are more related than technological classes which belong to different technology fields (Jacquemin, 1975, pp. 835-838; Jacquemin/Berry, 1979, p. 361 f.; Palepu, 1985, p. 244; Stephan, 2003, p. 192 f.; Krafft/Quatraro/Saviotti, 2009, p. 7 f.).

The *unrelated diversification (UD)* can be computed as:

$$UD_k = \sum_{j=1}^{M} P_{jk} log\left(\frac{1}{P_{jk}}\right)$$

(II.3)

where P_{jk} is country k's share of patent applications in technology field j.

Let RD be the *related diversification* arising out of technological activities within a technological field. First, the technological diversity TD_{jk} across the technological fields j has to be computed. TD_{jk} can be written as:

$$TD_{jk} = \sum_{i=1}^{N} P_{ijk} log\left(\frac{1}{P_{ijk}}\right)$$

(II.4)

where P_{ijk} is the country k's share of patents in technology class i in total patent applications in technology field j. The total related diversification RD_k which arises out of the technological activities in several technological fields is defined as:

$$RD_k = \sum_{j=1}^{M} TD_{jk} P_{jk}$$

(II.5)

where P_{jk} is country k's share of patent applications in technology field j in total patent applications (Jacquemin, 1975, pp. 836-838; Palepu, 1985, p. 252 f.). The sum of the related and unrelated diversity equals the total diversity of country k across all technology classes (Jaquemin/Berry, 1979, p. 362):

$$TD_k = RD_k + UD_k. \tag{II.6}$$

Based on the technological co-occurrences, the evolution of the knowledge base can be analysed with regard to the path dependence in the accumulation of technological knowledge. For this purpose, the following knowledge base indicators can be used: technological relatedness (coherence) and cognitive distance.

b) Technological relatedness (Coherence):

The coherence index measures the degree of relatedness of the existing knowledge base. Coherent knowledge bases are characterised by complementary pieces of knowledge and therefore represent the country's ability to combine or integrate different pieces of knowledge (Krafft/Quatraro/Saviotti, 2009, p. 9). The knowledge coherence index was originally introduced by Teece et al. (1994) to measure the coherence in firm's industry profiles. The index is based upon the following statistics:

$$r_{ij} = \frac{C_{ij} - \mu_{ij}}{\sigma_{ij}} \tag{II.7}$$

where C_{ij} indicates the number of patents that can be assigned to technology i and j, μ_{ij} is the expected number of patents attributed to technology i and j, if the patents were randomly assigned to technologies. Thus, r_{ij} measures the extent to which the observed linkage between two technologies exceeds the level which would be expected if the assignments of patents to technologies were random. The weighted average relatedness WAR_i^k measures the degree to which country k's technological activities in technology i are related to all other technologies i′ of country k's technology base.

$$WAR_i^k = \frac{\sum_{i \neq i'} r_{ii'} \, p_{i'k}}{\sum_{i \neq i} p_{ik}} \tag{II.8}$$

where p_{ik} measures the number of patents country k holds in technology i (Teece et al., 1994, p. 5 f.; Breschi/Lissioni/Malerba, 2004, p. 70 ff.). Positive (negative) values of the WAR_i^k measure indicate that technology i is closely (weakly) related to all other technologies of the respective country. The coherence of the knowledge base is then defined as the weighted average of the WAR_i^k measure (Krafft/Quatraro/Saviotti, 2009, p. 9):

$$Coh_k = \sum_{i=1}^{N} WAR_i^k \times \frac{p_{ik}}{\sum_i p_{ik}}. \tag{II.9}$$

Positive values of the coherence *(Coh)* measure indicate that the country's technology base is characterised by high relatedness and complementarity. A negative value of the measure reveals low complementarity of the technologies.

c) Cognitive distance:

A further important factor is *the cognitive distance (CD)* among different pieces of knowledge which measures the degree of dissimilarity among technologies. New technologies *'[...] require a 'cognitive distance' which is sufficiently small to allow for understanding but sufficiently large to yield non-redundant, novel knowledge'* (Nooteboom, 2000, p. 72).

The greater the cognitive distance of new technologies, the greater the merit of novelty. However, greater cognitive distance also entails the problem of incomprehensibility. Thus, in order to reduce the cognitive distance the new types of knowledge should be complementary to the existing knowledge base. This means that the new knowledge should – to a certain degree – share a common language (Nooteboom, 2000, p. 72; Nooteboom et al., 2007, p. 1017 f.).

The *similarity index* or *cosine index* was originally introduced by Jaffe (1986) to measure the similarity of technology profiles. Breschi/Lissoni/Malerba (2004) adapted the index to investigate the relatedness between two technologies based on technological co-occurrences. The underlying assumption can be formulated as follows:

> 'If [two technologies] i and j are frequently found to be jointly assigned to patent documents with other classes, and those classes are the same for both i and j, then i and j are said to be similar, i.e. they are supposed to share a common knowledge base or to be complementary to the same set of other technologies.' (Breschi/Lissoni/Malerba, 2004, p. 77)

The similarity index of technology i and j is computed as follows:

$$s_{ij} = \frac{\sum_{i=1}^{N} c_{ii'} \, c_{ji'}}{\sqrt{\sum_{i=1}^{N} c_{ii'}^2} \, \sqrt{\sum_{i=1}^{N} c_{ji'}^2}}$$

(II.10)

where c is the vector of technological co-occurrences. The cognitive distance of two technologies is then defined as the complement of the index of similarity (Krafft/Quatraro/Saviotti, 2009, p. 8 f.):

$$d_{ij} = 1 - s_{ij}.$$

(II.11)

To obtain a synthetic index of technological distance, the distance measure is applied at the aggregated country level. First, the average distance of technology i from all other technologies is computed. The weighted average distance is defined as follows:

$$WAD_i^k = \frac{\sum_{i \neq i'} d_{ii'} \, p_{ik}}{\sum_{i \neq i'} p_{ik}}$$

(II.12)

where p_{ik} is, for a given country k, the number of patents in technology i. Second, the average cognitive distance is obtained as follows (Krafft/Quatraro/Saviotti, 2009, p. 8 f.):

$$CD_k = \sum_{i=1}^{N} WAD_i^k \times \frac{p_{ik}}{\sum_i p_{ik}}$$

(II.13)

Increasing values of the *CD* measure indicate rising cognitive distance and vice versa.

In the following the knowledge base characteristics of the sample countries are presented with regard to the above mentioned indicators. For each country the evolution of these characteristics during the four periods under investigation are illustrated in three different charts (Figure 19).

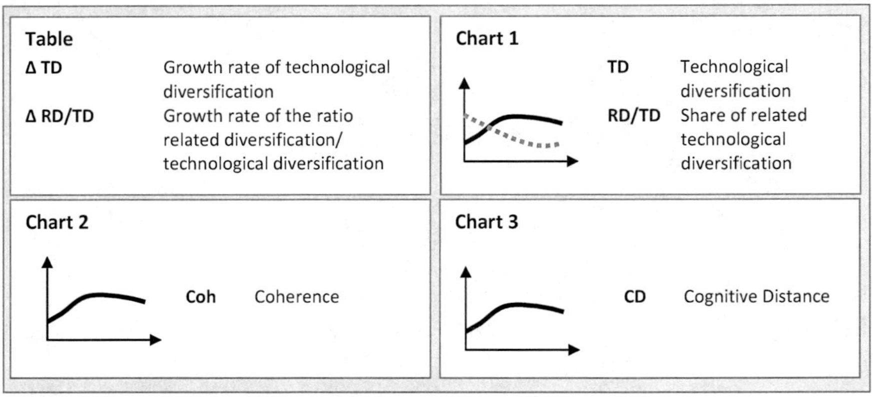

Figure 19: Illustration of knowledge base characteristics
Source: own illustration

The first chart shows the evolution of technological diversification taking into account the diversification type. The respective growth rates between the four periods of investigation are reported in a separate table.[24] The second and the third chart illustrate the evolution of the coherence (technological relatedness) and the cognitive distance.

Based on the knowledge base indicators, the different countries will be characterised according to their technology accumulation strategy (exploitative vs. explanatory research). While exploitation refers to refinement and extension of the existing technology base, the term exploration refers to the increasing variety of the technology base and the experimentation with new technological solutions (March, 1991, p. 71; Nooteboom et al., 2007, p. 1019).

The country specific patterns of Switzerland, France, Germany, Italy, the Netherlands and the United Kingdom are described in the following.

Switzerland

During the period of investigation Switzerland has continuously reduced its technological diversification as indicated by falling values of the TD measure (Figure 20). The strongest decline (about 7%) can be observed between the last two periods.

24 For the time periods the following abbreviations are used: P1=1986/90, P2=1991/95, P3=1996/00, P4=2001/05.

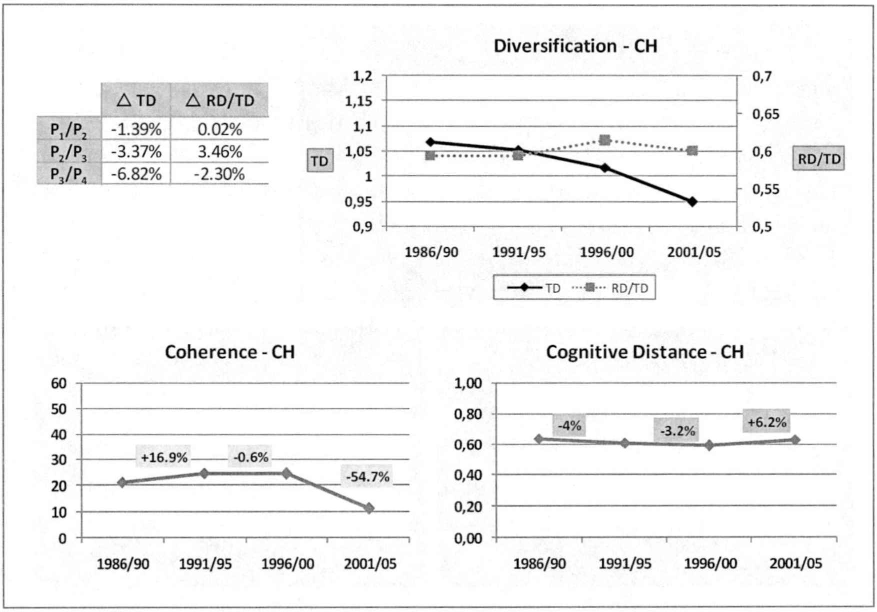

Figure 20: Knowledge base characteristics - CH

Source: PATSTAT October 2007, own computations

Taking into account the diversification type shows that the share of related technological diversification increases steadily during the first three periods. At the same time the technological relatedness increases. This holds especially for the period 1986/90 to 1991/95 where the growth rate accounts for nearly 17%. Furthermore, there is a slight decrease in the cognitive distance. I.e. between 1986/90 and 1996/00 the knowledge base of Switzerland is characterised by increasing technological relatedness and growing similarity among the technologies in the portfolio. As a result, it can be stated that new pieces of knowledge are mainly accumulated through the recombination of the existing competences (exploitation strategy).

After the period 1996/00 the picture changes: The share of related technological diversification decreases slightly. Additionally, a strong decrease in the technological relatedness (about 55%) and an increase in the cognitive distance can be observed. This trend could be interpreted as the evolution of new technological knowledge concepts, arising from the differentiation of the existing pieces of knowledge (characterised by growing cognitive distance and falling coherence), i.e. there is a transition from the exploitation driven to an exploration driven knowledge path.

Germany

Figure 21 illustrates the characteristics of Germany's knowledge base. Although Germany is the most diversified country in the sample, a slight decrease in the degree of technological diversification can be observed during the period of investigation. I.e. there is a tendency towards more specialisation.

Taking into account the diversification type may provide an indication on the relatedness of the knowledge base. It can be observed that the related variety is at a high level during the whole period of investigation, i.e. the knowledge base mainly consists of pieces of knowledge which are technologically related. Furthermore, Figure 21 shows that the share of related variety has continuously increased during the first three periods. At the same time a rise in the technological relatedness and a fall in the cognitive distance can be observed. Thus, there is a trend towards more technological coherence due to the growing relative relatedness or low cognitive distance of the new pieces of knowledge. I.e. it can be assumed that the new technological knowledge is mainly obtained by the recombination of the existing technology portfolio (exploitation strategy).

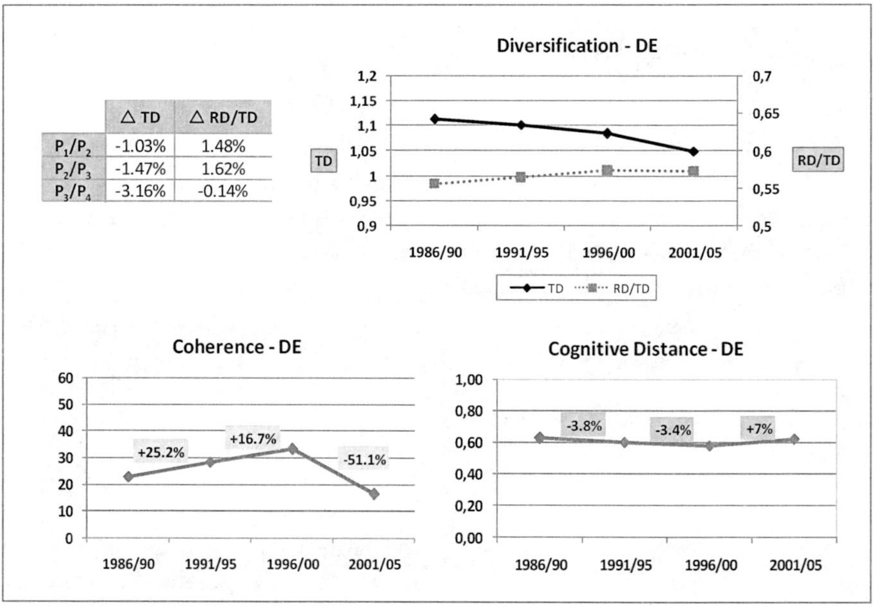

Figure 21: Knowledge base characteristics - DE

Source: PATSTAT October 2007, own computations

Between 1996/00 and 2001/05 the share of related technological diversification remains roughly stable, while technological coherence decreases and cognitive distance rises. Thus, there is a transition from exploitation to exploration. The knowledge base is now characterised by the introduction of completely new pieces of knowledge. This knowledge discontinuity is marked by an increase in the cognitive distance and a fall in the technological relatedness.

France

Figure 22 illustrates the evolution of the knowledge base in France. Technological diversification (TD) is falling during the period of investigation indicating a trend towards more specialisation.

Turning the analyses to the diversification type it shows that the share of related technological diversification increases only between 1986/90 and 1991/95 and then falls continuously. The initial rise in the share of the related variety goes hand in hand with an increase of the technological relatedness and a decrease of cognitive distance. Thus, this time period seems to be characterised by the exploitation of the existing knowledge.

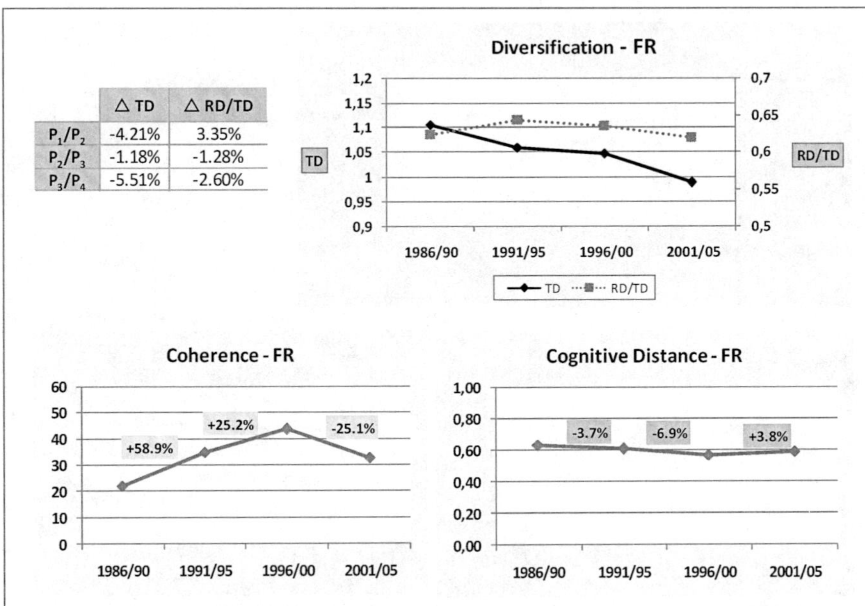

Figure 22: Knowledge base characteristics - FR

Source: PATSTAT October 2007, own computations

In the following period the trends of increasing technological relatedness and falling cognitive distance are continued, while the share of the related variety begins to fall. This trend could be interpreted as the evolution of new knowledge concepts, arising from the differentiation of the existing pieces of knowledge (characterised by low cognitive distance and high coherence), i.e. there is a transition from the exploitation driven to the exploration driven knowledge path. Between 1996/00 and 2001/05 the exploration of new technological knowledge dominates the research activities in France. The relative fall in related variety (as indicated by falling shares of related technological diversification) points towards the accumulation of new forms of knowledge outside the existing competencies. This interpretation is confirmed by the falling technological coherence and the growing cognitive distance.

Italy

During the first three periods of investigation the knowledge base of Italy is characterised by a slight decrease in the degree of total diversification. Between 1986/90 and 1991/95 this development is accompanied by an increasing share of related technological diversification, rising technological coherence and falling cognitive distance (Figure 23). Thus, the research strategy seems to consist of the exploitation of the existing knowledge base.

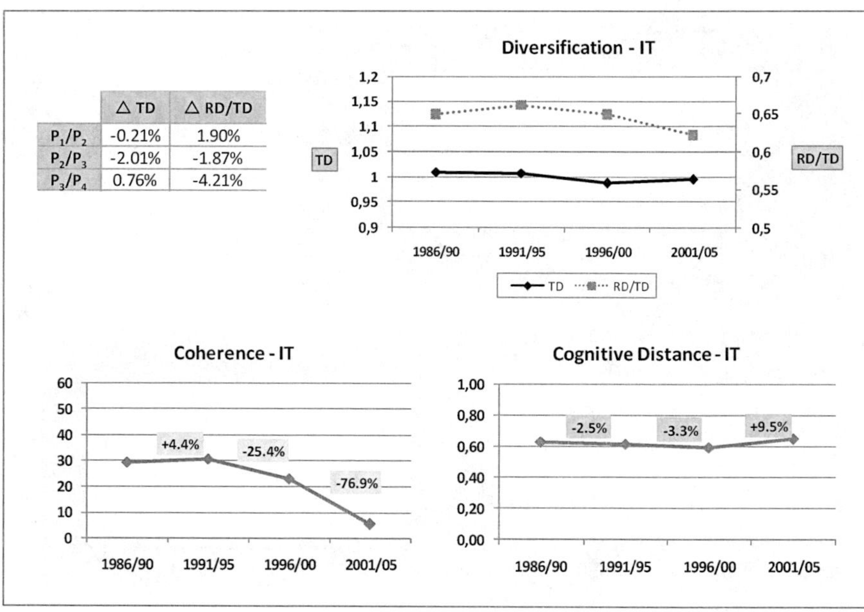

Figure 23: Knowledge base characteristics - IT
Source: PATSTAT October 2007, own computations

In the following, the technology portfolio is characterised by a falling share of the related variety, decreasing technological relatedness and slightly decreasing cognitive distance. The simultaneous decrease of total variety and cognitive distance seems to be contradictory at a first glance. However, it has to be noted that the inverse relationship between falling shares of total variety and increasing cognitive distance does not necessarily appear. In this context the distinction between related and unrelated diversification is important. Related variety can also grow through the differentiation of the previous technological knowledge present in a country and therefore leads not automatically to a rise in cognitive distance (Krafft/Quatraro/Saviotti, 2009, p. 14). At the same time falling shares of related variety can indicate increasing discontinuities in the knowledge base. There is a shift in the knowledge base from exploitation driven to exploration driven research. Between 1996/00 and 2001/05 a slight increase of technological diversification and a falling share of the related variety can be observed. Thus, the research strategy is now oriented towards the exploration of new technological fields. This interpretation is confirmed by the strongly decreasing knowledge coherence and the increasing cognitive distance.

The Netherlands

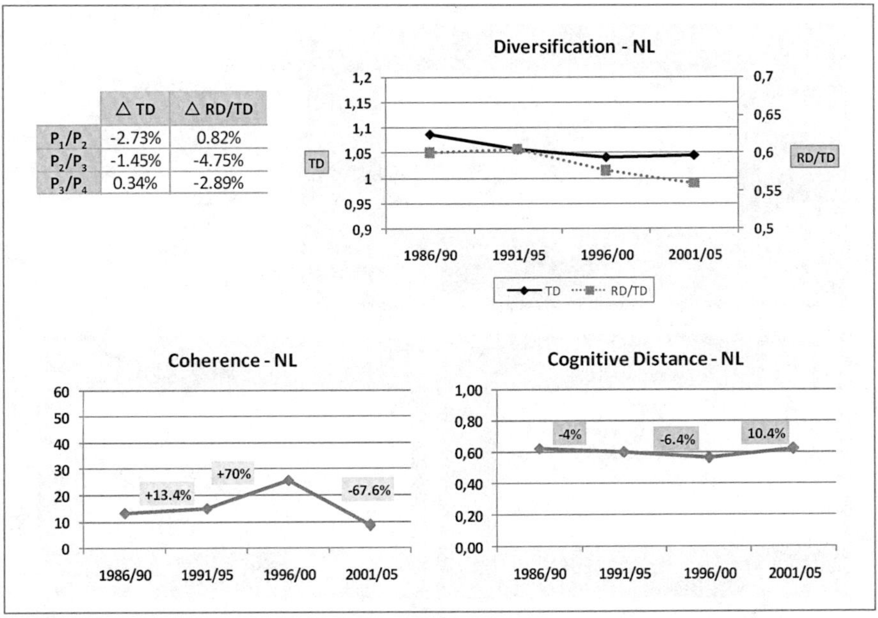

Figure 24: Knowledge base characteristics - NL

Source: PATSTAT October 2007, own computations

During the first three periods the Netherlands show a slight decrease in their degree of technological diversification. Between 1986/90 and 1991/95 this trend is accompanied by an increasing share of related variety, a rise in the knowledge coherence and a fall in the cognitive distance. Thus, at this time an exploitative research strategy, which is characterised by the recombination of existing pieces of knowledge, can be observed (Figure 24).

In the following a transition from exploitative to explanatory research takes place as indicated by rising knowledge relatedness and falling cognitive distance, accompanied by a decreasing share of the related variety. Between 1996/00 and 2001/05 the transition to an explorative strategy seems to be completed. The technological activities are now characterised by the integration of new pieces of knowledge (characterised by strongly falling coherence and increasing cognitive distance) and lead to a slight increase of technological diversification.

United Kingdom

The developments in the United Kingdom are similar to those which took place in Germany and Switzerland.

	Δ TD	Δ RD/TD
P_1/P_2	-2.70%	5.17%
P_2/P_3	-3.54%	1.61%
P_3/P_4	-0.91%	0.58%

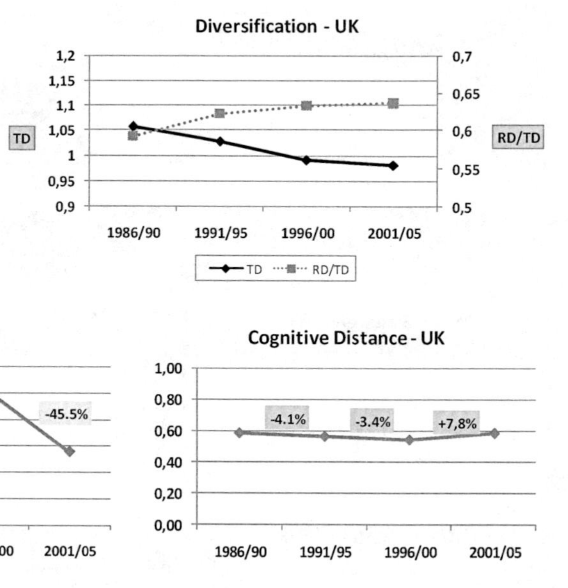

Figure 25: Knowledge base characteristics - UK

Source: PATSTAT October 2007, own computations

The technological diversification is falling during the whole period of investigation (Figure 25). Thereby, the greatest decrease can be observed between 1986/90 and 1996/00. The trend towards more specialisation is accompanied by a continuous increasing share of the related technological diversification. Furthermore, technological relatedness increases during the first three periods, while cognitive distance decreases. I.e. the underlying knowledge processes mainly consist of the recombination of existing pieces of knowledge indicating an exploitative research strategy. Between 1996/00 and 2001/05 the decrease in technological relatedness and the rise in cognitive distance indicate the transition from exploitation to exploration. This interpretation is confirmed by the comparably lower growth rate of the share of the related variety. Moreover, the fall in the degree of technological diversification is now negligibly small.

General patterns in the knowledge base characteristics

The analysis of the knowledge base characteristics exhibits the research strategies of the sample nations. The main results are summarised in Figure 26.

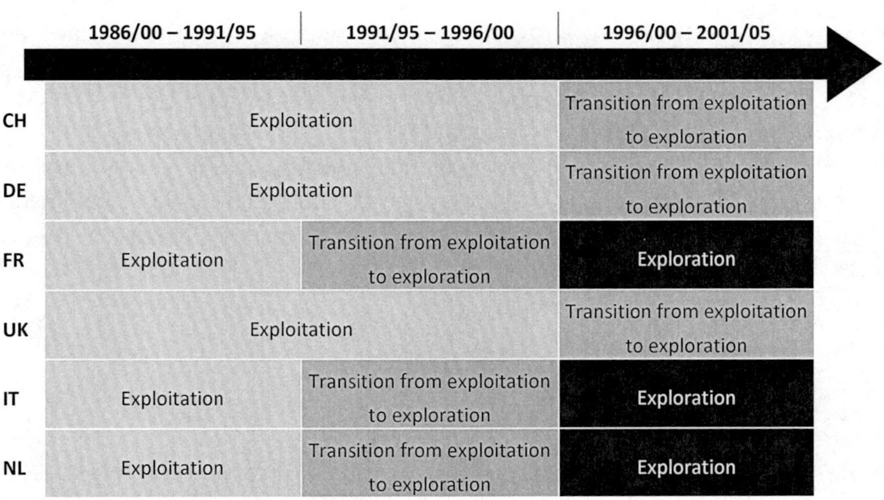

Figure 26: Development of research strategies

Source: own illustration

Initially, the six analysed European countries are characterised by an exploitative research strategy. I.e. the knowledge base consists mainly of related technologies which have a low cognitive distance. During the 1990s the transition from exploitative to explorative research can be observed. Thus, there is a tendency to create new pieces of knowledge through differentiation of the existing technological competencies. This transition leads to a decreasing share of the related variety. The entry into the exploratory research phase (indicated by falling technological relatedness, growing cognitive distance and a decrease in the share of related variety or an increase in total variety) could only be observed for France, Italy and the Netherlands. Thus, the different countries are in various stages of the industry lifecycle.

Concerning the breadth of the knowledge base there is a tendency towards more specialisation among all countries until the end of the 1990s (expressed by a slight decrease of the technological diversification). In the following years Italy and the Netherlands are the only ones who are expanding their knowledge base as indicated by a rise in the total diversification.

II.6.4 Patterns of technological specialisation in the life sciences

The aim of this sub-section is to illustrate the patterns of technological specialisation in the life sciences at the country level. The absolute numbers of patents provide only a rough overview of the technological performance in the sample countries. In order to control for systematic biases, which are caused by the differences in the propensity to patent, the indicator of *Relative Technological Advantage (RTA)* is used.

Technological profiles and their evolution over time can be analysed on the basis of technological specialisation patterns (Bachmann, 1998; Patel/Pavitt, 1994a). The Relative Technological Advantage determines the specialisation in a particular technology and is defined as follows:

$$RTA_{ik} = \frac{p_{ik}/p_i}{p_k/p_{total}} \tag{II.14}$$

where p_{ik} is the number of country k’s patent applications in technology class i, p_k the number of country k’s patent applications in total, p_i the total number of patent applications in technology i and p_{total} the total number of patent applications. The RTA takes values between zero and infinite. Values above one indicate the relative technological advantage of country k in the respective technological class in comparison to all other countries. In like manner values between zero and one point at a relative low competitive position in the respective technology (Bachmann, 1998, p. 597; Stephan, 2003, p. 193; Cantwell, 2004, p. 273).

The index has been criticised because it is not symmetric, i.e. the index is not comparable at both sides of unity (Laursen, 1998, p. 2), taking values between zero and infinity. To tackle the symmetry problem the symmetric and bounded form of the RTA index – the hyperbolic tangent of the RTA (RTA_h) – is used. It is defined as:

$$RTA_{h_{ik}} = 100\, tanh\, ln\, (RTA_{ik}). \tag{II.15}$$

The RTA_h takes values between −100 and +100 (Grupp, 1994, p. 187; Grupp, 1997, p. 212). Values above (below) zero indicate the technological advantage/specialisation (disadvantage/despecialisation) of the country. The higher (lower) the values of the index, the greater the country's technological specialisation (despecialisation) compared to all other sample countries.

Figure 27 illustrates the evolution of the relative technological advantages in the life sciences technologies measured by RTA_h-values. All countries have specific specialisation profiles which comprise two or three classes of relative technological advantage.

Switzerland

In Switzerland the fields of technological specialisation are *Food chemistry, Basic materials chemistry* as well as *Medical technology.* Thus, the comparative advantages lie in product and process technologies. The technological advantages in the generic technology *class Other special machines* are only present until the mid-1990s.

Germany

Germany has relative technological advantages in *Basic materials chemistry*, *Environmental technology* and *Other special machines* during the whole period of investigation. Thus, the focus is mainly on generic classes which have a variety of applications and can be used in different product areas. While there is a slight decline in the RTA_h-values in *Environmental technology*, there is an increase in the RTA_h-values in *Other special machines.* In the class *Basic materials chemistry* a moderate level of technological advantage is maintained during the whole period of investigation.

France

The developments in France are similar to those in Germany. *Environmental technology* as well as *Other special machines* are the main fields of technological advantage. However, while Germany is also specialised in *Basic materials chemistry,* France shows strong technological disadvantages in this technological class. Moreover, the RTA_h-values indicate growing relative strength in *Environmental technology* until the end of the 1990s and declining specialisation in *Other special machines*. Additionally, in the new millennium France has lost its comparative technological advantages in *Food chemistry*.

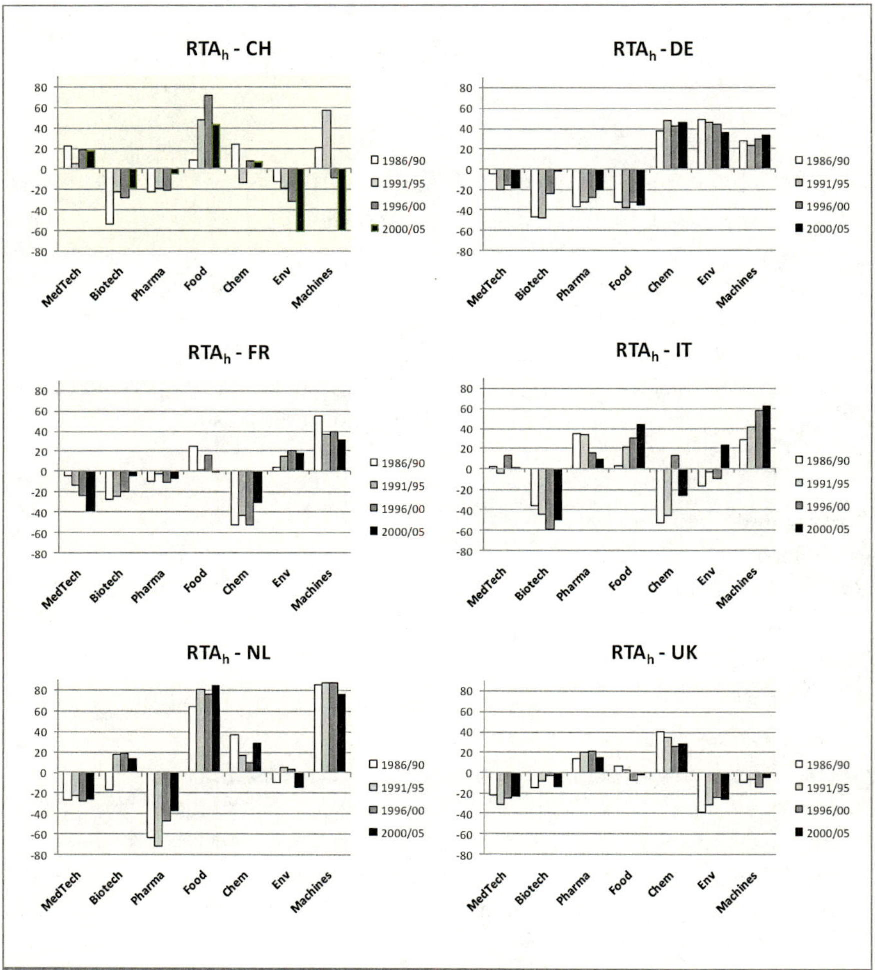

Legend:

MedTech	Medical technology	**Biotech**	Biotechnology
Pharma	Pharmaceuticals	**Food**	Food chemistry
Chem	Basic materials chemistry	**Env**	Environmental technology
Machines	Other special machines		

Figure 27: Technological specialisation in the life sciences industry
Source: PATSTAT October 2007, own computations

Italy

For Italy the RTA_h-values indicate rising specialisation in *Food chemistry* and *Other special machines* and falling specialisation in *Pharmaceuticals*. Thus, Italy has comparative advantages in product and process technologies as well as in generic technological areas like *Other special machines*.

The Netherlands

The Netherlands are highly specialised in *Food chemistry* and *Other special machines* and can be seen as the technological leader in these classes. The other fields of relative technological strength are *Biotechnology* and *Basic materials chemistry*.

United Kingdom

The United Kingdom is characterised by technological advantages in *Pharmaceuticals* and *Basic materials chemistry*. Furthermore, during the first two periods slight technological advantages are observed for the *Food chemistry* sector.

The specialisation profiles of the sample countries seem to be rather stable over time. Although there are fluctuations in the RTA_h-values, it can be shown, that the core competences which were already present in the 1980s could be maintained until the new millennium. To measure the stability in the technological advantages and disadvantages of the sample countries, the pairwise correlations of the RTA_h-values in the life sciences technologies are calculated (*Annex IX*). For all countries a positive relationship between the specialisation patterns of subsequent periods can be observed. The strength of the correlation in the RTA_h-values during the period 1986-2005 further confirms *Thesis 1*. Thus, it can be assumed that the technology profile in the life sciences changes only slowly and is characterised by high path dependence. One exception to this is Switzerland. Significant correlations between the RTA_h-profiles can only be observed between 1996/00 and 2001/05. This fact is caused by the changing competitive positions in *Basic materials chemistry* and *Other special machines*. Especially the sector *Other special machines* is characterised by profound changes: The strong specialisation of the early 1990s has turned to a strong despecialisation in the new millennium.

Figure 28 summarises the specialisation patterns of the sample nations. RTA_h-values between 0 and 50 (moderate specialisation) are marked with light grey colour, RTA_h-values above 50 (high specialisation) are illustrated with dark grey colour.

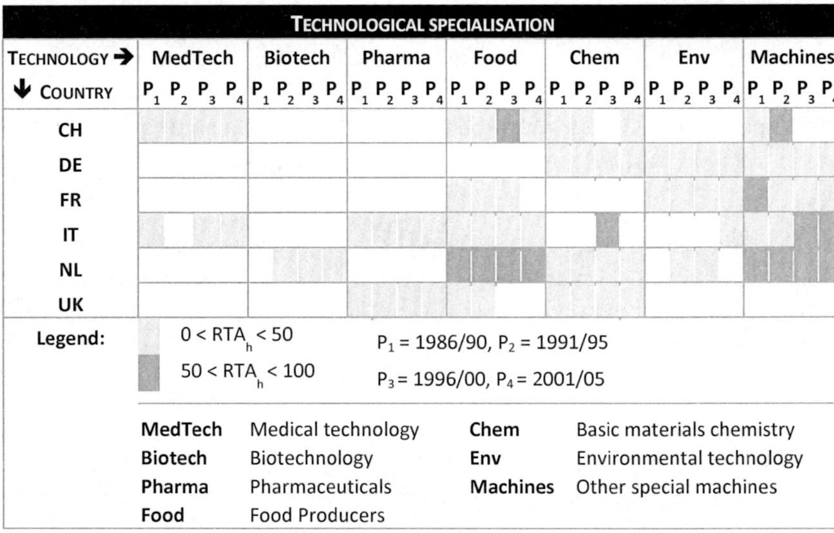

Figure 28: Overview of the technological specialisation patterns in the life sciences industry

Source: PATSTAT October 2007, own illustration

The figure reveals that the sample countries are characterised by distinct technological profiles. Thus, during the period of investigation the sample countries have developed country specific technological trajectories. This supports *Thesis 2a* predicting that the national environment favours the evolution of country-specific technological specialisation patterns.

Focusing on the specific fields of specialisation the empirical analyses show that the technological advantages in *Food chemistry* are mostly accompanied by a specialisation in *Other special machines*. This may be caused by the fact, that machines for food production are classified as part of the technological class *Other special machines* (Schmoch, 2008, p. 13 f.). Furthermore, most countries have comparative technological advantages in *Basic materials chemistry*. This technological field includes typical mass chemicals and may therefore be used for a wide range of applications. Specialisation in *Biotechnology* can only be observed in the Netherlands.

II.7 Concluding remarks to Chapter II

In this chapter the technological trajectories in the life sciences were investigated. The knowledge bases of six European countries were mapped using patent applications during the period 1986-2005. The analyses of the technological activities show that Germany, France, Italy, the Netherlands, Switzerland and the

United Kingdom are Europe's dominating countries in the life sciences. During the period of investigation these nations have continuously increased their patent output. Concerning the technological breadth and depth of the knowledge bases country specific differences can be observed.

Different properties of the knowledge base were measured: technological specialisation, technological diversification, technological coherence and cognitive distance. While the specialisation measure RTA_h determines the fields of comparative technological advantage, the three other indicators make it possible to determine the research strategies of the nations, distinguishing between exploitation and exploration. Based on the different indicators, the evolution of the technological trajectories in the sample nations was determined.

The technological diversification indicator measures the breadth of the knowledge base, i.e. the extent of differentiation. The analyses show that until the end of the 1990s all countries are characterised by slight decreases in their technological diversification. Thus, there is a tendency towards more specialisation. Since the mid-1990s Italy and the Netherlands have expanded their technology base. Additionally, the coherence and the cognitive distance of the knowledge base were calculated to determine the research strategy of the sample nations. The coherence indicator measures the closeness degree of the existing knowledge base. I.e. it represents the extent to which a country is able to combine or integrate different pieces of knowledge. The cognitive distance measure shows the dissimilarity among the technologies of the knowledge bases. During the period of investigation the sample countries have entered different stages of the industry life cycle. Initially, all countries are pursuing an exploitative research strategy based on the existing pieces of knowledge. During the 1990s the transition from exploitative to exploratory research could be observed in all six countries. Finally, the entry into the exploratory research phase took place only in France, Italy and the Netherlands. I.e. the countries have reached different stages of the industry lifecycle.

The analysis of the technological specialisation patterns reveals that all sample nations are characterised by distinct technological profiles. Furthermore, high path dependence in the specialisation profiles could be observed. Thus, the core competences which were already present in the 1980s could be maintained until the new millennium. The fields of relative technological advantage are mainly technologies like *Other special machines*, *Environmental technology* and *Basic materials chemistry* which cover a wide range of applications and can be used for different product lines. Furthermore, the analysis shows that nations with comparative technological advantages in *Food chemistry* are also specialised in *Other special machines*. This seems to be caused by the fact that machines for food production are classified as part of the technology field *Other special machines*. Although *Biotechnology* has been one of the emerging technology classes in the life sciences during the last decades, only the Netherlands could gain technological advantages in this class. The same holds for the more 'traditional' technology class: *Pharmaceuticals*, where only Italy and the United Kingdom show relative technological advantages.

The results confirm *Thesis 1*. The technological activities in the life sciences are highly path dependent. Changes in the knowledge base are incremental and cumulative. The technological strengths of the 1980s were still present in the period 2001/2005. Furthermore, the analysis of the knowledge bases reveals that the technology portfolios of the sample nations evolved in a coherent way. New technological activities are related to the existing pieces of knowledge and have a comparably low cognitive distance.

Thesis 2a argues that the national environment shapes the direction of national technological trajectories. The analysis of the technological specialisation patterns clearly confirms *Thesis 2a*. The sample countries have developed country specific specialisation patterns comprising several fields of technological advantage. Concerning the degree and the specific mix of their fields of technological advantage the sample countries show different developments.

Thesis 2b will be investigated in *Chapter III* and *IV*. As a precondition, *Chapter III* investigates the development patterns in the technological profiles of R&D-intensive life science companies. The findings elaborated in *Chapter II* and *Chapter III* then build the ground for the analyses in *Chapter IV*. The empirical analyses of *Chapter IV* aim to determine the main factors influencing the technology decisions of firms by linking the national technological trajectories with the technological profiles of the life sciences companies.

Chapter III Tracing technological diversification patterns

> 'The advance of knowledge depends upon a cumulative interaction between the process of differentiation (the focus associated with specialization) and integration (the new combinations or new applications that result from utilizing a diversification of activity through discovering or exploiting complementarities between different fields).' (Cantwell/Gambardella/Granstrand, 2004, p. 3)

This chapter introduces the phenomenon of technological diversification and provides a detailed synopsis of the relevant literature.[25] Furthermore, the diversification trends of European life sciences companies are analysed in depth.

III.1 Increasing technological diversification

Since the 1770s specialisation and the division of labour among countries, regions and firms have attracted researchers from different areas. Following Adam Smith (1776) specialisation in knowledge production through division of labour increases productivity. Smith's approach considers the creation of knowledge and specialisation as a co-evolving concept (Cantwell/Gambardella/Granstrand, 2004, p. 3). The specialisation in certain technologies is said to lead to economies of scale in R&D. In this line the competence based theory suggests that firms should focus on a set of core competences to build competitive advantages (Prahalad/Hamel, 1990). However, in the last decades there seems to be a trend towards moderate degrees of diversification. These observations led to an ongoing debate whether technological specialisation (i.e. the concentration on specific core competences) or diversification increases the competitiveness (Teece, 1988). Although this question is not definitely answered, current research provides empirical evidence about the increasing technological diversification of large multi-technology corporations (MTCs) in the Triads since the beginning of the 1980s. The pioneering works of Kodama (1986) and Pavitt/Robson/Townsend (1989) show the increased technological diversity in Japan and the United Kingdom. Additonally, Granstrand/Oskarsson (1994) observed that MTCs in Japan, Sweden and the United States have continuously expanded their technology portfolio. The highest technological diversity is observed in

25 For an overview of this topic see also Stohr (2007) and Fornahl/Stohr (2008). The theoretical approach of the mentioned publications is further developed in *Chapter III.1* of this dissertation.

Japan. Thus, there are national differences in the degree of technological diversification (ibid., p. 357). Furthermore, as pointed out by Gerybadze/Stephan (2002), the growing trend to expand the technology base has not continued since the beginning of the 1990s.

In general the term diversification stands for expanding activities into new areas and defines a wide-ranging topic. Two fundamental types of diversification can be distinguished: *business diversification* at the output level and *resource diversification* at the input level (Figure 29).

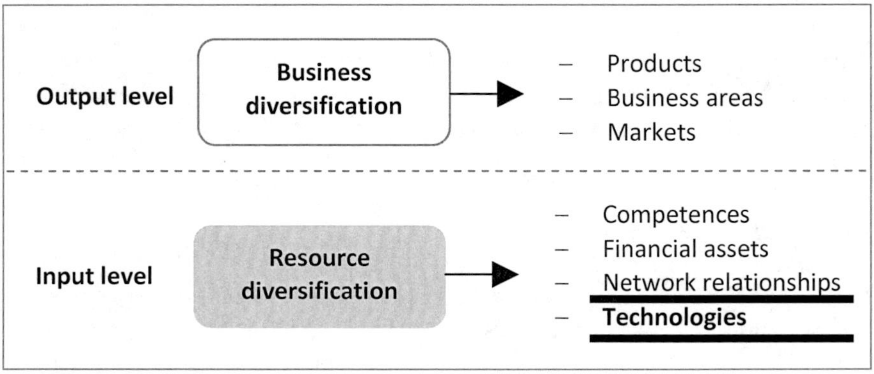

Figure 29: Diversification types
Source: own illustration

Business diversification typically refers to the expansion of the product range of firms and the diversification of services, markets and business areas as special cases. The concept of resource diversification focuses on the range and the distribution of input factors such as technologies or competences (Granstrand, 1998, p. 481; Stephan, 2003, pp. 6-9; Torrisi/Granstrand, 2004, p. 51).

The term *'technological diversification'* refers to the dynamic act of expanding the technology base into a broader range of technological areas. As a result, an increase in the variety of the technological competences and, hence, also the rising technological diversity can be observed. *'Technological diversity'* refers to the degree of technological diversification, i.e. the scope of the technological activities at a specific point of time (Granstrand/Oskarsson, 1994, p. 355).

Based on the technological interrelations, which exist between the new developed technologies and the established knowledge base, a further distinction can be made between two different directions of diversification: *'related and unrelated technological diversification'* (Figure 30).

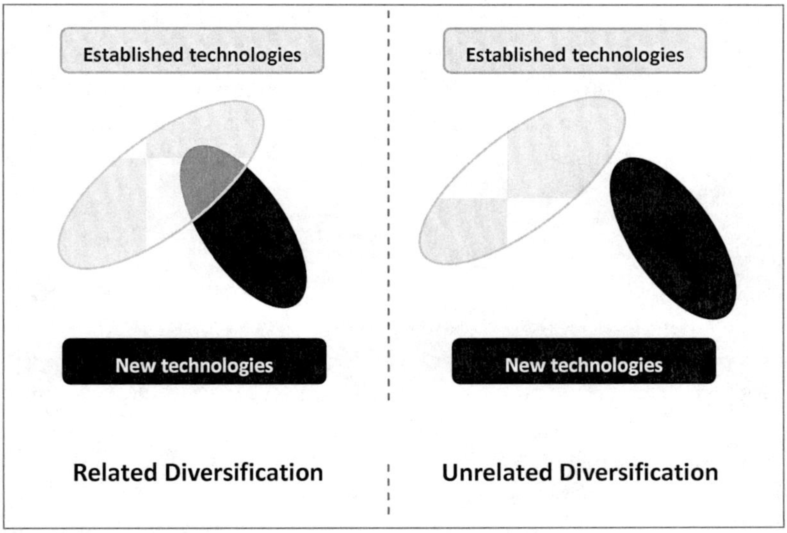

Figure 30: Direction of diversification
Source: own illustration

Related diversification is characterised by high degrees of relatedness between the old technologies and the new technologies. Contrary to this, unrelated technological diversification entails the development of new technologies, which have nothing in common with the established technological competences (Teece, 1982, p. 59; Stephan, 2003, p. 8).

III.1.1 Determinants of technological diversification

In this sub-section the different reasons, why firms accumulate technological competences outside their core business, are presented.[26]

a) Development of new business areas:
The development of new business areas can lead to substantial competitive advantages for the firm. New customer requirements (‘*demand-pull*’) as well as new technological opportunities (‘*technology-push*’) may create a need for modifications in the technology base of products (Dosi, 1982, pp. 148-151). The development or acquisition of new technologies makes it possible to provide products and processes with new functionalities to improve their

26 For an overview see also: Stephan, 2003, pp. 156-163; Garcia-Vega, 2006, p. 230 f.

performance. In this context, the term 'product-related technological diversification' is used. The introduction of new technologies leads to an increase in technological diversification. Through economies of scale and scope firms may then have an incentive to engage in 'technology-related product diversification' (Grandstand/Patel/Pavitt, 1997, p. 9; Granstrand, 1998, p. 473; Stephan, 2003, p. 157 f.).

b) *Reduction of uncertainties:*
In the early development stages there is a high uncertainty about the future application areas of new technological competences, i.e. new technologies may evolve in unexpected directions (Rosenberg, 1996, p. 97 f.). Hence, large MTCs explore and experiment with emerging technologies in order to assess their business applications in the future. As a result, firms need to build up and maintain a broad technology base. This often requires investments in technological classes outside the established core competences. Furthermore, competences in so called *'platform technologies'* or *'generic technologies'* such as 'Materials' or 'Computing' are becoming more important. These technologies can be applied in a wide range of products and sectors. As a consequence, large MTCs should also invest in generic classes in order to anticipate the emergence of new technologies (Granstrand/Patel/Pavitt, 1997, p. 13; Stephan, 2003, p. 160 f.; Cesaroni, 2004, p. 177).

c) *Increasing technological complexity:*
There is empirical evidence that technologies are becoming more complex. In many industries the number of distinct technologies involved in the manufacturing of products has increased. Exemplarily, Granstrand/Oskarsson (1994) show that the technology base of cellular phones, telecommunication cables and refrigerators has grown with each new generation of products. While the first product generation of cellular phones consisted of five sub-technologies, the third generation was based on 14 sub-technologies (ibid., pp. 360-362). New technologies often do not substitute established technologies. In many cases a combination of old and new technologies is required to develop new products or to improve the existing ones (Granstrand/Patel/Pavitt, 1997, p. 13). Besides the pure combination of technological competencies, the fusion of previously independent technologies can be observed. Examples for such linkages are the technological classes mechatronics (i.e. the fusion of materials, electronics and mechanics (see Figure 31)) and optoelectronics (i.e. the fusion of optics and electronics). The fusion of technologies is a nonlinear and complementary approach which brings forth new technological areas with own knowledge bases.

Thus, to understand the inner-logic of such a technological area, companies must build up and maintain technological competencies in all underlying technologies (De Bresson, 1987, pp. 754-757; Granstrand/Sjölander, 1990, p. 38; Kodama, 1992, p. 70; Granstrand/Oskarsson, 1994, p. 356; Kodama, 1995, p. 201).

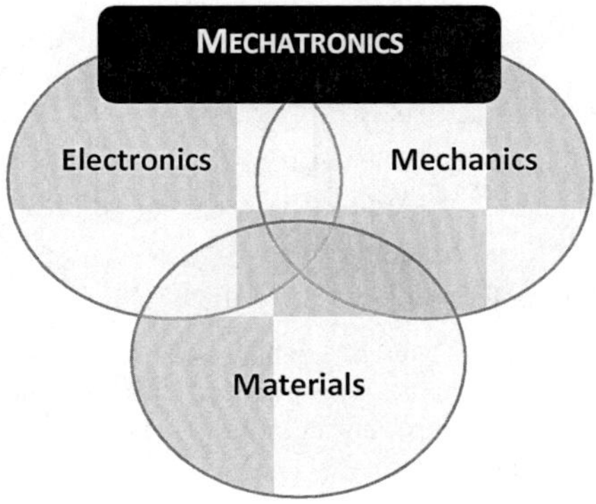

Figure 31: Technology fusion
Source: own illustration

A further distinction must be drawn between technology fusion and the technological interdependencies which arise from the complementary use of technologies from unrelated areas. Especially in the development of technological complex products, changes in one technological area often cause changes in complementary used technologies (Stephan, 2003, p. 160). To summarise, it should be emphasised that the increasing technological complexity as well as the fusion of formerly independent technologies lead to an increase in the degree of technological diversification.

d) Coordination of the supply chain:

Empirical evidence shows that the degree of technologicial diversification often exceeds the degree of product diversification (see among others: Granstrand/Oskarsson, 1994, p. 357; Granstrand/Patel/Pavitt, 1997, p. 10; Gambardella/Torrisi, 1998, p. 446). For instance, electronic companies which have focused their downstream activities did further expand their technological competences (Gambardella/Torrisi, 1998). This is caused by the fact that technologically complex products embody a number of distinct components and technologies. Furthermore, the development and manufacturing of these components is often carried out by external suppliers. But does the outsourcing of products also result in the outsourcing of technological competences? Analyses in technology-intensive industries show that the breadth and depth of the technological competence base is not affected by these outsourcing activities. A study of aircraft engine makers reveals that decisions to outsource components are not accompanied by an increasing technological specialisation. I.e. these companies maintain a broad range of in-house technological competences (Prencipe, 2004, p. 253 f.). Thus, the outsourcing of products or components does not result in the outsourcing of the corresponding technological competences. But why do firms invest in broadening their technology base while narrowing down their production bases? The transaction cost theory and the resource-based view (RBV) offer the explanations for this paradox. The transaction cost theory argues that firms develop technological competences alongside the outsourcing of production to protect themselves against the opportunistic behaviour by suppliers and the uncertain future (Stephan, 2010, pp. 309-315).

'[…], often coordination with external suppliers requires significant flows of proprietary knowledge that is difficult to protect (e.g., knowledge about processes or software) and the risk of opportunistic behaviour is high due to the small number of available suppliers.' (Torrisi/Granstrand, 2004, p. 49)

Purchased technologies are often characterised by high specificity and an idiosyncratic character. Furthermore, technologies are proprietary goods so that the market for technologies is inefficient. To assess the value of technological competences, firms rely partly on the disclosure of the supplier's knowledge. However, when the knowledge is sufficient codified and adapted to the recipient, the transfer of technological knowledge is irreversible. For this reason, the external suppliers will reveal only parts of their knowledge and the buyers risk the opportunistic behaviour of the suppliers. As a consequence, the firms keep in-house technological competences of their outsourced parts (Pavitt/Robson/Townsend, 1989, p. 91 f.; Granstand, 1998, pp. 478-480; Stephan, 2003, p. 96; Torrisi/Granstrand, 2004, p. 49). The resource-based view distinguishes between two concepts: absorptive capacity and dynamic capabilities. Cohen/Levinthal (1989) introduce the absorptive capacity concept. It describes the development of technological knowledge outside the core competences which makes it possible for firms to identify, assimilate and exploit external knowledge from suppliers, customers etc. Thus, these technological competences have an interface character. On the one hand they make it possible to evaluate the external knowledge, on the other hand they form the prerequisite for the successful integration of external knowledge (Cohen/Levinthal, 1989, 1990). The dynamic capabilities concept focuses on the firm's ability to renew and refine the existing knowledge base in order to address the changing environmental conditions. To face the changes which take place in the domains of the suppliers, firms need to possess technological knowledge outside their core competences. Consequently, the concept includes the integration and reconfiguration of internal as well as external knowledge (Teece/Pisano/Shuen, 1997, p. 516; Stephan, 2010, pp. 309-315). The arguments delivered by the transaction cost theory and the resource-based view offer explanations, why the outsourcing of technologies does not result in the reduction of the technological knowledge base of firms. On the contrary, outsourcing of technological competences can lead to increasing technological diversification.

e) *Licensing of technologies:*
The previous determinants of technological diversification have an 'internal' justification. I.e. firms expand their knowledge base in order to improve the competitiveness of existing products and processes, to develop new business areas or to reduce uncertainties. Despite this, the technological diversification also offers an 'external' justification: the licensing out of technologies (Cesaroni, 2004, p. 177 f.). This means that companies can license out their technologies to other firms in order to generate additional values from their innovative activities. Taking into account that the diversification of technologies is associated with high cost, the licensing out is a feasible strategy to increase the returns from innovation. This is particular true for technological classes which are marginal to the company's core competencies (ibid., p. 197). Cesaroni (2004) shows that corporations in the chemical processing industry use their in-house developed technological competences internally as well as for external licensing.

> 'Indeed, in the case of the chemical industry, the technological surplus generated by processes of technological diversification according to the needs of business diversification, provided an incentive to chemical corporations to license their technologies to other firms'. (Cesaroni, 2004, p. 176 f.)

In sum, it can be stated that the licensing out of technologies represents a strategy to gain additional values from innovative activities. It offers a further incentive for technological diversification, especially in industries with a high propensity to license out technologies (Cesaroni, 2004, p. 177).

Figure 32 summarises the determinants of technological diversification which have been discussed within this sub-section.

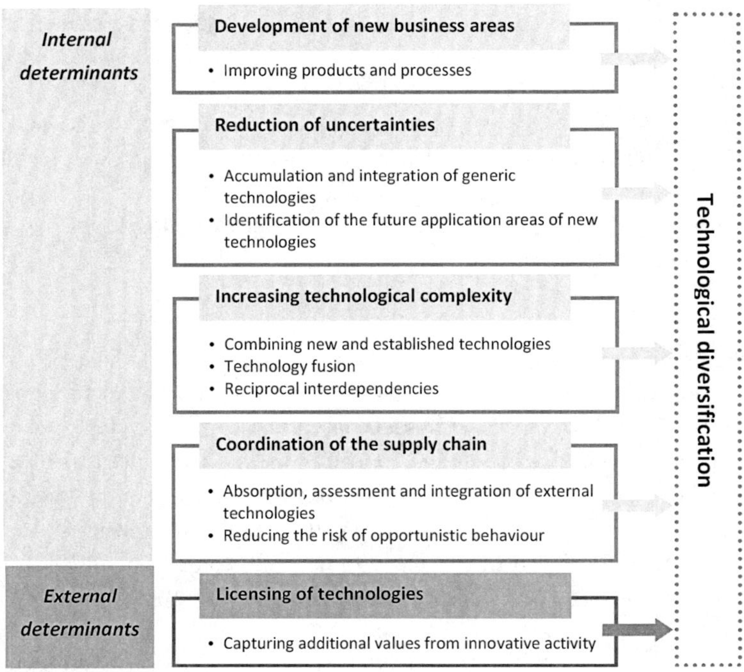

Figure 32: Determinants of technological diversification
Source: own illustration

III.1.2 Effects of technological diversification

The previous sub-section shed light on the determinants of technological diversification. In the following the main advantages of technological diversification will be presented.

- Technological diversification can give rise to economic benefits in the form of *static economies of scope*. These scope economies refer to the advantages arising when the technological knowledge of a company could be used across several product areas with minor adaption costs. This is especially true for generic technologies which can be applied in a wide range of sectors and products. Compared to the costs of acquiring technologies the costs of additional applications are small. Furthermore, technological knowledge can be used without deterioration. This means that knowledge is limitlessly reusable and not worn out when applied several times. The technological knowledge is improved through learning processes arising from the repeated application and therefore gives rise to *dynamic economies of scope* (Granstrand/Oskarsson, 1994, p. 356; Granstrand, 1998, p. 474).

- In addition, technological diversification creates synergy effects trough the complementary use of technologies. I.e. different technologies can cross-fertilise each other when combined.[27] The *cross-fertilisation of technologies* leads to increased product and process performance, new functionalities of existing products or completely new inventions (Granstrand/Oskarsson, 1994, p. 356; Granstrand, 1998, p. 474).

- The transfer of technological knowledge is – under certain conditions – associated with high costs. In this regard, the intra-firm technology transfer may be preferred if the external knowledge sourcing is surrounded by difficulties (see also *Chapter III.1.1*). Thus, the technology transfer within a multi-technology company is faster and more effective and can therefore give rise to time advantages – labelled as *economies of speed* (Teece, 1980, p. 226; Granstrand, 1998, p. 474).

- The diversification of the technology portfolio leads as already mentioned to the growth of R&D expenditures. However, as argued by the portfolio theory concept, variety reduces risks by reducing the variances associated with the returns from R&D investments. Therefore, technological diversification can *reduce the uncertainties in R&D projects*. Moreover, a diversified technology portfolio also *avoids lock-in effects* in declining technologies. Companies with a richer technology base can respond to unpredictable environmental changes with more flexibility and sustain their competitive position (Garcia-Vega, 2006, p. 231; Chiu et al., 2010, p. 39 f.).

- There is empirical evidence that technological diversification has also a *positive impact on firm performance*. The relationship between technological diversification and innovativeness of European companies is investigated by Garcia-Vega (2006). Those MTCs which have continuously expanded their technology bases are more innovative than others. Gambardella/Torrisi (1998) found a positive relationship between the technological diversification and the performance of the 32 largest US and European electronics firms. For a sample of 24 Swedish companies Granstrand/Sjölander (1990) recognised the positive correlations between corporate R&D intensity, sales growth and technological diversification. This perspective is confirmed by recent empirical studies (Miller, 2006; Chiu et al., 2007; Leten/Belderbos/van Looy, 2007). Taking into account that growing technological diversification is also associated with increasing coordination and integration costs, it

27 Diversified companies have a higher propensity to patent resulting from the cross-fertilisation of different technologies (Scherer, 1983, p. 117).

can be argued that the expansion of the knowledge base may only be economically meaningful until a certain degree. I.e. the positive impacts of technological diversification can only be achieved if the diversification of the technology base does not exceed a certain threshold (see Figure 33). It can be assumed that there is an inverted U-shaped relationship between technological diversification and firm performance (Granstrand/Sjölander, 1990, p. 59; Leten/Belderbos/van Looy, 2007, p. 575).

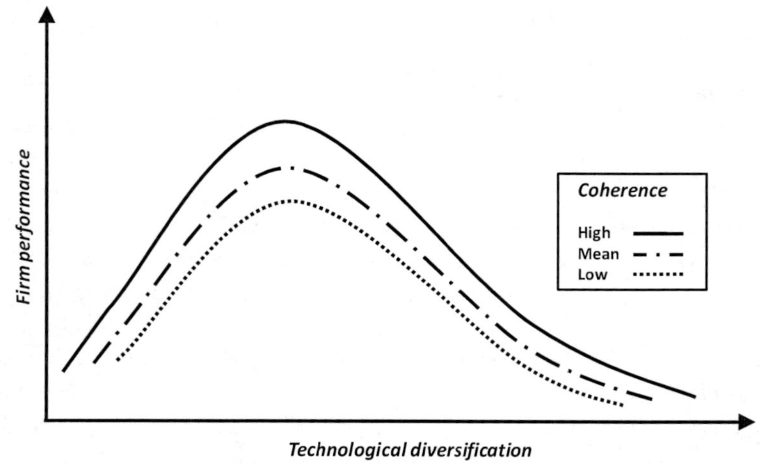

Figure 33: Relationship between technological diversification and firm performance

Soucrce: cf. Leten/Belderbos/van Looy, 2007, p. 575, own illustration

Another important success factor is the technological coherence in the technology base. The benefits resulting from a diversified technology portfolio seem to be higher, when the underlying technologies are related. Thus, investments in related technologies, which share partly a common knowledge base, provide sufficient levels of scale economies and favour the cross-fertilisation of technologies. Furthermore, the integration and coordination costs are reduced. However, it has to be noted that the investment in related technological areas may also promote path dependence and lower the opportunity to exploit new technologies. Thus, there is also an inverted U-shaped relationship between technological relatedness and the future technological performance (Nesta/Saviotti, 2005; Leten/Belderbos/van Looy, 2007; Shin/Jalajas, 2010).

In conclusion, the positive effects of technological diversification are summarised in Figure 34.

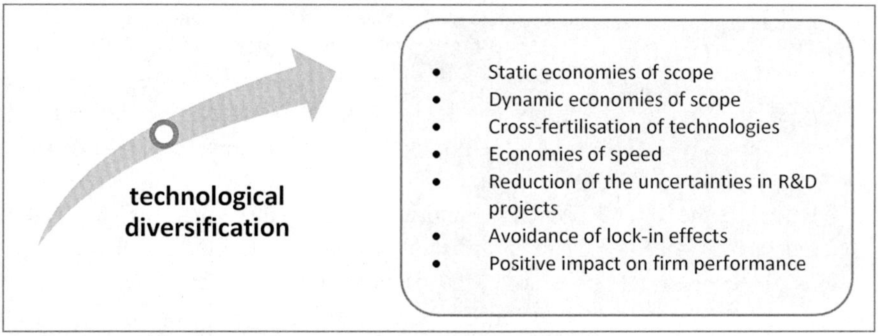

Figure 34: Positive effects of technological diversification
Source: own illustration

III.2 Technological change at the firm level

This section elaborates the nature of technological change at the firm level. First, the process of technological change is discussed from an evolutionary perspective focusing on the role of routines by shaping the technological search space of firms. Second, the accumulation of new technological knowledge is explored from the perspective of the resource-based view of the firm.

III.2.1 Evolutionary theory of the firm

In the Nelson-Winter framework organisational routines are described as follows:

> 'It may refer to a repetitive pattern of activity in an entire organization, to an individual skill, or, as an adjective, to the smooth uneventful effectiveness of such an organizational or individual performance.' (Nelson/Winter, 1982, p. 97)

They are used to understand the forces of change at the micro-level. The organisational routines help to identify the sources of change that affect the behaviour of firms. Furthermore, organisational routines represent the repository of the organisation's capabilities (Nelson/Winter, 1982, pp. 96-136; Becker, 2004; Becker et al., 2005, pp. 775-780).

> 'A routine, as a way of doing something in an organization, has two aspects. One is like a recipe or a program. The other is the way the work is divided up among individuals and organizational sub-units, and coordinated and managed.' (Becker et al., 2005, p. 778)

Routines reflect recurrent patterns of activity. They represent rules on how things should be done or improved (Dosi, 1988, p. 1133).

> '[...], through practice, repetition, and more or less incremental improvements [routines] make certain firms "good" at exploring certain technical opportunities and translating them into specific marketable products.' (ibid., p. 1133)

The collective nature of activity is a key characteristic of routines. In general, routines are carried out through the interaction of multiple actors which can be located in different places or organisational units. However, the routines are embedded in the organisational structures and are, therefore, highly context specific. As a consequence, it is difficult to transfer routines to other organisations or contexts. Furthermore, the context-specificity and embeddedness favours the path dependence of routines. The learning processes take place close to previous activities. They are characterised by trial, feedback and evaluation. Moreover, historically developed solutions to problems are stored in the organisational memory. Therefore, it is difficult to 'reset' routines and enter alternative search paths (Teece/Pisano/Shuen, 1997, p. 522 f.; Becker, 2004, pp. 646-653; Dominquez Lacasa, 2005, pp. 29-31.). Hence, to avoid lock-in effects in declining technologies and to renew the knowledge base, firms have to build up new and promising technologies.

III.2.2 Resource-based view of the firm

There are two different processes of resource accumulation which have to be distinguished: *exploitation* and *exploration*[28]. I.e. firms can draw on their established competencies and exploit the existing knowledge base or explore the external environment for new technological opportunities (see also *Chapter II.6.3.2*).

The *exploitative search strategy* leverages the existing resources. Thus, the knowledge base is refined and expanded through the recombination of the existing pieces of knowledge. As a consequence, this strategy is characterised by low costs and risks. An important disadvantage is that the chance of discovering new technological opportunities is very low. The repeated exploitation and the associated local search constrict the research space in coming periods. In the long term this may endanger the firm's competitive position. To avoid such lock-in effects new and promising technologies have to be developed. The *exploratory search strategy* is oriented towards the development of competences in new technological domains. Thus, the external environment is the nucleus for new opportunities. Exploration includes things captured by terms such as experimentation and risk taking. In contrast to exploitation, the exploratory

28 For a more detailled overview of this topic see also: Praest (1998), Stephan (2003, 2004), Stohr (2007).

strategy is time consuming and involves also higher costs because the outcomes of the process are highly uncertain. Moreover, in most cases the gap between the existing competences and the new developed technologies is comparably high. Thus, it is also difficult to integrate and adapt the new knowledge into the existing knowledge base. Summing up it can be said, that exploitation relies on the existing resources and entails the refinement and extension of the established knowledge base. The exploratory research strategy increases the technological diversity of the knowledge base (March, 1991, pp. 71-73; Praest, 1998, pp. 11-20; Stephan, 2003, pp. 147-150; Leten/van Looy/Belderbos, 2008, p. 2 f.).

In general, most firms do not solely rely on one research strategy, but face a trade-off between exploitation and exploration. *'In sum a balance between exploration and exploitation seems a viable strategy for sustained firm survival* (Praest, 1998, p. 20).

The resource accumulation strategies can be linked to two different diversification types: related and unrelated diversification. The related diversification uses the existing technological capabilities to build up new technological competences. As a consequence, the new technologies show a high similarity to the existing technology base. I.e. the related diversification captures the characteristics of the exploitative research strategy. The unrelated diversification strategy opens up new technologies that have nothing in common with the existing knowledge base. I.e. it captures the characteristics of the exploratory research (Stephan, 2003, p. 151; Stephan, 2004, pp. 242-247).

III.3 Research theses

The preceding theoretical contributions of *Chapter III* state the increasing technological diversification of MTCs in the Triads since the 1980s. However, there are only few studies investigating the developments in the following decades. An exception is the study of Gerybadze/Stephan (2002) which stresses the decline in technological diversification of MTCs since the beginning of the 1990s. Hence, it is questionable if the diversification trend of the 1980s has continued or not.

Taking into account the inverted U-shaped relationship between technological diversification and firm performance, *Thesis 3* argues that the expansion of the technological portfolios has come to a halt during the 1990s. Furthermore, it is assumed that MTCs have begun to refocus their technology base in the new millennium.

Thesis 3: **The trends in technological diversification have changed.** Since the 1980s multi-technological companies have continuously increased their technological diversification. However, it is assumed that this trend has reversed in the new millennium.

Chapter III

By expanding their technological portfolios firms can draw on their established competencies and exploit the existing knowledge base or search for new technological opportunities. The unrelated technological diversification entails the development of new technologies, which have nothing in common with the established technological competences and are therefore associated with high risks and costs. In contrast to this, the diversification in related areas is characterised by high degrees of relatedness between the old technologies and the new technologies.

Thesis 4 argues that the benefits resulting from the expansion of the technology base are higher, when the underlying technologies are related. Hence, it is assumed that MTCs show higher shares of related diversification.

Thesis 4: **Firms tend to diversify into related technological areas.** Thus, it can be assumed, that large MTCs will be characterised by comparably higher shares of related technological diversification than unrelated technological diversification.

Chapter III

III.4 Selection of the firm sample

This sub-chapter introduces the company data set which has been collected to investigate the technology base of large European MTCs. The sample covers companies, whose ultimate parent company is located in Germany, France, Italy, the Netherlands, the United Kingdom or Switzerland. The list of sample companies was identified in two ways. The first group – *Scoreboard companies* – consists of those firms which were among the top R&D spending companies between 2008 and 2009. The second group – *Top applicants* – comprises those firms which have accounted for the highest level of life sciences patents during the period 1986-2005.

a) *Scoreboard companies:*

Firms were selected from the *'2008 EU Industrial R&D Investment Scoreboard'* (European Commission, 2009) and *'2009 EU Industrial R&D Investment Scoreboard'* (European Commission, 2010) published by the European Commission. The list of Swiss firms was obtained from the *'2008 R&D Scoreboard'* (Department for Innovation, University and Skills, 2009) and the *'2009 R&D Scoreboard'* (Department for Business, Innovations and Skills, 2010) provided by the British government. These scoreboards list the top R&D spending companies in the world and contain information about their R&D expenditures, sales, employees, market capitalisation etc. Furthermore, the scoreboards report the sectors and countries of the top R&D spenders.

Based on their main economic activity, the firms were assigned to appropriate ICB sectors.[29] Actual the scoreboards cover more than 30 sectors at the three digit-level. Thus, in order to extract the relevant sample of life sciences companies an adequate subset of ICB sectors has to be determined. Thus, analogous to the technology-based definition of the life sciences industry introduced in *Chapter II.6.1* an ICB sector-based definition of the life sciences industry is created. However, it has to be noted that the technological classes of the *WIPO IPC Technology Concordance* cannot be directly translated into the industrial sectors of the ICB. Although there have been numerous attempts at linking technology and industry classifications, a satisfactory solution to this problem does not exist (Schmoch et al., 2003, pp. 1-4). In the context of this thesis the technology-based definition of the life sciences was used as basis for the sector-based definition (Figure 35).

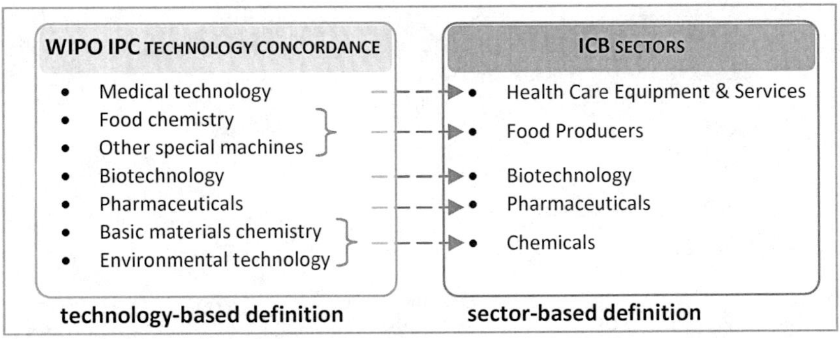

Figure 35: Life sciences sectors
Source: own illustration

29 Industry Classification Benchmark (ICB)

The following sectors of the ICB are suitable for representing the life sciences industry: Health Care Equipment & Services, Food Producers, Biotechnology, Pharmaceuticals and Chemicals.

b) *Top applicants:*
The scoreboards cover only information about the actual top R&D spenders. Taking into account only the companies listed in R&D scoreboards may, therefore, neglect the 'real' distribution of the applicant structure at the patent offices (Frietsch, 2006, p. 159 f.). The scoreboards do not take into account small firms which spent comparably lower sums in R&D, but are not necessarily little innovative. Furthermore, the scoreboards report only the actual top R&D spenders. Thus, those companies who have invested large sums in R&D in the past – i.e. during the period 1986-2005 – are not necessarily listed in the actual scoreboards.

To tackle this problem the list of sample companies was expanded taking also into consideration the top patent applicants of the sample countries during the period 1986-2005. Using the country data set presented in *Chapter II*, for each country a list of the 'Top30' patent applicants was compiled. From this list, initially, all research faculties and private persons (inventors) were excluded. Second, those companies, who were already listed in the respective scoreboard or whose ultimate parent is not headquartered in the considered countries, were eliminated. Based on the information about the main economic activity, these firms were classified to one of the life sciences sectors.[30] Those companies which could not be assigned to one of these sectors were excluded.[31]

Figure 36 summarises the proceeding. By bringing together the selected scoreboard companies and the selected top applicants the preliminary company sample consists of 178 firms (Annex X).

30 Information on the sector of main economic activity was extracted from annual reports and the LexisNexis database by using the following sources: *Extel Cards Database, Hoppenstedt Konzernstrukturen, The Major Companies Database, LexisNexis(R) Corporate Affiliations (TM).*

31 For example, Siemens was one of Germany's top patent applicants due to its technological know-how in the field of Medical technology. However, the company has its main economic activity in the fields Electrical Components & Equipment and was therefore excluded from the sample.

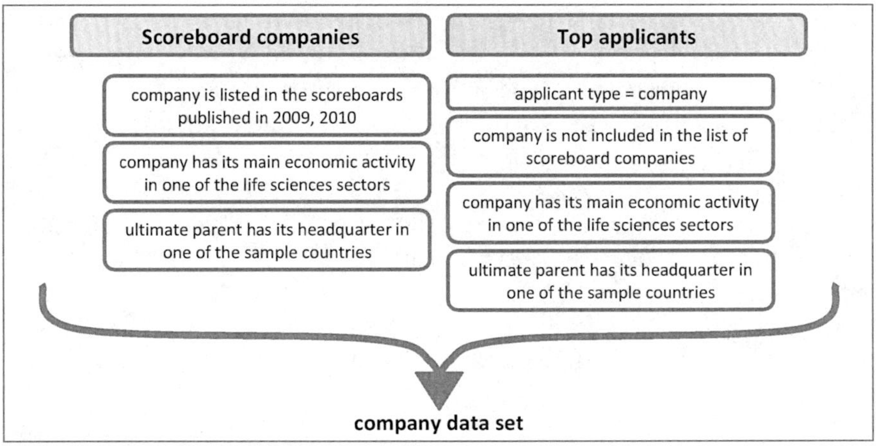

Figure 36: Selection of the company data set
Source: own illustration

III.5 Data extraction and processing

The technological activities of the sample firms are constructed using patent data. In this context one major problem is that company names in patent databases are not unified. I.e. company names may appear under different names due to typing errors (e.g. 'Eppendorf' and 'Ependorf'), acronyms ('LFB' and 'Laboratoire Français de Fractionement et des Biotechnologies') and different spellings of the names (e.g. BioMérieux and Bio Merieux). To deal with this problem keywords as distinctive as possible were used.

Furthermore, patents are also applied for under the names of subsidiaries or divisions of the parent company. Thus, to collect the patent data at the consolidated parent level, the corporate structure of each sample company has to be determined.[32] This includes the determination of subsidiaries or affiliates as well as the consideration of mergers and acquisitions. The consolidation was conducted based on the corporate structure in the year 2009. Concerning the mergers this means that the companies were regarded as merged from the beginning of the observation period.[33] In total, more than 3,000 different keywords have been linked to the sample firms.

32 The consolidated data were constructed based on the information on the corporate structure provided by LexisNexis using the following sources: *Extel Cards Database, Hoppenstedt Konzernstrukturen, The Major Companies Database, LexisNexis(R) Corporate Affiliations (TM)*. If necessary, these data were supplemented by information available in the firm's annual reports.

33 A detailed discussion on this topic is provided by Frietsch (2006), p. 178 f.

The location of the technological activities was proxied as follows: Patents were assigned to the countries in which the applicant has his residence. If a patent has more than one applicant, a proportional fraction of the patent is assigned to each applicant's country of residence. For the consolidated company level the following data were extracted from the EPO Worldwide Statistical Patent Database (PATSTAT October 2007): priority date (1986-2005)[34], IPC classes, name and location of the applicant, name and location of co-applicants. The patent data set covers the patent applications at the EPO and WIPO.

III.6 Technological diversification patterns of European life sciences companies

The following empirical analyses provide an overview of the breadth and depth of the technology bases in the life sciences. First, the depth of the technological portfolios, i.e. the classes of technological specialisation, is analysed using the index of Relative Technological Advantage (RTA). Second, the breadth of the technology base, i.e. the degree of technological diversification, is investigated. Different diversification measures are used in order to show the rates and directions of corporate technological diversification. Additionally, the dynamics in the technology bases are assessed by taking into account the exploration of new technological classes.

Furthermore, this chapter aims at providing a first impression of the firm-external factors which shape the patterns of technological diversification. For this purpose, the evolution of the technological profiles of the life sciences companies is assessed at the national and sectoral level. At the national level, the analyses are provided at the level of the six different sample countries. At the sectoral level the study distinguishes between the different life sciences sectors.

III.6.1 Technological performance in the life sciences industry

The aim of this sub-section is to provide an initial overview of the technological activities of the sample firms. For this purpose, the technological profiles of the sample companies were compiled based on the patent applications during the period 1986-2005.

34 The delimitation of the time period is based on the priority date of the patent applications. The priority date is appropriate for patent statistics because it is close to the date of the invention (Schmoch, 1999, p. 120).

By performing the patent analysis it appeared that for some companies no patent applications were found. This is due to the following reasons: First, some of these firms have applied for patents, but these patents did not cover the life sciences technologies. Second, the companies have applied for patents at the national patent offices and not at the EPO or WIPO. Third, some of the firms may rely on other protection instruments (Frietsch, 2006, p. 179). The ten companies[35] of the sample which have not applied for life sciences patents during the period of investigation were excluded from the following analyses.

Furthermore, the analyses contain only those firms which show technological activities during at least two of the four time periods considered (see *Annex XI*). Firms that have applied for less than 20 patents during the period of investigation were also excluded from the sample. The final sample then consists of 114 firms.[36] Table 3 lists the number of sample firms by sector and nation of origin. It shows that the number of life sciences companies is unevenly distributed across the sample nations. More than 50% of the companies are located in Germany and the United Kingdom. Turning the focus on the sectoral distribution reveals that the life sciences industry is dominated by pharmaceutical companies. Food producers represent the lowest share of life sciences companies and are mainly headquartered in the Netherlands and the United Kingdom.

Table 3: Distribution of sample firms by sector and nation of origin
Source: own compilation

		Nation of origin						
		CH	DE	FR	IT	NL	UK	Σ
Sector	Biotechnology	3	7	4	0	3	7	**24**
	Chemicals	5	9	3	1	2	3	**23**
	Food Producers	1	1	2	2	4	5	**14**
	Health Care & Equipment Services	2	7	2	2	0	5	**18**
	Pharmaceuticals	4	10	3	7	2	9	**35**
	Σ	**15**	**34**	**14**	**12**	**11**	**29**	**114**

During the period 1986-2005 the sample firms have applied for a total of 72,186 patents. On average the life sciences companies hold 633 patents. The standard

35 Balda, Fuchs Petrolub, Uzin Utz, Franz Haniel & Cie, LFB, Dynaction, Unibel, Polynt, Lectus Therapeutics and Dechra Pharmaceuticals.

36 Please note that Unilever has two parent companies: *Unilever NV* located in the Netherlands and *Unilver PLC* located in the UK. As a consequence, the patent profiles of Unilever are assigned to both countries.

deviation of 1,476 patents indicates that the number of patents has a high dispersion about the mean. While 56 sample companies have applied for less than 100 patents, the chemical company Bayer shows the highest technological activities (7,883 patents). Thus, the sample companies differ in their propensity to patent.

The concentration of the patent applications is indicated by the Lorenz curve in Figure 37. When the patent applications are uniformly distributed, the Lorenz curve coincides with the 45-degree line. For the sample data set the Lorenz curve in Figure 37 shows that the patents are unevenly distributed across the firms. The 'Top15' applicants account for about 70% of the total patent stock.

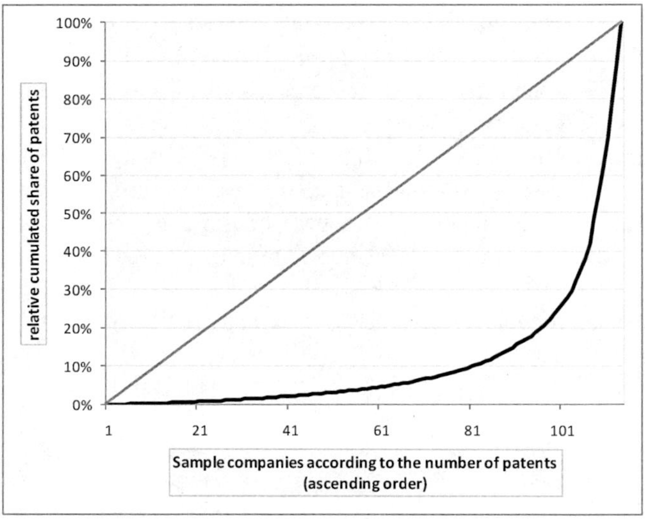

Figure 37: Concentration of patent applications
Source: PATSTAT October 2007, own computations

In the following the technological profiles of the sample companies are investigated in detail. To control for cyclical fluctuations the technological activities are produced for four time periods (P_1 = 1986/1990, P_2 = 1991/1995, P_3 = 1996/2000, P_4 = 2001/2005) based on the priority years.

Figure 38 provides a general overview of the technological activities in the different life sciences sectors during the period 1986-2005. The highest shares of the life sciences patents have been applied for in the sectors Pharmaceuticals and Chemicals. Turning the focus on the evolution of the patent output the figure reveals that the amount of patents has continuously increased in all sectors (except Pharmaceuticals and Food Producers). The highest growth rates are achieved during the periods P_1, P_2 and P_3. The lowest patent activity is observed in the sectors Health Care Equipment & Services and Biotechnology.

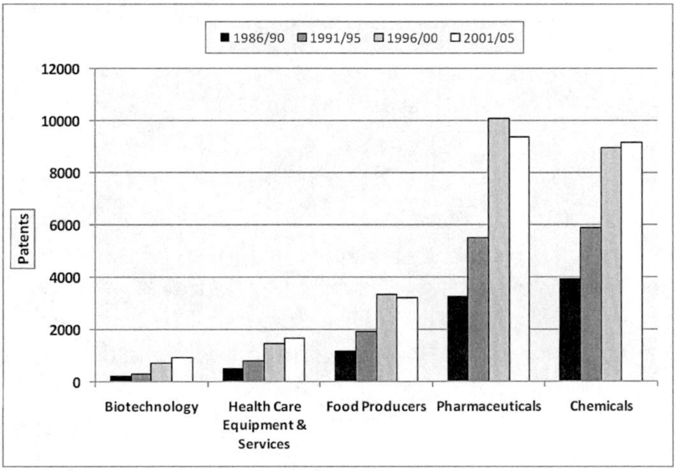

Figure 38: Sectoral distribution of patent activities
Source: PATSTAT October 2007, own computations

Next, the breadth and depth of the corporate technological portfolios are examined in detail. *Chapter III.6.2* analyses the fields of technological advantage. The patterns of technological diversification are elaborated in *Chapter III.6.3*.

III.6.2 Patterns of technological specialisation

The aim of this sub-section is to illustrate the patterns of technological specialisation. The technological profiles of the companies were analysed using the index of *Relative Technological Advantage (RTA)* introduced in *Chapter II.6.4*. The *Relative Technological Advantage (RTA)* determines the specialisation in a particular technology and is defined as follows:

$$RTA_{ix} = \frac{p_{ix}/p_i}{p_x/p_{total}} \tag{III.1}$$

where p_{ix} is the number of company x's patent applications in technology class i, p_x the number of company x's patent applications in total, p_i the total number of patent applications in technology i and p_{total} the total number of patent applications (Cantwell, 2004, p. 273).

The hyperbolic tangent of the RTA is defined as:

$$RTA_{\mathrm{h}_{\mathrm{ix}}} = 100 \tanh \ln \left(RTA_{ix}\right).$$

(III.2)

Figure 39, Figure 40, Figure 41, Figure 42 and Figure 43 illustrate the technological specialisation patterns of the sample companies, measured by RTA_h-values, at the sectoral level. The figures clearly show that the companies from different industrial sectors have developed specific specialisation profiles.

a) Biotechnology:

Companies from the Biotechnology sector have their relative technological advantages mainly in the technological classes *Biotechnology* and *Pharmaceuticals* (see Figure 39). Thus, at a first glance, the technology profile of these companies seems to be highly focused, as indicated by the high specialisation in *Biotechnology* as well as *Pharmaceuticals*. Turning the analysis to the country level shows slight differences in the specialisation patterns. Companies from Germany, France and the Netherlands are characterised by high specialisation in *Biotechnology* and moderate specialisation in *Pharmaceuticals*. In contrast to this, for biotechnology firms from Switzerland and the United Kingdom the patterns are reverse (high specialisation in *Pharmaceuticals*, moderate specialisation in *Biotechnology*).

b) Chemicals:

In the Chemicals sector the technology class *Basic materials chemistry* is the field of main technological advantage (see Figure 40, p. 120). Despite this, the specialisation patterns of the chemical companies are less homogenous. A large amount of companies is also specialised in *Food chemistry*. Chemical companies from Germany, France and the United Kingdom have additionally gained technological advantages in *Environmental technology*. A few companies are also specialised in *Biotechnology* or *Pharmaceuticals*. Summarising it can be said that the technological knowledge base is more diverse than those of the other life sciences sectors.

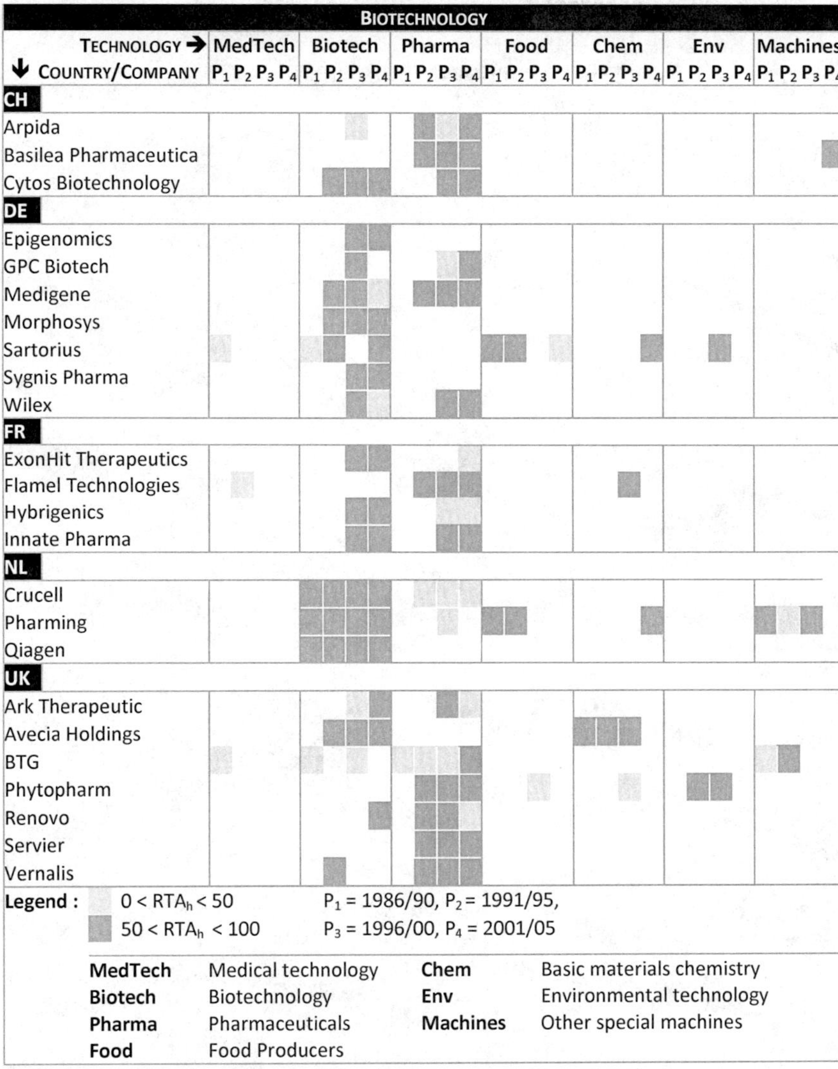

Figure 39: Technological specialisation patterns - Biotechnology

Source: PATSTAT October 2007, own computations

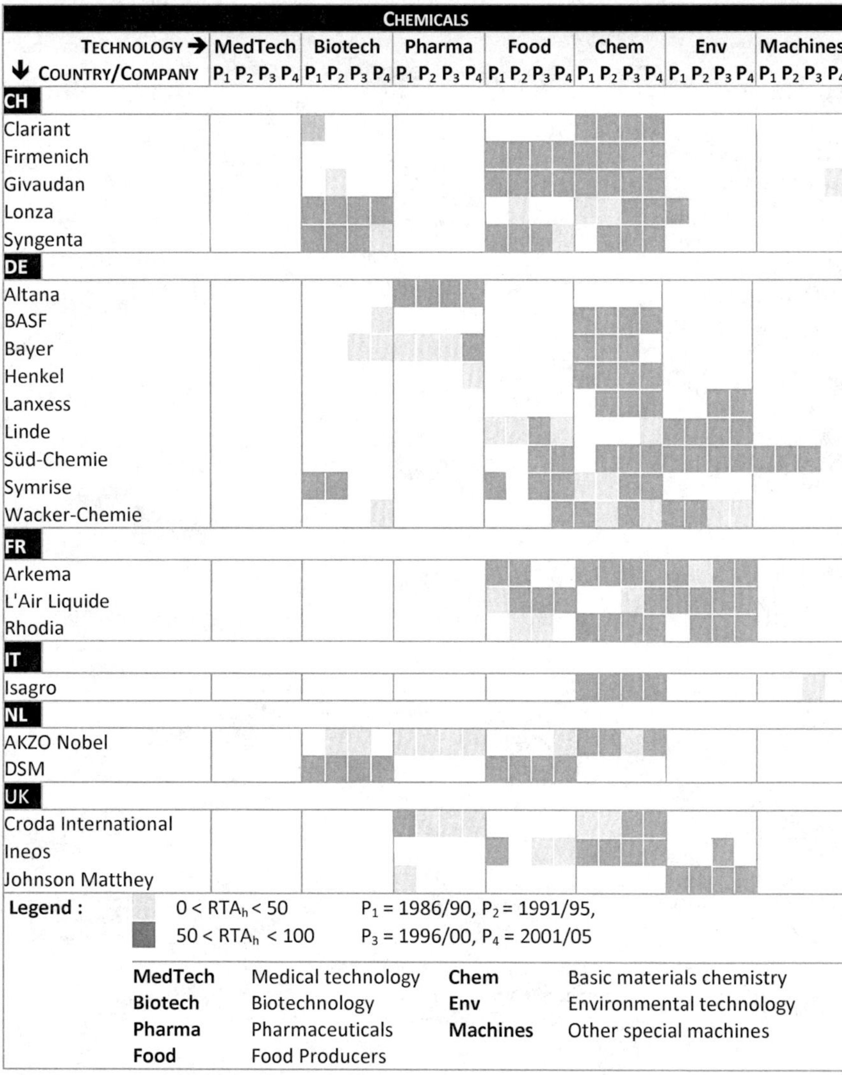

Figure 40: Technological specialisation patterns - Chemicals

Source: PATSTAT October 2007, own computations

c) Food Producers:

In the Food Producers sector the comparative technological advantages lie primarily in the technological class *Food chemistry*. Additionally, most companies are specialised in the technology class *Other special machines*. This may be caused by the fact, that machines for food production are classified as part of the technology field *Other special machines* (Schmoch, 2008, p. 13 f.). Especially firms from Italy and the Netherlands are characterised by technological advantages in this technological class. In the remaining life sciences technologies only few companies could gain relative technological advantages.

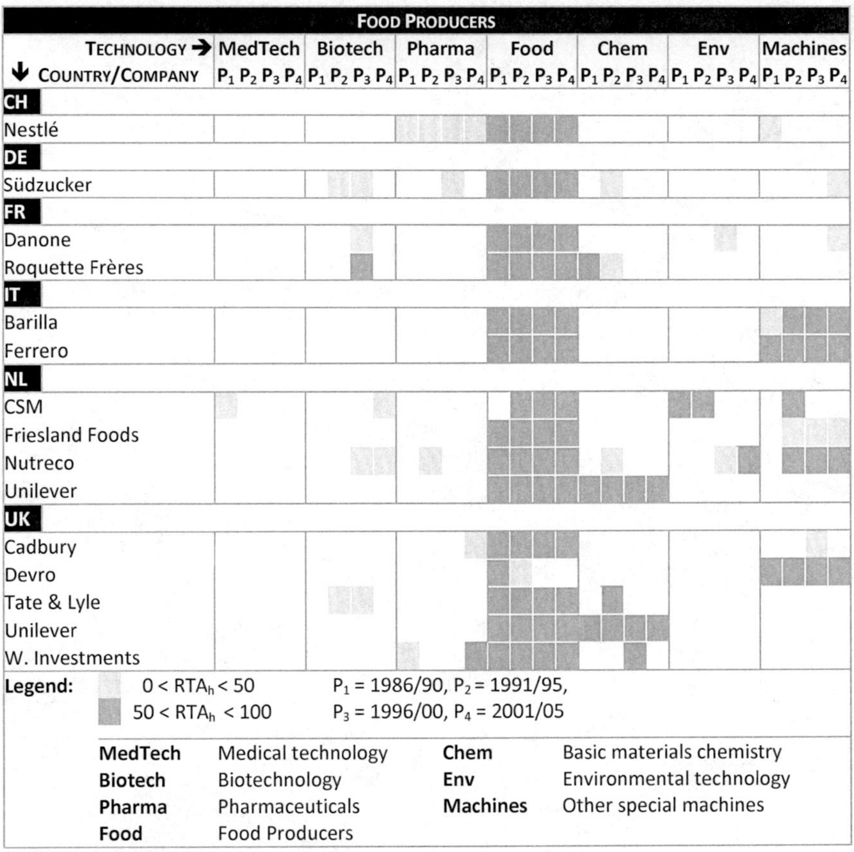

Figure 41: Technological specialisation patterns - Food Producers

Source: PATSTAT October 2007, own computations

d) Health Care Equipment & Services:

In the sector Health Care Equipment & Services the relative technological advantages lie almost exclusively in the class *Medical technology*. Thus, the technology profile in this sector is very focused and characterised by high specialisation in *Medical technology*. Despite this, a few companies could gain comparative advantages in *Biotechnology*, *Pharmaceuticals* or *Basic materials chemistry*.

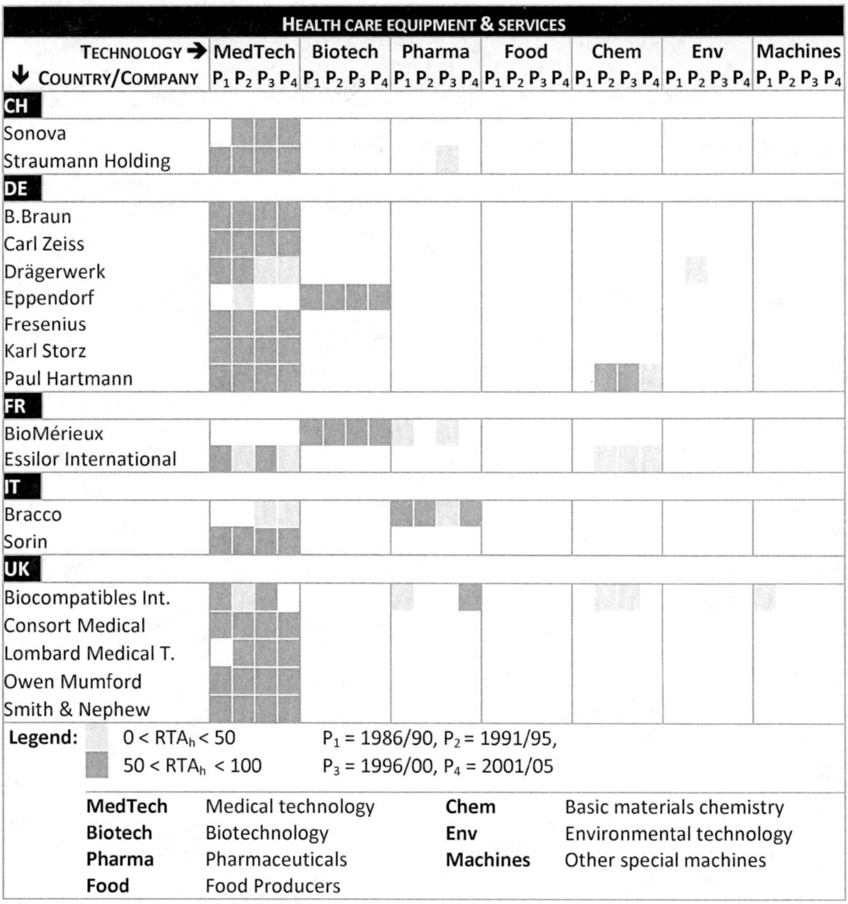

Figure 42: Technological specialisation patterns - Health Care Equipment & Services

Source: PATSTAT October 2007, own computations

e) Pharmaceuticals:

Companies from the Pharmaceuticals sector are highly specialised in the technology class *Pharmaceuticals*. Approximately half of the companies could also gain relative technological advantages in *Biotechnology*. Thus, the technology base in this sector is also comparably focused.

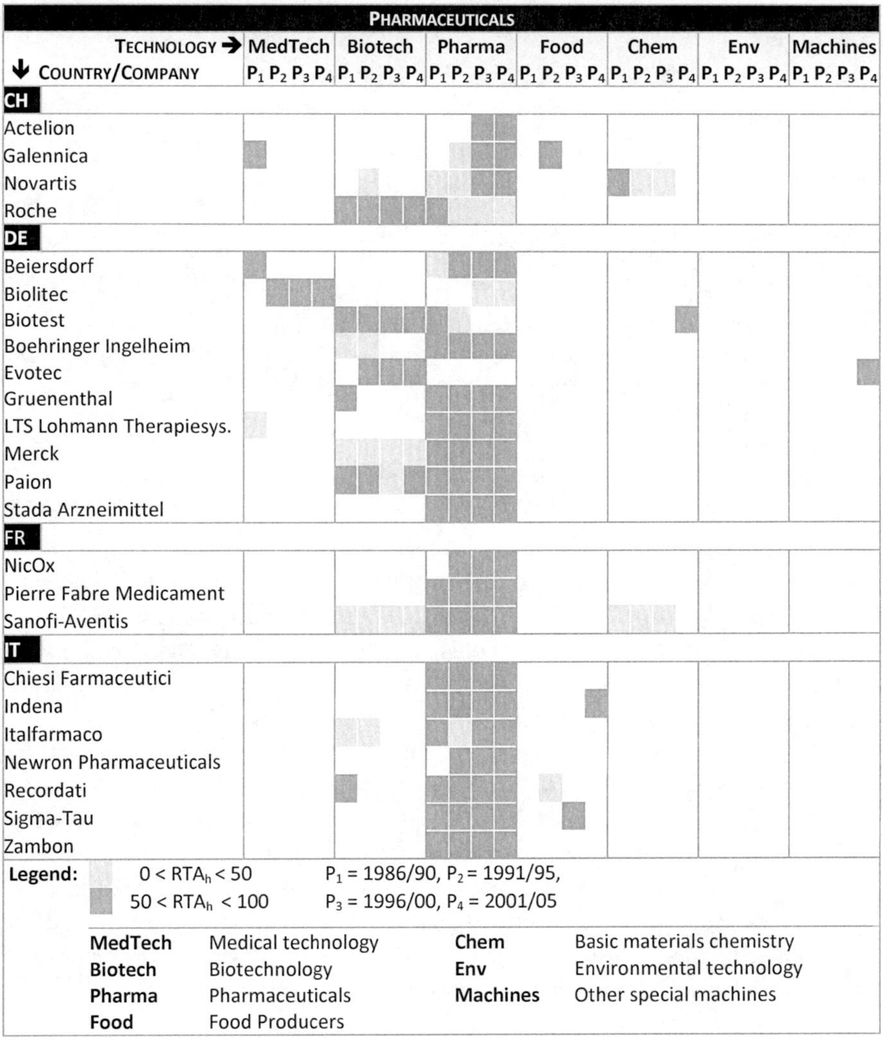

Figure 43: Technological specialisation patterns - Pharmaceuticals

Source: PATSTAT October 2007, own computations

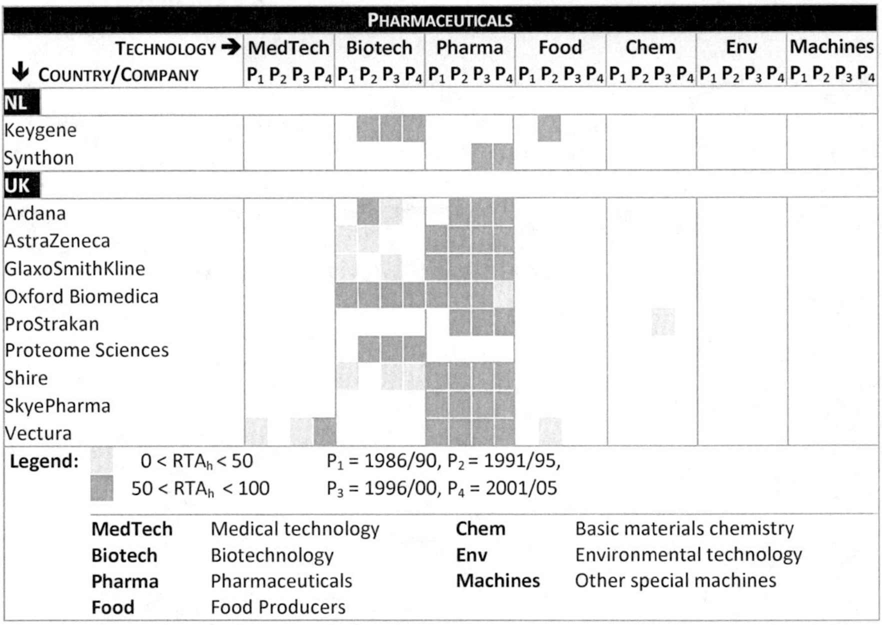

Figure 43: Technological specialisation patterns - Pharmaceuticals (continued)
Source: PATSTAT October 2007, own computations

Comparison of the sectoral technological specialisation patterns

The analysis of the specialisation patterns shows that companies from different sectors have developed distinct patterns of technological strength. While the specialisation patterns in Biotechnology, Pharmaceuticals and Health Care Equipment & Services are comparably focused, Food Producers and Chemical companies could gain technological advantages in a wide range of technological fields. Despite this, the analysis exhibits that technological advantages in *Biotechnology* seem to be important in all sectors (with the one exception: Health Care Equipment & Services). Country specific patterns of specialisation can be observed in the Biotechnology, Food Producers and Chemicals sectors. Furthermore, the figures reveal that the corporate technological specialisation patterns are rather persistent over time. Thus, the evolution of the firm specific technological capabilities is an incremental and cumulative process. This is in line with the observations of *Chapter II* showing the path dependent evolution of technological competences.

In conclusion, the analysis of the technological specialisation patterns exhibits that the life sciences sectors are characterised by distinct, path dependent technological profiles. Additionally, biotechnology represents the platform technology of the life sciences sectors which is applied in nearly all sectors except Health Care Equipment & Services. Similar results are obtained by Patel/Pavitt (1997) and Fai/Tunzelmann (2001): On the one hand they stress the evolution of distinct sectoral technological profiles. On the other hand the importance of platform technologies that develop across sectoral borders is emphasised (Patel/Pavitt, 1997, p. 144 ff.; Fai/Tunzelmann, 2001, p. 166 f.).

Thesis 2b predicts the influence of the technological, sectoral and national environment on the technological profiles of firms. The recent findings seem to support this thesis. The analysis of the RTA_h-profiles reveals the presence of sectoral and national technological diversification patterns. Furthermore, the increasing importance of the technological class *Biotechnology* for nearly all life sciences sectors has been shown. This indicates that the technological system of biotechnology has an influence on the sectors of the life sciences industry.

III.6.3 Patterns of technological diversification

The technological diversification is calculated using the entropy measure introduced in *Chapter II.6.3.2*. At the firm level *technological diversification (TD)* is defined as:

$$TD_x = \sum_{i=1}^{N} P_{ix} log\left(\frac{1}{P_{ix}}\right) \qquad \text{(III.3)}$$

where P_{ix} is company x's share of patent applications in technology class i (i = 1, …, N; N ≤ 35).

Table 4 summarises the trends in technological diversification differentiated by home countries and industrial sectors of the sample companies. At the beginning of the 1990s the sample companies have slightly decreased their degree of technological diversification. In the mid-1990s this trend has come to a halt. The technological diversification of the sample companies now remains quite stable. However, at the beginning of the new millennium, there is a strong decrease in technological diversification by 10%. Thus, the trend of diversifying the technology portfolio has not continued. These observations support *Thesis 3*. The trend of increasing technological diversification is reversed in the new millennium. The life sciences companies have begun to refocus their technology base.

Table 4: Technological diversification of the sample firms

Source: PATSTAT October 2007, own computations

	Technological diversification (TD)							
Industrial Sectors		**Period**	**Mean**	**△ TD**	Countries	**Period**	**Mean**	**△ TD**
	Biotech-nology	**1986/90**	0.440		**CH**	**1986/90**	0.745	
		1991/95	0.453	3.02%		**1991/95**	0.549	-26.39%
		1996/00	0.473	4.50%		**1996/00**	0.571	4.04%
		2001/05	0.399	-15.65%		**2001/05**	0.567	-0.68%
	Chemicals	**1986/90**	0.724		**DE**	**1986/90**	0.586	
		1991/95	0.754	4.08%		**1991/95**	0.580	-1.02%
		1996/00	0.789	4.72%		**1996/00**	0.599	3.26%
		2001/05	0.757	-4.08%		**2001/05**	0.528	-11.86%
	Food Producers	**1986/90**	0.490		**FR**	**1986/90**	0.675	
		1991/95	0.566	15.31%		**1991/95**	0.633	-6.18%
		1996/00	0.536	-5.29%		**1996/00**	0.608	-4.00%
		2001/05	0.496	-7.46%		**2001/05**	0.566	-6.89%
	Health Care Equipment & Services	**1986/90**	0.459		**IT**	**1986/90**	0.386	
		1991/95	0.426	-7.19%		**1991/95**	0.434	12.52%
		1996/00	0.471	10.59%		**1996/00**	0.413	-4.82%
		2001/05	0.373	-20.84%		**2001/05**	0.377	-8.78%
	Pharma-ceuticals	**1986/90**	0.507		**NL**	**1986/90**	0.484	
		1991/95	0.452	-10.95%		**1991/95**	0.537	10.89%
		1996/00	0.441	-2.33%		**1996/00**	0.511	-4.74%
		2001/05	0.405	-8.10%		**2001/05**	0.475	-7.02%
Total		**1986/90**	0.547		**UK**	**1986/90**	0.480	
		1991/95	0.530	**-3.23%**		**1991/95**	0.473	-1.49%
		1996/00	0.534	0.93%		**1996/00**	0.472	-0.09%
		2001/05	0.481	**-10.00%**		**2001/05**	0.396	-16.27%

(shaded) Total diversification is above average

The table also reveals that there exist considerable differences between the sample companies according to their home countries or industrial sectors. Figure 44 provides an overview of the trends in total diversification differentiated at the sectoral level.

Companies from the Chemicals sector show by far the highest degree of diversification. Furthermore, these companies have expanded their technology base until the beginning of the new millennium. The Food Producers are also characterised by a relatively broad technological base as indicated by the entropy measure. Since the beginning of the 1990s their degree of technological diversification is above average. Companies from the Biotechnology, Health Care Equipment & Services and Pharmaceuticals sector manage a technology portfolio that is comparatively less diversified.

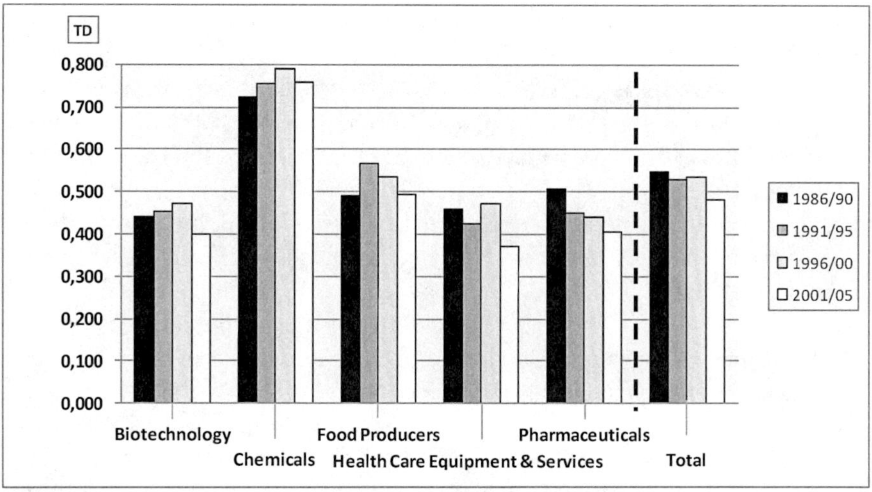

Figure 44: Development of technological diversification (sectoral level)
Source: PATSTAT October 2007, own computations

Figure 44 also reveals that there exist differences concerning the development of technological diversification. While companies from the Chemicals and Biotechnology sector have expanded their technology base until the end of the 1990s, companies from the Pharmaceuticals sector have continuously refocused their technological portfolio. At the country level the trends in total diversification are illustrated in Figure 45.

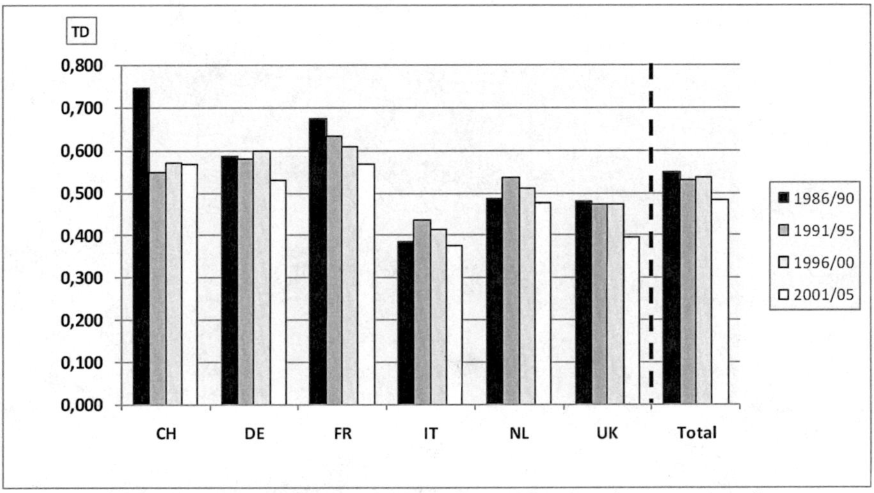

Figure 45: Development of technological diversification (country level)
Source: PATSTAT October 2007, own computations

Although the companies from Germany, France and Switzerland are the most diversified ones, they have significantly reduced the breadth of their knowledge base. Italy, the Netherlands and the United Kingdom are characterised by comparably low degrees of technological diversification. Furthermore, companies from Italy and the Netherlands have slightly increased the breadth of their technology base until the middle of the 1990s. While companies from Switzerland have already dramatically refocused their technology portfolio at the beginning of the 1990s, most countries have not significantly reduced their degree of technological diversification until the beginning of the new millennium.

Focusing on the rates of technological diversification, the analyses revealed that R&D intensive companies in the life sciences have not continued to increase the range of their technological competences in the 1990s. In the following subchapters the direction of technological diversification is analysed in depth by using three different indicators. First, the evolution of related technological diversification is investigated. Second, based on the share of related technological diversification, the prevalent diversification type is determined. Third, the share of patent applications, which involved the exploration of new technological classes, is calculated.

III.6.3.1 Related technological diversification

The *related diversification (RD)* can be computed as follows. First, the technological diversity TD_{jx} across the technological fields j has to be calculated. TD_{jx} can be written as:

$$TD_{jx} = \sum_{i=1}^{N} P_{ijx} log\left(\frac{1}{P_{ijx}}\right) \tag{III.4}$$

where P_{ijx} is the company x's share of patents in technology class i in total patent applications in technology field j.

The total related diversification RD_x which arises out of the technological activities in several technological fields is defined as:

$$RD_x = \sum_{j=1}^{M} TD_{jx} P_{jx} \tag{III.5}$$

where P_{jx} is company x's share of patent applications in technology field j in total patent applications.

Table 5 summarises the trends in related technological diversification (RD) differentiated by home countries and industrial sectors of the sample companies. At the beginning of the 1990s the sample companies have slightly increased their degree of related technological diversification. However, since the mid-1990s the degree of related technological diversification remains quite stable. Furthermore, at the beginning of the new millennium, the sample firms are characterised by a decrease in the degree of related diversification.

Table 5: Related technological diversification of the sample firms
Source: PATSTAT October 2007, own computations

RELATED TECHNOLOGICAL DIVERSIFICATION (RD)

Industrial sectors	Period	Mean	Δ RD	Countries	Period	Mean	Δ RD
Biotechnology	**1986/90**	0.247		CH	**1986/90**	0.521	
	1991/95	0.305	23.14%		**1991/95**	0.433	-16.79%
	1996/00	0.306	0.51%		**1996/00**	0.444	2.58%
	2001/05	0.268	-12.43%		**2001/05**	0.394	-11.39%
Chemicals	**1986/90**	0.433		DE	**1986/90**	0.191	
	1991/95	0.450	4.09%		**1991/95**	0.179	-6.46%
	1996/00	0.452	0.30%		**1996/00**	0.201	11.99%
	2001/05	0.427	-5.55%		**2001/05**	0.175	-12.79%
Food Producers	**1986/90**	0.323		FR	**1986/90**	0.530	
	1991/95	0.394	22.05%		**1991/95**	0.519	-2.12%
	1996/00	0.379	-3.83%		**1996/00**	0.486	-6.30%
	2001/05	0.371	-2.11%		**2001/05**	0.457	-6.01%
Health Care Equipment & Services	**1986/90**	0.231		IT	**1986/90**	0.131	
	1991/95	0.213	-7.54%		**1991/95**	0.121	-7.63%
	1996/00	0.231	8.42%		**1996/00**	0.129	7.26%
	2001/05	0.189	-18.11%		**2001/05**	0.137	5.61%
Pharmaceuticals	**1986/90**	0.244		NL	**1986/90**	0.358	
	1991/95	0.231	-5.51%		**1991/95**	0.418	16.73%
	1996/00	0.238	3.34%		**1996/00**	0.392	-6.20%
	2001/05	0.214	-10.09%		**2001/05**	0.403	2.66%
Total	**1986/90**	0.305		UK	**1986/90**	0.328	
	1991/95	0.310	1.51%		**1991/95**	0.361	10.14%
	1996/00	0.312	0.72%		**1996/00**	0.346	-3.97%
	2001/05	0.284	**-9.00%**		**2001/05**	0.298	-13.84%

(shaded) Related technological diversification is above average

Figure 46 visualises the trends in related technological diversification differentiated by industrial sectors. The companies from the sectors Chemicals and Food Producers are characterised by their above average degree of related technological diversification. In the Pharmaceuticals, Health Care Equipment & Services and Biotechnology sector the RD values are under average. Furthermore, these sectors are characterised by a strong decrease of the related technological diversification since the end of the 1990s.

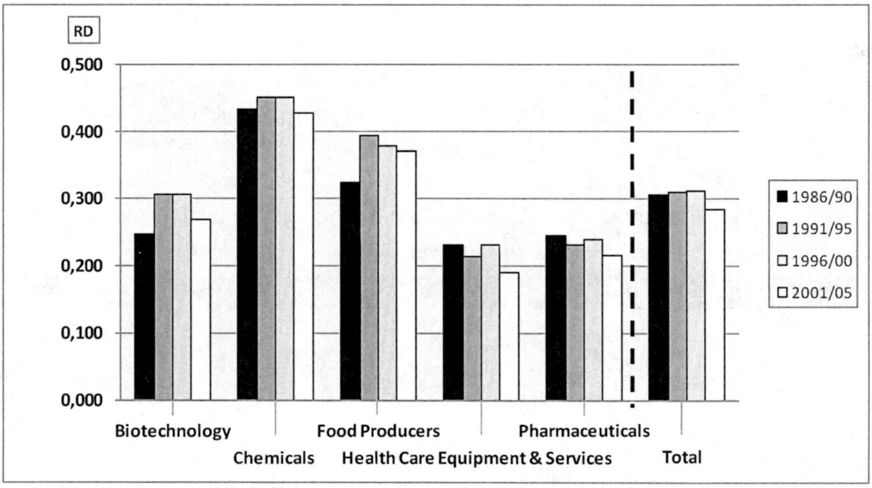

Figure 46: Development of related technological diversification (sectoral level)
Source: PATSTAT October 2007, own computations

The trends at the country level are illustrated in Figure 47. The sample companies differ in their degree of related technological diversification.

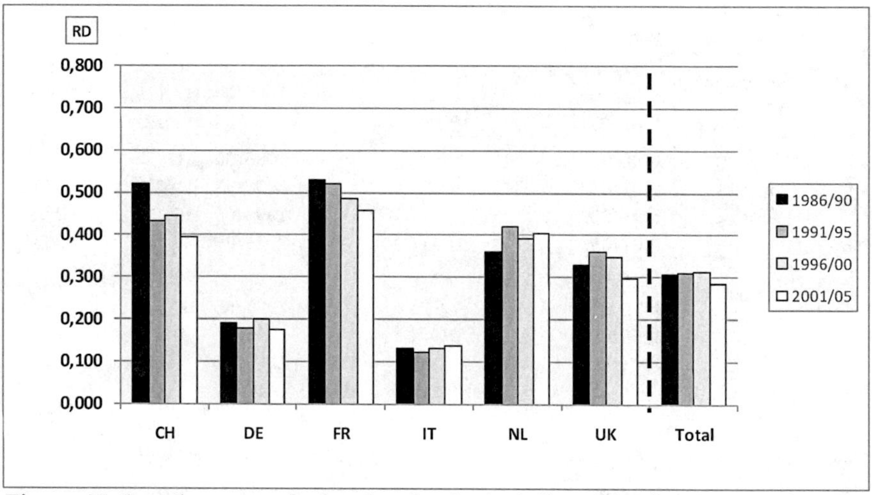

Figure 47: Development of related technological diversification (country level)
Source: PATSTAT October 2007, own computations

The highest degrees of related technological diversification are observed in France, Switzerland, the Netherlands and the United Kingdom. Companies from Germany and the Italy manage a technology portfolio that is characterised by comparatively low degrees of related technological diversification.

III.6.3.2 Prevalent diversification type

The prevalent *diversification type (DT)* of firm x can be determined by calculating the share of the related technological diversification (RD):

$$DT_x = RD_x / TD_x \tag{III.6}$$

The index takes values between zero and one. When related technological performance is more important than unrelated technological diversification the index takes values close to one. Otherwise if the unrelated technological diversification is prevalent the index takes values close to zero.

Table 6 reports the evolution of the technological diversification type (DT) differentiated by home countries and industrial sectors of the sample companies.

Table 6: Technological diversification type

Source: PATSTAT October 2007, own computations

TECHNOLOGICAL DIVERSIFICATION TYPE (DT)

Industrial sectors	Period	Mean	Δ RD	Countries	Period	Mean	Δ RD
Biotechnology	1986/90	0.629		CH	1986/90	0.692	
	1991/95	0.704	12.06%		1991/95	0.748	8.05%
	1996/00	0.645	-8.49%		1996/00	0.777	3.86%
	2001/05	0.676	4.82%		2001/05	0.684	-11.99%
Chemicals	1986/90	0.587		DE	1986/90	0.343	
	1991/95	0.572	-2.41%		1991/95	0.320	-6.55%
	1996/00	0.567	-0.88%		1996/00	0.351	9.74%
	2001/05	0.554	-2.31%		2001/05	0.355	0.98%
Food Producers	1986/90	0.665		FR	1986/90	0.769	
	1991/95	0.685	3.03%		1991/95	0.815	5.93%
	1996/00	0.727	6.11%		1996/00	0.757	-7.06%
	2001/05	0.747	2.71%		2001/05	0.811	7.16%
Health Care Equipment & Services	1986/90	0.503		IT	1986/90	0.321	
	1991/95	0.507	0.93%		1991/95	0.270	-15.66%
	1996/00	0.469	-7.50%		1996/00	0.308	13.91%
	2001/05	0.461	-1.69%		2001/05	0.331	7.40%

Table 6: Technological diversification type (continued)
Source: PATSTAT October 2007, own computations

TECHNOLOGICAL DIVERSIFICATION TYPE (DT)							
	Period	Mean	△ RD		Period	Mean	△ RD
Pharma-ceuticals	1986/90	0.458		NL	1986/90	0.752	
	1991/95	0.512	11.79%		1991/95	0.795	5.72%
	1996/00	0.538	5.19%		1996/00	0.785	-1.16%
	2001/05	0.530	-1.50%		2001/05	0.860	9.56%
Total	1986/90	0.546		UK	1986/90	0.679	
	1991/95	0.578	5.90%		1991/95	0.768	13.07%
	1996/00	0.579	0.11%		1996/00	0.700	-8.89%
	2001/05	0.580	0.27%		2001/05	0.693	-0.94%
Share of related technological diversification is above average							

At the aggregated industry level the values of the DT-measure (accounting for more than 0.500) reveal that related diversification is more prevalent than unrelated diversification during the whole period of investigation. Furthermore, until the mid-1990s the life sciences industry is characterised by a slight increase in the share of related diversification. In the following periods the share of related technological diversification remains almost stable.

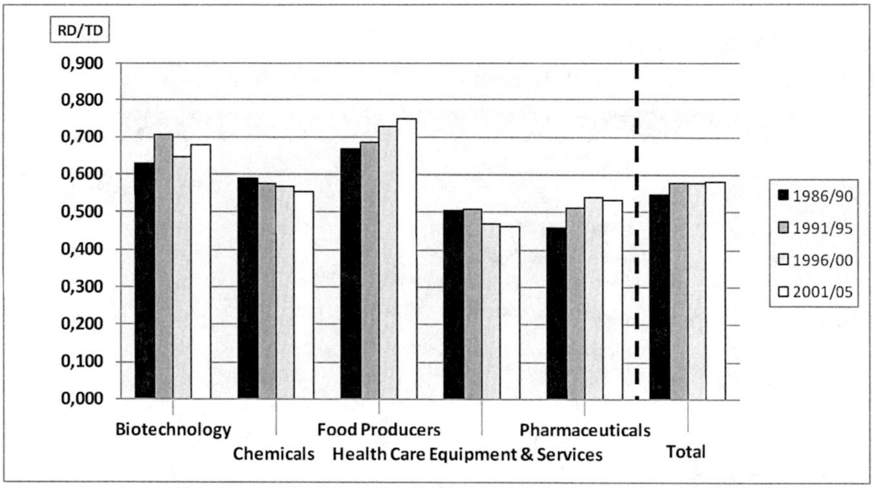

Figure 48: Development of technological diversification type (sectoral level)
Source: PATSTAT October 2007, own computations

Turning the analysis to the sectoral level shows that related technological diversification is prevalent during almost the whole period of investigation. Especially in the Biotechnology and Food Producers sector the share of related technological diversification is above average. However, while companies from the Food Producers sector have steadily increased their share of related variety, companies from the Chemicals sector have reduced their share of related variety (Figure 48).

By turning the analysis to the national level no general trend can be observed (Figure 49). There are considerable differences between the sample companies from different countries. While companies from Switzerland, France, the Netherlands and the United Kingdom show high shares of related diversification, in Germany and Italy the share of related diversification is under average. Thus, unrelated diversification is more prevalent than related diversification.

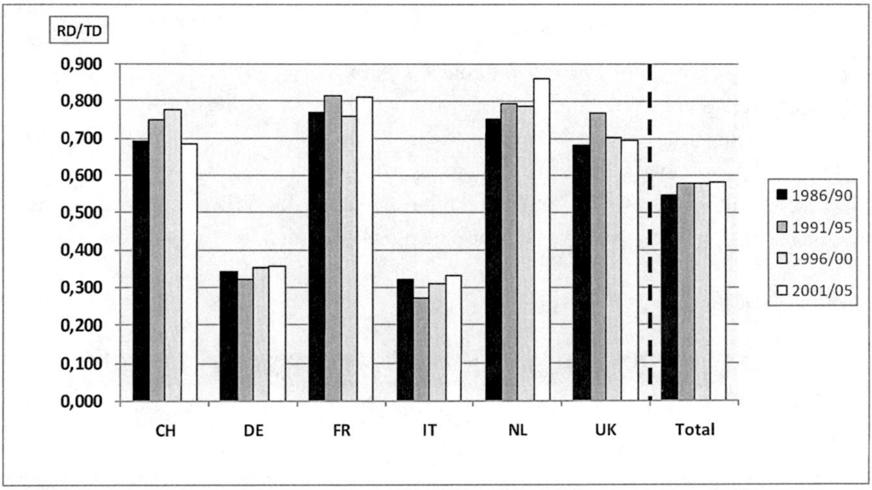

Figure 49: Development of technological diversification type (country level)
Source: PATSTAT October 2007, own computations

The observations partly confirm *Thesis 4*. Focusing on the aggregated industry or national level reveals that related technological diversification is the dominating diversification type. The same holds if the analysis is turned to the sectoral level. However, at the disaggregated country level Figure 49 illustrates that the diversification into related technological areas is not always prevalent. Firms from Italy and Germany seem to open up new, technologically unrelated areas.

III.6.3.3 Exploration of new technological fields

The entropy index is a static measure which captures the breadth of the knowledge base (i.e. the technological diversity) at specific time points. However, the dynamic dimension of diversification, the exploration of new technological fields, is not reflected in the entropy measure. For this purpose, the patent scope measure which indicates the level of new technology exploration is introduced (Chen/Jang/Wen, 2010, p. 269). This index compares the number of patent applications in new technological fields during a reference period *t* with the technology portfolio of the previous period *t-1*. The *patent scope (PS)* is defined as follows:

$$PS_{tx} = \frac{p_{new,tx^{[t-1]}}}{p_{tx}} \tag{III.7}$$

$p_{new,tx^{[t-1]}}$ is the number of company x's patents, which have been applied in new technological classes during period *t* (based on 4-digit IPCs in the life sciences technology classes) in comparison with the patent stock in *t-1*, and p_{tx} is the total patent stock of the firm in period t.

Table 7 summarises the trends in the patent scope (PS) differentiated by home countries and industrial sectors of the sample companies.

Table 7: Patent scope of the sample firms
Source: PATSTAT October 2007, own computations

Industrial Sector			Countries		
PATENT SCOPE (PS)					
Biotechnology	$PS_{1991/95}$	14.72%	CH	$PS_{1991/95}$	12.37%
	$PS_{1996/00}$	8.76%		$PS_{1996/00}$	11.97%
	$PS_{2001/05}$	4.97%		$PS_{2001/05}$	2.65%
Chemicals	$PS_{1991/95}$	10.21%	DE	$PS_{1991/95}$	10.26%
	$PS_{1996/00}$	6.03%		$PS_{1996/00}$	5.76%
	$PS_{2001/05}$	2.90%		$PS_{2001/05}$	2.61%
Food Producers	$PS_{1991/95}$	18.48%	FR	$PS_{1991/95}$	7.96%
	$PS_{1996/00}$	16.71%		$PS_{1996/00}$	3.25%
	$PS_{2001/05}$	6.20%		$PS_{2001/05}$	4.33%
Health Care Equipment & Services	$PS_{1991/95}$	7.88%	IT	$PS_{1991/95}$	5.27%
	$PS_{1996/00}$	7.53%		$PS_{1996/00}$	2.42%
	$PS_{2001/05}$	1.72%		$PS_{2001/05}$	1.69%
Pharma-ceuticals	$PS_{1991/95}$	8.60%	NL	$PS_{1991/95}$	17.25%
	$PS_{1996/00}$	4.51%		$PS_{1996/00}$	8.73%
	$PS_{2001/05}$	2.83%		$PS_{2001/05}$	12.58%
Total	$PS_{1991/95}$	10.97%	UK	$PS_{1991/95}$	12.93%
	$PS_{1996/00}$	7.70%		$PS_{1996/00}$	11.30%
	$PS_{2001/05}$	3.53%		$PS_{2001/05}$	1.90%
(shaded) Patent scope over average					

On average the patent scope measure takes values between 4% ($PS_{2001/05}$) and 11% ($PS_{1991/95}$). Thus, during the whole period of investigation the sample companies were engaged in the exploration of new technological fields.

Turning the analysis to the sectoral level shows that the patent scope of the companies from the Biotechnology and Food Producers sector is above average (Figure 50). Until the beginning of the new millennium, between 17% and 18% of the innovative activities of the food companies involved the exploration of new technological fields. In the Biotechnology sector about 15% of the patents have been applied for in new technological fields at the beginning of the 1990s. The remaining sectors differ only slightly in their patent scope, ranging from about 2% in the Health Care Equipment & Services sector (at the beginning of the new millennium) to about 11% (at the beginning of the 1990s) in the Chemicals sector.

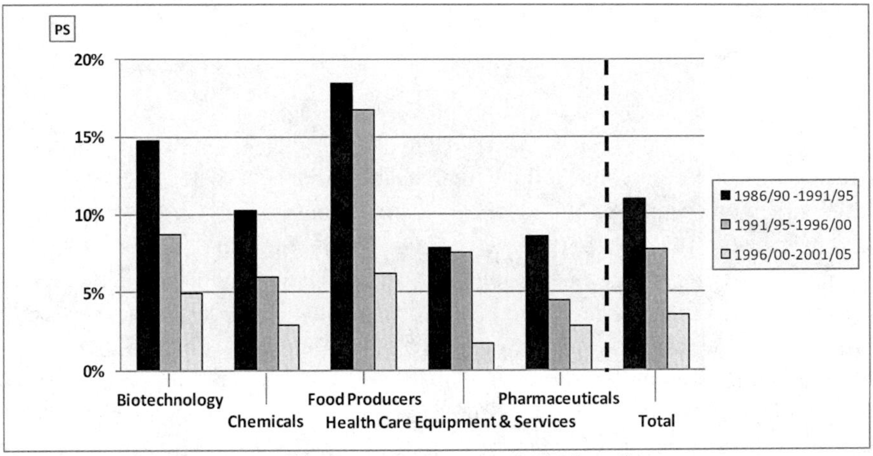

Figure 50: Development of the patent scope (sectoral level)
Source: PATSTAT October 2007, own computations

There are also considerable differences between the sample companies from different countries (see Figure 51). The Dutch companies have the highest level of new technology exploration. In the 1990s about 20% of the innovative activities involved the exploration of new technological areas. Until the beginning of the new millennium also the sample companies from Switzerland and the United Kingdom are characterised by a patent scope over average (ranging from 11% to 13%). The lowest patent scope is observed for the sample firms from Italy and France. On average less than 10% of the firms' total patents have been applied for in new technological areas.

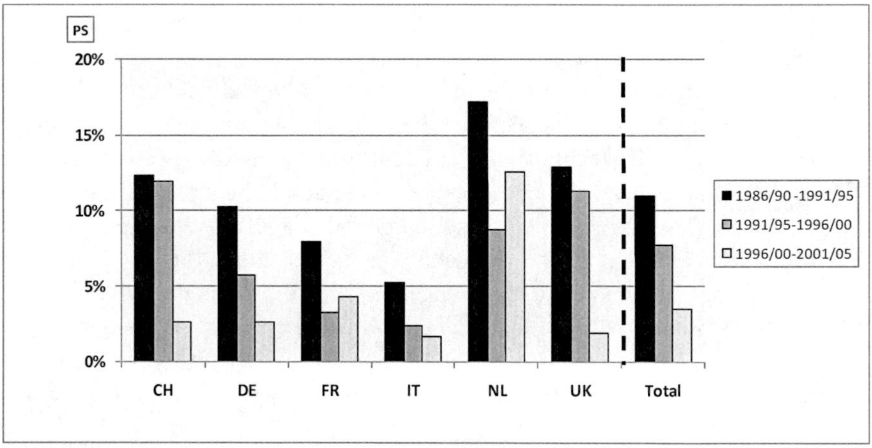

Figure 51: Development of the patent scope (country level)
Source: PATSTAT October 2007, own computations

III.7 Concluding remarks to Chapter III

Recent theoretical contributions emphasise the increasing technological diversification of large multi-technology corporations (MTCs) in the Triads since the beginning of the 1980s (see among others Stephan, 2003). However, differences in the degree of technological diversification can be observed across different industries and nations. This thesis examines the technological specialisation and diversification patterns of large MTCs in the life sciences. The analyses distinguish between five different life sciences sectors and comprise 114 companies from six European countries. The analysis of the technological specialisation patterns showed that the different life sciences sector are characterised by distinct fields of technological advantage. Furthermore, the findings reveal that companies from different nations and sectors show varying rates and directions of technological diversification. This section summarises the trends in technological specialisation and diversification by taking into account the results in the previous sections.

Table 8 reports the evolution of technological diversification of the sample firms at the sectoral level.

The Biotechnology sector is characterised by a comparably low patent intensity. On average the technology portfolio of the biotechnology companies comprises between five and eight technologies. The relatively low degrees of technological diversification further confirm that the technology base in this sector is relatively focused. Turning the analysis to the diversification type shows that the related diversification is more prevalent than unrelated diversification. This also goes in line with the results obtained in *Chapter III.6.2* showing a specialisation in the fields of *Biotechnology* and *Pharmaceuticals*.

Table 8: Evolution of technological diversification based on different indicators (sectoral level)[37]

Source: PATSTAT October 2007, own computations

		Patents	Tech	TD	RD	RD/TD	PS
Biotech-nology	**1986/90**	33	8	0.440	0.247	0.629	---
	1991/95	18	5	0.453	0.305	0.704	14.72%
	1996/00	29	6	0.473	0.306	0.645	8.76%
	2001/05	38	5	0.399	0.268	0.676	4.97%
Chemicals	**1986/90**	177	12	0.724	0.433	0.587	---
	1991/95	255	14	0.754	0.450	0.572	10.21%
	1996/00	390	16	0.789	0.452	0.567	6.03%
	2001/05	399	16	0.757	0.427	0.554	2.90%
Food Producers	**1986/90**	82	8	0.490	0.323	0.665	---
	1991/95	136	9	0.566	0.394	0.685	18.48%
	1996/00	238	9	0.536	0.379	0.727	16.71%
	2001/05	228	8	0.496	0.371	0.747	6.20%
Health Care Equipment & Services	**1986/90**	32	9	0.459	0.231	0.503	---
	1991/95	44	8	0.426	0.213	0.507	7.88%
	1996/00	81	11	0.471	0.231	0.469	7.53%
	2001/05	92	10	0.373	0.189	0.461	1.72%
Pharma-ceuticals	**1986/90**	130	9	0.507	0.244	0.458	---
	1991/95	166	8	0.452	0.231	0.512	8.60%
	1996/00	289	9	0.441	0.238	0.538	4.51%
	2001/05	268	9	0.405	0.214	0.530	2.83%

Above average

Strongly above average

Companies from the Chemicals sector show the highest propensity to patent. On average, these companies applied between 177 patents (1986/90) and 399 patents (2001/05). Their technology portfolio comprises between twelve and 16 technologies. Furthermore, this sector has the highest degrees of technological diversification. Considering the diversification type shows that the chemical companies have a comparably moderate share of related diversification. Thus, the diversification strategy seems to be very balanced and does not solely rely on one diversification type.

The Food Producers have continuously increased their technological activities. Since the mid-1990s their propensity to patent is above average. The

37 The table reports the average values.

companies of this sector manage on average between eight and nine technologies. The RD and TD values indicate that technological diversity is above average. Although the related diversification is prevalent, these companies have the highest shares of new technology exploration. Thus, it seems that new technological opportunities mainly arise in the neighbourhood of the established technological competencies.

In the Health Care Equipment & Services sector the propensity to patent is below average. Although the absolut number of technological classes increases during the period of investigation, the comparably low degrees of technological diversification indicate that the technology base is relatively focused. Moreover, the exploration of new technological areas is at a low level during all time periods considered. There is a slight decrease in the share of related technological diversification. Companies from this sector are highly specialised in the field of *Medical technology* (see *Chapter III.6.2*).

The pharmaceutical companies of the sample are characterised by a comparably high propensity to patent. In contrast to this, the degree of technological diversification is under average. The technology portfolio comprises on average eight or nine technological classes. The fields of relative technological specialisation are mainly concentrated in the fields *Pharmaceuticals* and *Biotechnology*. Taking into account the share of related diversification shows that the diversification strategy seems to be very balanced and does not solely rely on one diversification type. Furthermore, the exploration of new technological classes is comparably low. Summarising it can be said that the technology base of the pharmaceutical companies is relatively focused. Furthermore, the companies of the Pharmaceuticals sector have continuously decreased their degree of technological diversification.

In Table 9 the evolutions of corporate technological diversification are reported at the country level. The sample companies from Germany, France and Switzerland show the highest degrees of technological diversification. On average their technology portfolio comprises between ten and 13 technologies. Differences can be observed regarding the diversification type. In France and Switzerland the related diversification strategy is clearly prevalent. Furthermore, the Swiss firms are characterised by high degrees of new technology exploration. Thus, it can be assumed that new technological developments arise in the neighbourhood of the established competences. For Germany the ratio RD/TD reveals that unrelated diversification is more prevalent than related diversification.

Firms from Italy and the United Kingdom show the lowest degree of technological diversification. Their technology portfolio comprises on average between three and nine technologies. The Italian firms are characterised by low degrees of related diversification, the ratio RD/TD further indicates that unrelated diversification is prevailing. Taking into account the patent scope shows, that the exploration of new technological areas is negligibly low. In contrast to this, companies from the United Kingdom show high degrees of related diversification. Furthermore, during the 1990s these firms have invested comparably high shares of their innovative activities in the exploration of new technologies.

Table 9: Evolution of technological diversification based on different indicators (country level)[38]

Source: PATSTAT October 2007, own computations

		Patents	Tech	TD	RD	RD/TD	PS
CH	1986/90	121	13	0.745	0.521	0.692	---
	1991/95	143	10	0.549	0.433	0.748	12.37%
	1996/00	271	11	0.571	0.444	0.777	11.97%
	2001/05	297	12	0.567	0.394	0.684	2.65%
DE	1986/90	161	11	0.586	0.191	0.343	---
	1991/95	205	11	0.580	0.179	0.320	10.26%
	1996/00	296	13	0.599	0.201	0.351	5.76%
	2001/05	332	12	0.528	0.175	0.355	2.61%
FR	1986/90	158	12	0.675	0.530	0.769	---
	1991/95	180	11	0.633	0.519	0.815	7.96%
	1996/00	192	11	0.608	0.486	0.757	3.25%
	2001/05	132	10	0.566	0.457	0.811	4.33%
IT	1986/90	17	5	0.386	0.131	0.321	---
	1991/95	34	3	0.434	0.121	0.270	5.27%
	1996/00	48	7	0.413	0.129	0.308	2.42%
	2001/05	53	6	0.377	0.137	0.331	1.69%
NL	1986/90	141	8	0.484	0.358	0.752	---
	1991/95	173	7	0.537	0.418	0.795	17.25%
	1996/00	255	7	0.511	0.392	0.785	8.73%
	2001/05	268	6	0.475	0.403	0.860	12.58%
UK	1986/90	86	7	0.480	0.328	0.679	---
	1991/95	120	8	0.473	0.361	0.768	12.93%
	1996/00	214	9	0.472	0.346	0.700	11.30%
	2001/05	172	7	0.396	0.298	0.693	1.90%

Above average

Strongly above average

Although their propensity to patent is above average, the Dutch firms show comparably low degrees of technological diversification. Related technological

38 The table reports the average values.

diversification is clearly more prevalent than unrelated technological diversification. Furthermore, the degree of new technology exploration, as indicated by the patent share, is strongly above average. Thus, a high share of the technological activities involved the exploration of new technological classes.

This chapter shed light on the technological specialisation and diversification patterns of the life sciences companies. The empirical analyses of *Chapter III* demonstrate that firms from different sectors and nations are characterised by distinct diversification strategies. Furthermore, the increasing importance of the technological class Biotechnology has been shown. These findings indicate the impact of different innovation systems on the technological scope of companies (*Thesis 2b*). Moreover, the results confirm empirically *Thesis 3* and *Thesis 4*: The increasing technological diversification trend of the 1980s has reversed in the new millennium and related technological diversification is prevailing in most of the analysed sectors and nations. By bringing together the findings elaborated in *Chapter II* and *Chapter III*, in the following chapter the focus will be laid on the relationship between the diversification patterns of the sample firms and the national technological trajectories in the life sciences industry.

Chapter IV Linking national technological trajectories and technological diversification patterns

Aim of this chapter is to determine the technological similarity between the firms' technological diversification patterns and the national technological trajectories. Technological similarity is defined as the degree to which technological portfolios have similar patent shares in the different technological classes. Based on the insights from the systems of innovation approach, *Thesis 2b* argues that R&D intensive companies are embedded in different innovation systems. They span their technological activities over different countries, sectors and technologies. As a consequence, national as well as sectoral and technological frameworks can influence the technological developments of these companies. In order to determine the relationships between the corporate technological diversification patterns and the national technological trajectories, this thesis uses a clustering approach. *Chapter IV.1* provides the theoretical framework and presents the most common cluster techniques. In *Chapter IV.2* a partitional cluster approach, the k-means algorithm, is described in detail. Afterwards, in *Chapter IV.3* the cluster analysis is performed using the sample data elaborated in the context of this thesis.

IV.1 Cluster analysis

The cluster analysis divides data into groups (clusters) that share common characteristics (see Figure 52).

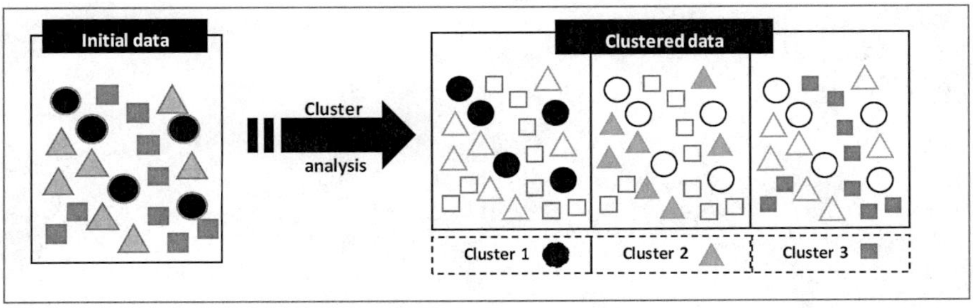

Figure 52: Cluster analysis
Source: own illustration

Thus, aim of the cluster analysis is to identify groups of objects that are similar to each other, but different from objects in other groups. The cluster analysis is used for assigning observed data into groups or clusters which comprise similar objects (Diday, 1971, p. 20; Bortz, 2005, p. 565). The proceeding is visualised in Figure 52.

IV.1.1 Similarity/distance measures

To determine the distance between two objects an appropriate similarity or dissimilarity (distance) measure has to be chosen.[39] Some of the available measures are suitable for continuous variables (e.g. the Euclidean distance), while others fit better for categorical variables (e.g. Kendall rank correlation coefficient) or binary variables (e.g. SMC-coefficient) (Bortz, 2005, pp. 566-571).

In this thesis the distance of two objects e_i and $e_{i'}$ is computed using the Euclidian distance (or L_2-norm) which is defined as follows:

$$d_{ii'} = \left[\sum_{j=1}^{p} \left(x_{ij} - x_{i'j}\right)^2\right]^{1/2} \tag{IV.1}$$

where x_{ij} ($x_{i'j}$) is the characteristic of object e_i ($e_{i'}$) concerning the variable (attribute, characteristic) j (Bortz, 2005, p. 568 f.).

The Euclidean distance measure is applied to the following example (Table 10). The objects A, B and C are represented by five attributes:

Table 10: Example – Euclidean distance
Source: own computations

		Attribute				
		x_{i1}	x_{i2}	x_{i3}	x_{i4}	x_{i5}
Object	A	1	1	2	3	0
	B	2	1	3	2	1
	C	1	0	2	3	0

39 For a detailed discussion of the most common similarity/distance measures see among others Backhaus et al., 2006, pp. 493-510 and Bortz, 2005, pp. 566-571.

Based on the five attributes the Euclidean distance is calculated as follows:

$$d_{AB} = \sqrt{(1-2)^2 + (1-1)^2 + (\cdots) + (0-1)^2}$$

$$= \sqrt{4} = 2$$

$$d_{AC} = \sqrt{(1-1)^2 + (1-0)^2 + (\cdots) + (0-0)^2}$$

$$= \sqrt{1} = 1$$

$$d_{BC} = \sqrt{(2-1)^2 + (1-0)^2 + (\cdots) + (1-0)^2}$$

$$= \sqrt{5} = 2.24$$

The smallest difference between two objects is the distance between the objects A and C ($d_{AC} = 1$). The largest difference ($d_{BC} = 2.24$) occurs between the objects B and C. Thus, while the objects A and C show the highest similarity based on the Euclidean distance measure, the objects B and C show the highest dissimilarity.

IV.1.2 Clustering algorithms

Of the numerous clustering approaches (for an overview see among others Backhaus et al., 2006, pp. 510-533; Bortz, 2005, pp. 571-580) this thesis exemplarily describes the procedure of hierarchical and partitional clustering techniques.

IV.1.2.1 Hierarchical Clustering

The hierarchical clustering approaches can be subdivided into agglomerative and divisive algorithms. Starting with individual objects as clusters, at each step, the agglomerative clustering approach merges the two closest objects. In contrast to this, the divisive approach starts with one cluster which comprises all objects. At each iteration step, the cluster is divided into successively smaller clusters, until only clusters of single objects remain. Thus, the hierarchical clustering algorithms result in a clustering structure (all objects are assigned to one cluster (agglomerative approach) or each object represents one cluster (divisive approach)). Therefore, based on the characteristics of the clusters at successive iteration steps, a reasonable number of clusters has to be determined by the user (Bortz, 2005, p. 571 f.; Backhaus et al., 2006, p. 511).

IV.1.2.2 Partitional clustering (Non-Hierarchical Clustering)

The partitional clustering approach divides the set of objects into k clusters. Thus, before running the partitional clustering algorithm the number of desired clusters has to be chosen. The clusters are then produced by optimising a certain criterion. The algorithm terminates if a further reassignment of objects does not improve the clusters. One of the most popular partitional algorithms is the k-means algorithm which is discussed in detail below (Bortz, 2005, p. 573 f.; Backhaus et al., 2006, p. 511).

IV.2 Partitional clustering: k-means approach

The hierarchical approaches are computationally very expensive because all possible distances between all pairs of objects have to be computed. As a conseqence, these approaches are not suitable for large data sets. In such cases the application of partitional algorithms (like k-means) is preferable (see among others Bühl, 2006, p. 543). Furthermore, they are characterised by a higher variability. While the hierarchical algorithms create clusters which cannot be rearranged, the partitional approaches can also reassign objects to clusters. This means that objects can repeatedly change their clusters (Bortz, 2005, p. 578; Backhaus et al., 2006, p. 514).

IV.2.1 k-means algorithm

One of the main disadvantages of the k-means algorithm is that the resulting clusters may depend on the initial ranking of the objects. It is therefore recommendable to run the algorithm with different start states. In practice, the configuration which is confirmed by different start rankings is chosen as initial partition (Bortz, 2005, p. 580). The proceeding of the k-means algorithm is visualised in Figure 53.

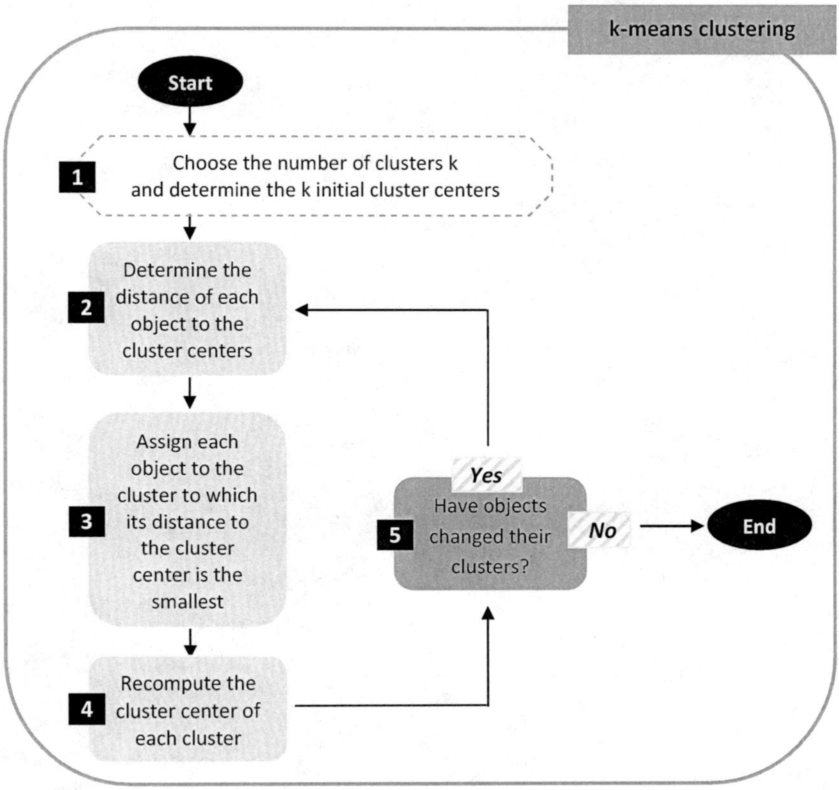

Figure 53: Flow chart – k-means algorithm
Source: own illustration

IV.2.2 Example – Proceeding of k-means algorithm

The operation of the k-means algorithm is described in the following example. For this purpose, 13 objects (here: points) are assigned to three clusters (see Figure 54). Each object is characterised by two attributes x_1 and x_2.

Initial cluster centers:
The k-means algorithm starts by assigning the objects to the initial cluster centers. The start ranking of the objects is visualised in Figure 54. The objects within one cluster have the same marker colour (light grey = Cluster 1, grey = Cluster 2, dark grey = Cluster 3). The means of the objects are used as the cluster centers. Hence, the initial cluster centers are $Z_1(0.813/2.5)$, $Z_2(2.417/1.667)$ and $Z_3(2.167/4.667)$.

Cluster 1	x_1	x_2
	1	2
	0.5	1
	0	5
	1.75	2
Cluster center	**0.813**	**2.5**

Cluster 2	x_1	x_2
	2.5	3
	3	0
	2	0
	3	3
	2	3
	2	1
Cluster center	**2.417**	**1.667**

Cluster 3	x_1	x_2
	3	5
	2	5
	1.5	4
Cluster center	**2.167**	**4.667**

Figure 54: Example data set - k-means
Source: own illustration

1. Iteration:

At the beginning of the first iteration step, the Euclidean distance of all points to each of the three cluster centers ($D(P_j,Z_i)$, i = 1, … ,3; j = 1, ... ,13) is calculated (Table 11). The point $P_1(1/2)$ has the shortest distance to Z_1

- $D(P_1,Z_1) = 0.534 < D(P_1,Z_2) = 1.455$ and
- $D(P_1,Z_1) = 0.534 < D(P_1,Z_3) = 2.911$

and therefore remains in Cluster 1. The same holds for $P_2(0.5/1)$. By contrast, the point $P_3(0/5)$ has the shortest distance to Z_3:

- $D(P_3,Z_1) = 2.629 < D(P_3,Z_2) = 4.117$ but
- $D(P_3,Z_1) = 2{,}629 > D(P_3,Z_3) = 2.192$.

Thus, this point is now assigned to Cluster 3.

Analogically, the distances of all other points to the cluster centers are computed. As reported in Table 11, the points $P_4(1.75/2)$ and $P_9(2/3)$ also change their clusters. While $P_4(1.75/2)$ is now assigned to Cluster 2, $P_9(2/3)$ is assigned to Cluster 1.

Table 11: k-means clustering: 1. Iteration

Source: own computations

1. Iteration						
			Distance to cluster centers			
Cluster 1	x_1	x_2	$D(P_j, Z_1)$	$D(P_j, Z_2)$	$D(P_j, Z_3)$	
	1	2	0.534	1.455	2.911	
	0.5	1	1.532	2.029	4.028	
	0	5	2.629	4.117	2.192	→ Cluster 3
	1.75	2	1.063	0.745	2.699	→ Cluster 2
Cluster center	**0.812**	**2.5**				
Cluster 2	x_1	x_2	$D(P_j, Z_1)$	$D(P_j, Z_2)$	$D(P_j, Z_3)$	
	2.5	3	1.760	1.336	1.700	
	3	0	3.322	1.766	4.740	
	2	0	2.768	1.718	4.670	
	3	3	2.244	1.455	1.863	
	2	3	1.288	1.397	1.675	→ Cluster 1
	2	1	1.913	0.786	3.670	
Cluster center	**2.417**	**1.667**				
Cluster 3	x_1	x_2	$D(P_j, Z_1)$	$D(P_j, Z_2)$	$D(P_j, Z_3)$	
	3	5	3.322	3.384	0.898	
	2	5	2.768	3.359	0.373	
	1.5	4	1.650	2.507	0.943	
Cluster center	**2.167**	**4.667**				

2. Iteration - 5. Iteration:

After each object has been assigned to the cluster to which its distance to the clusters center is the smallest, the new centroids have to be computed. This is done by taking the mean of all objects in the respective cluster. Again the points are assigned to the closest centroid. The update and assignment steps are repeated until no object changes its cluster (Table 12).

After five iteration steps the algorithm terminates and the final cluster centers are determined. All objects are assigned to their permanent clusters.

Table 12: k-means clustering: 2. Iteration - 5. Iteration
Source: own computations

2. Iteration

Cluster 1	x_1	x_2	$D(P_j, Z_1)$	$D(P_j, Z_2)$	$D(P_j, Z_3)$	
			Distance to cluster centers			
	1	2	0.167	1.463	2.820	
	0.5	1	1.202	1.941	3.915	
	2	3	1.302	1.546	1.790	
Cluster center	**1.167**	**2**				
Cluster 2	x_1	x_2	$D(P_j, Z_1)$	$D(P_j, Z_2)$	$D(P_j, Z_3)$	
	2.5	3	1.667	1.505	1.957	
	3	0	2.713	1.625	4.945	
	2	0	2.167	1.546	4.765	
	3	3	2.088	1.625	2.226	
	2	1	1.302	0.625	3.769	
	1.75	2	0.583	0.800	2.753	→ Cluster 1
Cluster center	**2.375**	**1.5**				
Cluster 3	x_1	x_2	$D(P_j, Z_1)$	$D(P_j, Z_2)$	$D(P_j, Z_3)$	
	3	5	3.516	3.555	1.398	
	2	5	3.114	3.520	0.451	
	1.5	4	2.028	2.649	0.760	
	0	5	3.219	4.230	1.644	
Cluster center	**1.625**	**4.75**				

3. Iteration

Cluster 1	x_1	x_2	$D(P_j, Z_1)$	$D(P_j, Z_2)$	$D(P_j, Z_3)$	
			Distance to cluster centers			
	1	2	0.313	1.616	2.820	
	0.5	1	1.288	2.040	3.915	
	2	3	1.214	1.676	1.790	
	1.75	2	0.438	0.960	2.753	
Cluster center	**1.313**	**2**				
Cluster 2	x_1	x_2	$D(P_j, Z_1)$	$D(P_j, Z_2)$	$D(P_j, Z_3)$	
	2.5	3	1.552	1.600	1.957	→ Cluster 1
	3	0	2.617	1.487	4.945	
	2	0	2.115	1.487	4.765	
	3	3	1.962	1.676	2.226	
	2	1	1.214	0.640	3.769	
Cluster center	**2.5**	**1.4**				
Cluster 3	x_1	x_2	$D(P_j, Z_1)$	$D(P_j, Z_2)$	$D(P_j, Z_3)$	
	3	5	3.442	3.635	1.398	
	2	5	3.078	3.635	0.451	
	1.5	4	2.009	2.786	0.760	
	0	5	3.275	4.383	1.644	
Cluster center	**1.625**	**4.75**				

Table 12: k-means clustering: 2. Iteration - 5. Iteration (continued)
Source: own computations

4. Iteration

	x_1	x_2	$D(P_j, Z_1)$	$D(P_j, Z_2)$	$D(P_j, Z_3)$	
			Distance to cluster centers			
Cluster 1	1	2	0.585	1.803	2.820	
	0.5	1	1.595	2.000	3.915	
	2	3	0.918	2.062	1.790	
	1.75	2	0.283	1.250	2.753	
	2.5	3	1.242	2.000	1.957	
Cluster center	**1.55**	**2.2**				
Cluster 2	3	0	2.635	1.118	4.945	
	2	0	2.246	1.118	4.765	
	3	3	1.656	2.062	2.226	→ Cluster 1
	2	1	1.282	0.500	3.769	
Cluster center	**2.5**	**1**				
Cluster 3	3	5	3.153	4.031	1.398	
	2	5	2.836	4.031	0.451	
	1.5	4	1.801	3.162	0.760	
	0	5	3.200	4.717	1.644	
Cluster center	**1.625**	**4.75**				

5. Iteration

	x_1	x_2	$D(P_j, Z_1)$	$D(P_j, Z_2)$	$D(P_j, Z_3)$
			Distance to cluster centers		
Cluster 1	1	2	0.859	2.134	2.820
	0.5	1	1.856	1.951	3.915
	2	3	0.698	2.687	1.790
	1.75	2	0.336	1.766	2.753
	2.5	3	0.973	2.672	1.957
	3	3	1.380	2.749	2.226
Cluster center	**1.792**	**2.333**			
Cluster 2	3	0	2.628	0.745	4.945
	2	0	2.343	0.471	4.765
	2	1	1.350	0.745	3.769
Cluster center	**2.333**	**0.333**			
Cluster 3	3	5	2.928	4.714	1.398
	2	5	2.675	4.679	0.451
	1.5	4	1.692	3.760	0.760
	0	5	3.213	5.217	1.644
Cluster center	**1.625**	**4.75**			

Figure 55 visualises the procedure of the k-means algorithm. All points belonging to the same cluster have the same marker colour (light grey = Cluster 1, grey = Cluster 2, dark grey = Cluster 3). The cluster centers (Z_1, Z_2, Z_3) are indicated by black colour. Starting from the three initial chosen cluster centers, the final clusters are found in five iteration steps. Each subfigure shows the assignment of the objects to the cluster to which the distance to the cluster center is the smallest.

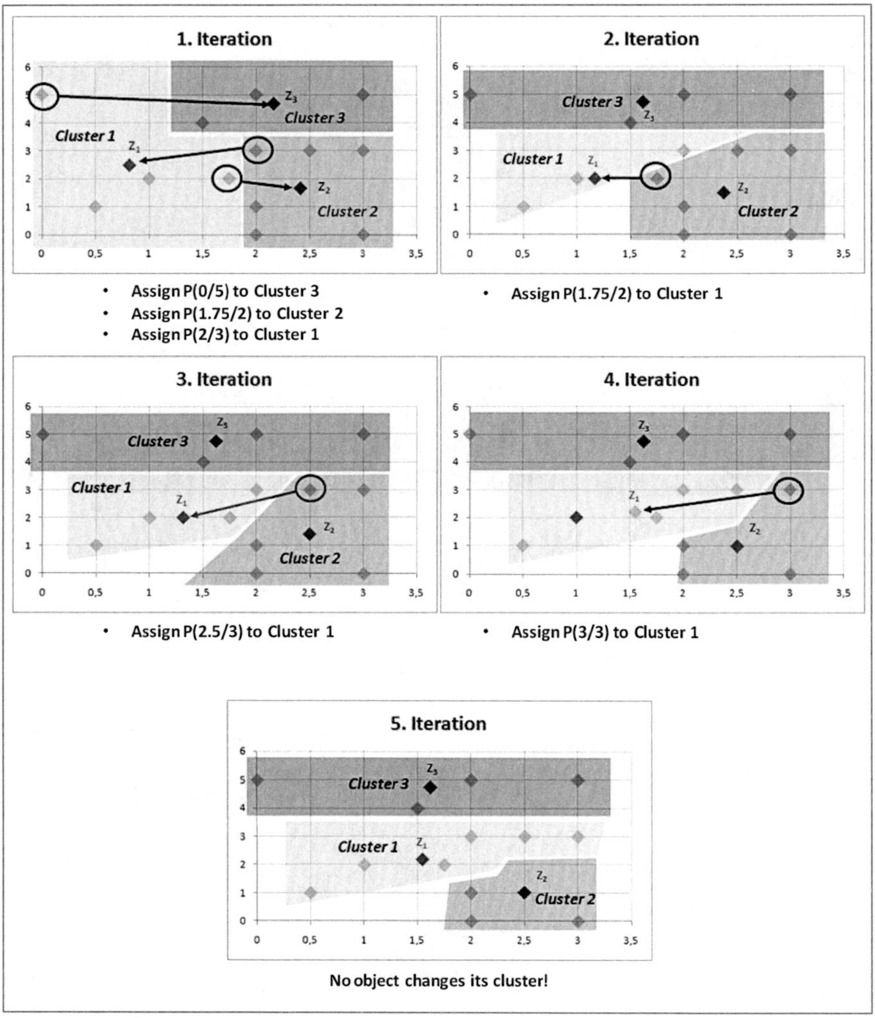

Figure 55: Operation of k-means clustering
Source: cf. Siegele (2010), p. 36, own illustration

IV.3 Linking national technological trajectories and technological diversification patterns in the life sciences industry

In the following the k-means clustering is applied to the sample data set of this dissertation. *Chapter IV.3.1* describes the data set and the proceeding. The empirical results of the k-means clustering are presented in *Chapter IV.3.2* and *Chapter IV.3.3*. The main results of the clustering procedure are summarised in *Chapter IV.3.4*.

IV.3.1 Data set and proceeding

In order to determine the similarities between the national technological profiles and the technological diversification patterns of the sample firms the k-means algorithm is applied. Aim of this chapter is to link the corporate technology base with the technological base of the sample nations.

The technological profiles of the sample nations have been determined in *Chapter II*. Based on the patent applications in the different technological classes, the technological competences of the countries can be represented as technology vectors:

$$T_{country} = \left(\overrightarrow{P_{i,k}}\right) = \begin{pmatrix} P_{1k} \\ P_{2k} \\ \vdots \\ P_{nk} \end{pmatrix} \tag{IV.2}$$

where P_{ik} is country k's patent share in technology i (i = 1, …, n; n ≤ 35).

Chapter III has investigated the technological profiles of the sample companies. Corresponding to the proceeding at the country level, the technological competencies of the companies can be represented as technology vectors:

$$T_{company} = \left(\overrightarrow{P_{i,x}}\right) = \begin{pmatrix} P_{1x} \\ P_{2x} \\ \vdots \\ P_{nx} \end{pmatrix} \tag{IV.3}$$

where P_{ix} is company x's patent share in technology i (i = 1, …, n; n ≤ 35).

By applying the k-means algorithm to the sample data set, the firms represent the objects (Table 13) which should be grouped according to their technology profile (attributes). Aim of the cluster analysis is to identify groups (clusters) of firms with homogenous characteristics (here: technology bases). Those companies which are characterised by similar technological profiles are assigned to the same cluster. If the national technological trajectories have an influence on the technological diversification patterns of the firms, it can be assumed that firms within the same cluster (i.e. the firms sharing similar technological profiles) have the country of origin as common characteristic.

Table 13: k-means clustering - Objects of the sample data
Source: own compilation

Objects	
1986/90	83 companies
1991/95	104 companies
1996/00	114 companies
2001/05	114 companies

The attributes P_{1x}, P_{2x}, ..., P_{35x} represent the patent shares of the companies in the respective technologies. The additional firm level attributes *'country of origin'* and *'industrial sector'* are not included in the cluster analysis (Table 14). These attributes will only be used to further characterise the resulting clusters.

Table 14: k-means clustering - Attributes of the sample data
Source: own compilation

Attributes	
P_{1x} P_{2x} ⋮ P_{35x}	Company x's patent share in the 35 technological classes *(with Tech 1 = Electrical machinery, apparatus, energy, ..., Tech 35 = Civil engineering)*[40]
Additional firm level attributes:	
Country of origin	Country, where the company has its headquarter *(CH, DE, FR, IT, NL or UK)*
Industrial sector	Sector of the companies' main economic activity *(Biotechnology, Chemicals, Food Producers, Health Care Equipment & Services, Pharmaceuticals)*

40 For an overview of the 35 technological classes of the *WIPO IPC Technology Concordance* see *Annex I*.

The technological profiles of the sample countries are used as initial cluster centers. If the sample companies follow the national technological trajectories, it can be assumed that the sample companies will be arranged around the cluster centers, which represent their home country. Hence, the firms which are assigned to the same cluster should have the same country of origin. *Annex XII* reports the initial centroids for all clusters and time periods.

In the following the k-means algorithm is applied for the different time periods. The k-means clustering is performed by using the statistical software SPSS.[41] The firms are assigned to the closest cluster, based on their Euclidean distance to the cluster centers. In the following iterations the cluster centers are recomputed and the objects are assigned to the closest cluster center until no cluster center changes significantly.[42] The final clusters are characterised with regard to the attributes *'country of origin'* and *'industrial sector'*. Furthermore, to determine the technological focus of the clusters, the final cluster centers are taken into account.

IV.3.2 Assignment to the clusters – national perspective

In the following the assignment of the companies to the clusters is presented. Aim is to determine the influence of the national technological trajectories on the technological diversification patterns of the firms. For this purpose, the allocation of the companies to the different clusters is investigated from the national perspective. If the national technological trajectories shape the technological profiles of the firms, it can be assumed that companies within the same cluster have the same country of origin. Figure 56 illustrates the results of the clustering procedure for each time period.

It shows that the different clusters are quite heterogeneous concerning the country of origin, i.e. the clusters are not dominated by firms of one specific country. During the whole period of investigation most clusters comprise firms from five or six different countries. Hence, the common attribute of the objects within the different clusters is not the country of origin. This means that the companies do not necessarily follow exclusively the national technological trajectories of their home country.

41 SPSS is a statistical software tool and stands for *Statistical Package for the Social Sciences*. The analyses are performed with version *PASW Statistics 18*. Here the k-means algorithm is called cluster center analysis.

42 The algorithm was performed with different start states in order to avoid that the resulting clusters depend on the initial ranking of the firms.

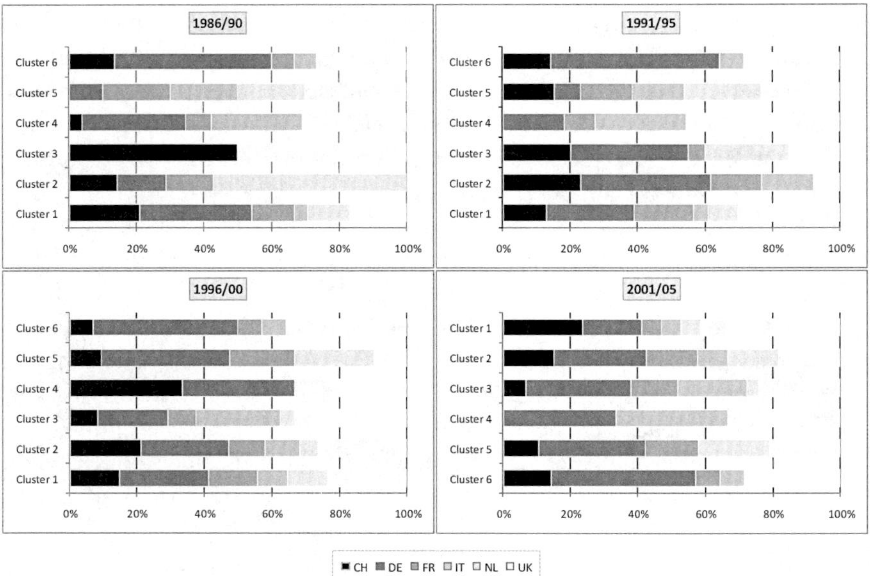

Figure 56: Cluster characteristics related to country of origin (cluster perspective)

Source: own computations

In the next step, the assignment to the clusters is investigated from the perspective of the firms. Figure 57 reports the allocation of the companies from the six European countries to the six clusters. It clearly shows that firms from the same country are not necessarily linked to the same cluster. During the whole period of investigation the companies of the most countries are present in five or six clusters. This further confirms the assumption that the companies do not necessarily follow exclusively the national technological trajectories of their home country. Furthermore, it can be stated that the influence of the national innovation environment may differ between the sample countries. Companies from Italy and the Netherlands seem to be more homogeneous concerning their technological profile and are mostly assigned to one specific cluster. During the whole period of investigation between 44% and 64% of the companies from Italy and the Netherlands are grouped within the same clusters. So, at a first glance, the companies operating in Italy and the Netherlands may be shaped by the national technological trajectories. However, in this context, the distribution of the sample firms by sector and nation (see *Chapter III*, Table 3) has to be taken into account. At least the sample of Italian firms is unevenly distributed across the different life sciences sectors. Here, nearly 60% of the sample firms are operating in the Pharmaceuticals sectors. For this reason, it may be assumed that the assignment to the different clusters is also shaped by the sectors.

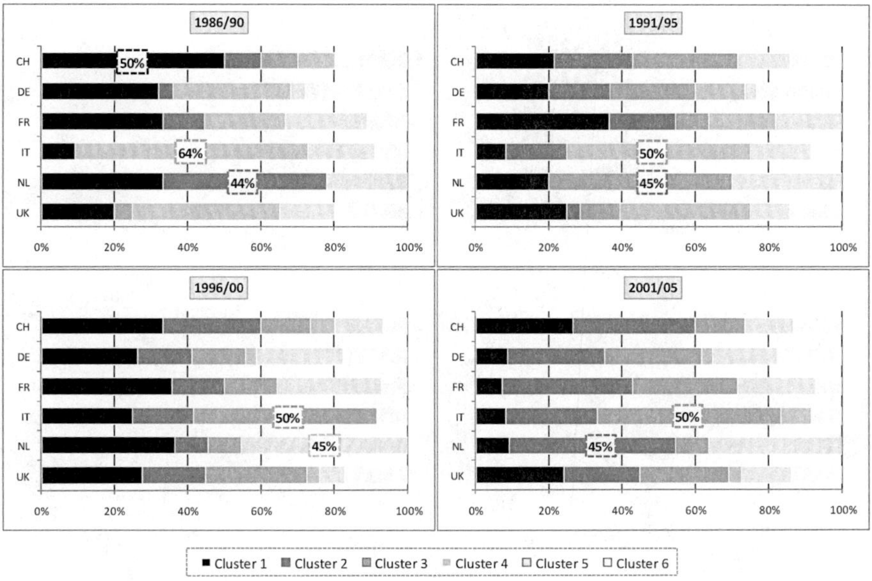

Figure 57: Cluster characteristics related to country of origin (country perspective)

Source: own computations

IV.3.3 Assignment to the clusters – sectoral perspective

In order to determine the influence of sectoral patterns on the technological profiles of companies, this section turns the analysis to the second firm level attribute: the industrial sector. Moreover, to determine the technological focus of the clusters, the final cluster centers are taken into account. Additional technology base characteristics are used in order to characterise the technological portfolios of the final clusters. The following sub-sections present the results of the k-means clustering for each of the four analysed time periods.

IV.3.3.1 Period 1986/90

Figure 58 clearly shows that companies within the same cluster are similar concerning their sector of economic activity. For instance, about 78% of the companies which are assigned to Cluster 1 operate mainly in the Chemicals sector. Cluster 3 and 5 are dominated by firms from the Food Producers sector. Firms of the Health Care Equipment & Services sector are primarily assigned to Cluster 6, while Cluster 4 mainly consists of companies which are active in the

Pharmaceuticals sector. Only the patterns in Cluster 2 are more heterogeneous. It comprises firms from the sectors: Biotechnology, Chemicals and Health Care Equipment & Services.

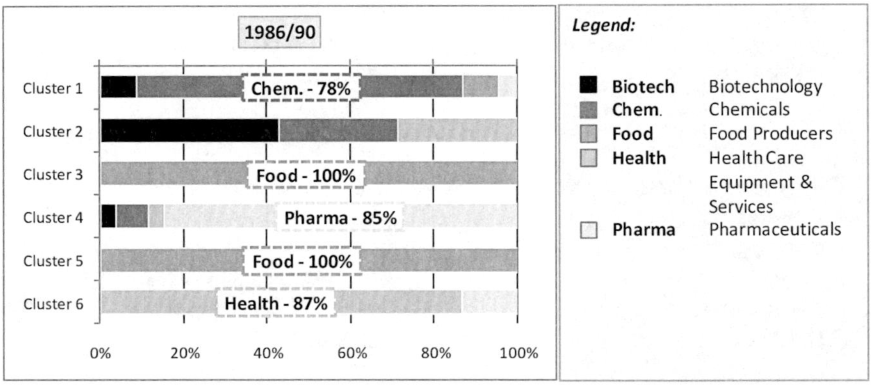

Figure 58: Cluster characteristics 1986/90 related to industrial sector
Source: *own computations*

The final cluster centers reported in *Annex XIII* can be used to characterise the clusters. The variables of the cluster centers represent the patent shares in each of the 35 technologies and provide information about the technological focus in the different clusters. The following table summarises the characteristics of the six clusters. For each cluster, the patent share in eight technological classes (the seven life sciences technologies and the class *Organic fine chemistry* which also accounts for relatively high patent shares in the life sciences) is put under investigation. The technological areas with the comparably highest patent shares are marked. Furthermore, additional characteristics of the technology base are taken into account.

Cluster 1 – Chemicals:

The technological portfolio of Cluster 1 is characterised by high patent shares in the technological classes *Organic fine chemistry*, *Basic materials chemistry* and *Environmental technology*. About 40% of the technological activities can be attributed to the chemical technological classes *Organic fine chemistry* and *Basic materials chemistry*. The class *Environmental technology* accounts for 11% of the technological activities within the Chemicals cluster. Table 15 further indicates that Cluster 1 comprises highly diversified companies with a high propensity to patent.

Table 15: Technology base characteristics of final clusters - 1986/90
Source: PATSTAT October 2007, own computations

		Cluster 1	Cluster 2	Cluster 3	Cluster 4	Cluster 5	Cluster 6
Patent focus							
Comparably high patent shares in ...	**Medical technology**						✔
	Organic fine chemistry	✔			✔		
	Biotechnology		✔		✔		
	Pharmaceuticals				✔		
	Food chemistry			✔		✔	
	Basic materials chemistry	✔					
	Environmental technology	✔					
	Other special machines			✔			

Technological diversification *(average values)*						
Patents	228	23	124	128	10	33
Technologies	13	6	13	8	5	9
Total Diversification (TD)	0.735	0.363	0.665	0.512	0.403	0.523
Prevalent diversification type (DT)	0.598	0.760	0.575	0.455	0.668	0.478

Cluster characteristics						
Cluster	**Cluster 1**	**Cluster 2**	**Cluster 3**	**Cluster 4**	**Cluster 5**	**Cluster 6**
Companies	27	7	2	26	10	15
Label	Chemicals	Biotech-nology	Food Producers *(Diversified)*	Pharma-ceuticals	Food Producers *(Specialised)*	Health Care Equipment & Services

Cluster 2 – Biotechnology:
The technology base of Cluster 2 is comparably focused. Here, technological diversification is on a comparably low level and the diversification into related areas is prevalent. The technological competences in *Biotechnology* clearly dominate. About 75% of the patents applications can be attributed to *Biotechnology*.

Cluster 3 – Food Producers (*Diversified*):
The third cluster comprises solely companies from the Food Producers sector with a broad technology base, comprising on average thirteen technologies. The highest patent shares are achieved in the classes *Food chemistry* and *Other special machines*.

Cluster 4 – Pharmaceuticals:
In Cluster 4 the technological competences in *Organic fine chemistry*, *Biotechnology* and *Pharmaceuticals* dominate. The highest patent shares are achieved in *Pharmaceuticals* accounting for nearly 50% of the total patent applications in

this cluster. The firms within this cluster show a comparably high propensity to patent and manage a technology portfolio which comprises on average eight technologies.

Cluster 5 – Food Producers (*Specialised*):

Also the second Food Producers cluster comprises solely firms from the Food Producers sector. The patent focus is clearly on *Food chemistry*. However, in contrast to Cluster 3 the patent share in the class *Other special machines* is negligible small. Thus, the patent portfolio of these companies is more focused as indicated by Table 15. On average the companies of Cluster 5 manage five technologies and are characterised by high shares of related diversification.

Cluster 6 – Health Care Equipment & Services:

The companies which are assigned to Cluster 6 are active in the Health Care Equipment & Services sector. The TD measure indicates that the degree of technological diversification is at a moderate level. On average, the technological portfolio of the companies within this cluster encompasses nine technological classes. The technological competencies in *Medical technology* clearly dominate the technology base. About 64% of the technological activities can be attributed to this technological class.

IV.3.3.2 Period 1991/95

For the Period 1991/95 the cluster analysis reveals that the companies within the clusters are more similar concerning their sector of economic activity than their country of origin (Figure 59).

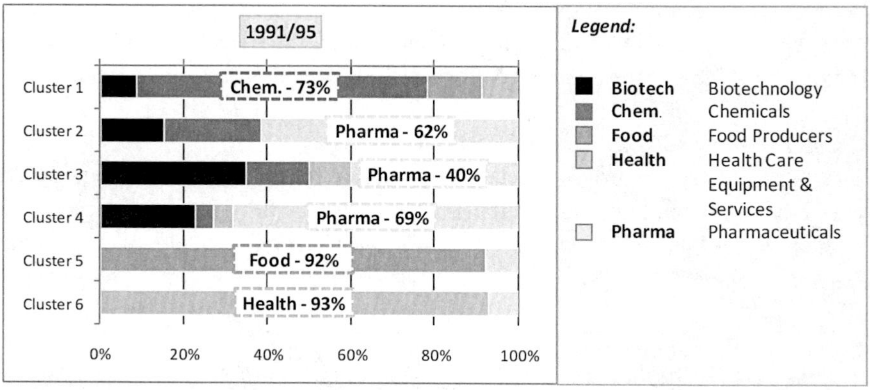

Figure 59: Cluster characteristics 1991/95 related to industrial sector
Source: own computations

About 70% of the companies which are assigned to Cluster 1 operate in the Chemicals sector. Cluster 2 and 4 are dominated by pharmaceutical companies. In contrast to this, Cluster 3 mainly consists of firms which are active in Pharmaceuticals and Biotechnology. While the Food Producers are mainly assigned to Cluster 5, Cluster 6 is clearly dominated by firms of the Health Care Equipment & Services sector.

To further determine the main characteristics of the six clusters, the final cluster centers are taken into account (see also *Annex XIII*). Table 16 summarises the technology base characteristics of the clusters. The technological areas with comparably high patent shares are marked.

Table 16: Technology base characteristics of final clusters - 1991/95
Source: PATSTAT October 2007, own computations

		Cluster 1	Cluster 2	Cluster 3	Cluster 4	Cluster 5	Cluster 6
Patent focus							
Comparably high patent shares in ...	**Medical technology**						✓
	Organic fine chemistry	✓	✓		✓		
	Biotechnology			✓			
	Pharmaceuticals		✓	✓	✓		
	Food chemistry					✓	
	Basic materials chemistry	✓					
	Environmental technology						
	Other special machines					✓	
Technological diversification *(average values)*							
Patents		225	345	69	105	49	43
Technologies		14	12	6	7	7	8
Total Diversification (TD)		0.777	0.582	0.444	0.428	0.525	0.378
Prevalent diversification type (DT)		0.637	0.508	0.635	0.506	0.663	0.480

Cluster characteristics						
Cluster	**Cluster 1**	**Cluster 2**	**Cluster 3**	**Cluster 4**	**Cluster 5**	**Cluster 6**
Companies	22	13	20	22	13	14
Label	Chemicals	Pharmaceuticals *(Diversified)*	Biotechnology	Pharmaceuticals *(Specialised)*	Food Producers	Health Care Equipment & Services

Cluster 1 – Chemicals:
This cluster comprises mainly companies from the Chemicals sector and has comparably high patent shares in the technological classes *Organic fine chemistry* and *Basic materials chemistry*. The cluster is characterised by a high propensity to patent and comparably high degrees in technological diversification. Related technological diversification is prevalent.

Cluster 2 – Pharmaceuticals *(Diversified)* and
Cluster 4 – Pharmaceuticals *(Specialised)*:
Both clusters are dominated by technological competences in the classes *Organic fine chemistry* and *Pharmaceuticals*. Especially in Cluster 2 the patent share in the field *Organic fine chemistry* is comparably high. However, compared to the firms in Cluster 2 those in Cluster 4 have a more focused technology base. On average they are active in seven technologies, while the firms of Cluster 2 manage twelve technological areas. Furthermore, in Cluster 2 the degree of technological diversification is comparably higher. Thus, it can be stated that Cluster 2 comprises large established pharmaceutical companies with a diversified technology base, while Cluster 4 contains new dedicated companies with a more focused technology base.

Cluster 3 – Biotechnology:
Cluster 3 is characterised by low degrees of technological diversification. The highest patent shares are achieved in the technological classes *Biotechnology* and *Pharmaceuticals* and related technological diversification is prevalent. The cluster comprises mainly established pharmaceutical and new dedicated biotechnology companies that manage on average six technologies.

Cluster 5 – Food Producers:
This cluster shows relatively high patent shares in the fields *Food chemistry* and *Other special machines* and comprises mainly firms from the Food Producers sector. Furthermore, the companies of this cluster are characterised by a comparably diversified technology base and high shares of related technological diversification.

Cluster 6 – Health Care Equipment & Services:
In this cluster the technological competences in *Medical technology* clearly dominate. Hence, not surprisingly, to this cluster almost solely firms from the Health Care Equipment & Services sector have been assigned. The technological activities are on a relatively low level and rooted towards unrelated technological areas.

IV.3.3.3 Period 1996/00

Figure 60 illustrates the cluster characteristics related to the industrial sectors during the period 1996/00. The companies which are assigned to Cluster 1 operate mainly in the Chemicals and Food Producers sector. Cluster 2 and 3 are dominated by pharmaceutical companies. In contrast to this, Cluster 4 consists mainly of firms which are active in Health Care Equipment & Services and Pharmaceuticals. Biotechnology companies are primarily assigned to Cluster 5. Additionally, Cluster 6 comprises exclusively firms from the Health Care Equipment & Services sector.

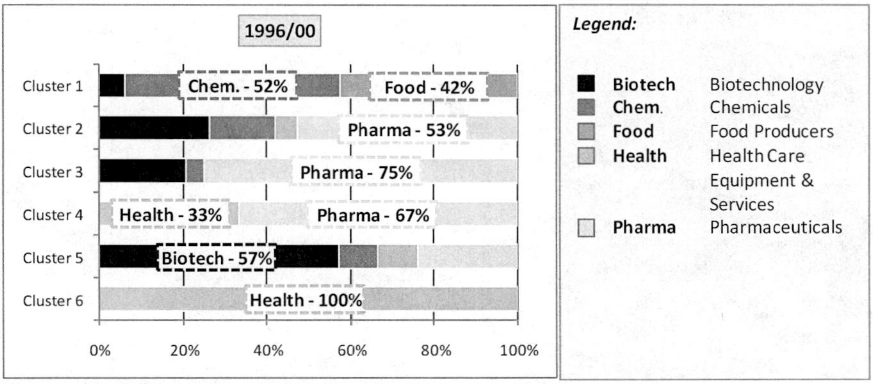

Figure 60: Cluster characteristics 1996/00 related to industrial sector
Source: own computations

The technological characteristics of the final clusters are summarised in Table 17 (see also *Annex XIII*).

Cluster 1 – Chemicals + Food Producers:
This cluster is dominated by Food Producers as well as companies from the Chemicals sector and has comparably high patent shares in *Organic fine chemistry*, *Basic materials chemistry* and *Food chemistry*. In this cluster the technological activities are on a high level and the technology base is characterised by high degrees of technological diversification. Related technological diversification is prevalent.

Cluster 2 – Pharmaceuticals *(Diversified)*:
Cluster 2 is characterised by relatively high patent shares in the classes *Organic fine chemistry*, *Pharmaceuticals* and *Biotechnology*. Hence, it can be assumed that this cluster mainly consists of established pharmaceutical companies with a diversified knowledge base (as indicated by high degrees of technological diver-

sification). The firms which are assigned to Cluster 2 seem to expand their technological portfolio by acquiring new technological knowledge in the field of biotechnology.

Table 17: Technology base characteristics of final clusters - 1996/00
Source: PATSTAT October 2007, own computations

	Cluster 1	Cluster 2	Cluster 3	Cluster 4	Cluster 5	Cluster 6
Patent focus						
Comparably high patent shares in …						
Medical technology				✔		✔
Organic fine chemistry	✔	✔	✔			
Biotechnology		✔			✔	
Pharmaceuticals		✔	✔	✔		
Food chemistry	✔					
Basic materials chemistry	✔					
Environmental technology						
Other special machines						
Technological diversification *(average values)*						
Patents	270	629	54	34	56	77
Technologies	12	15	6	6	7	11
Total Diversification (TD)	0.684	0.645	0.390	0.419	0.445	0.437
Prevalent diversification type (DT)	0.592	0.597	0.600	0.455	0.593	0.507

Cluster characteristics						
Cluster	**Cluster 1**	**Cluster 2**	**Cluster 3**	**Cluster 4**	**Cluster 5**	**Cluster 6**
Companies	34	19	24	3	22	13
Label	Chemicals + Food Producers	Pharma-ceutics *(Diversified)*	Pharma-ceuticals *(Specialised with focus on Pharma-ceuticals and Organic fine chemistry)*	Pharma-ceuticals *(Specialised with focus on Pharma-ceuticals and Medical technology)*	Biotech-nology	Health Care Equipment & Services

Cluster 3 – Pharmaceuticals *(Specialised with focus on Pharmaceuticals and Organic fine chemistry)*:
In contrast to Cluster 2, the knowledge base of Cluster 3 is more focused as indicated by the comparably low levels of technological diversification. The highest patent shares are achieved in the technological classes *Organic fine chemistry* and *Pharmaceuticals*. Related technological diversification is prevalent.

Cluster 4 – Pharmaceuticals (*Specialised with focus on Pharmaceuticals and Medical technology)*:
Cluster 4 is another Pharmaceutical cluster, with a focused technology portfolio comprising on average six technologies. The technological focus is on *Pharmaceuticals* and *Medical technology*. Accordingly, this cluster seems to consist of specialised pharmaceutical firms. However, it has to be noticed that this cluster comprises only three companies.

Cluster 5 – Biotechnology:
This cluster mainly contains firms from the Biotechnology and the Pharmaceuticals sector. The technology base of Cluster 5 is characterised by moderate shares of technological diversification. On average the companies of this cluster manage six technological classes which are characterised by comparably high degrees of relatedness. The technological activities in *Biotechnology* dominate the technology portfolio.

Cluster 6 – Health Care Equipment & Services:
Again there is one cluster which consists solely of firms from the Health Care Equipment & Services sector. These firms have a clear technological focus in the field of *Medical technology*. The degree of technological diversification is at a comparably low level.

IV.3.3.4 Period 2001/05

The cluster characteristics for the period 2001/05 are illustrated in Figure 61. Cluster 1, Cluster 3 and Cluster 4 are dominated by firms from the Pharmaceuticals sector. Furthermore more than 24% of the companies which are additionally assigned to Cluster 1 and Cluster 3 are operating in the Biotechnology sector. In contrast to this, Cluster 4 further includes firms from the Health Care Equipment & Services sector. Cluster 2 mainly comprises companies from the Chemicals and Food Producers sector. Cluster 5 primarily consists of biotechnology firms. As in the periods before, 100% of the companies which are assigned to Cluster 6 operate in the Health Care Equipment & Services sector.

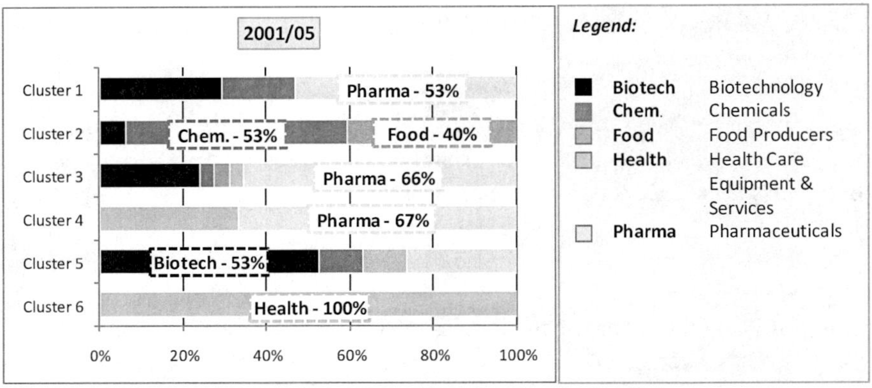

Figure 61: Cluster characteristics 2001/05 related to industrial sector
Source: own computations

The final cluster centers for the period 2001/05 are reported in *Annex XIII*. Summarising Table 18 reports the technological focus of the different clusters.

Cluster 1 – Pharmaceuticals *(Diversified)*:
The technological focus in this pharmaceutical cluster is mainly on *Organic fine chemistry*, *Biotechnology* and *Pharmaceuticals*. Hence, it can be assumed that the pharmaceutical companies which are assigned to this cluster are established companies with a diversified technology portfolio. The firms of this sector manage a portfolio of twelve technologies and are characterised by a comparably high degree of technological diversification. Related technological diversification is the dominant diversification type.

Cluster 2 – Chemicals + Food Producers:
This cluster is dominated by companies from the Chemicals and Food Producers sector and has a clear technology focus on *Organic fine chemistry*, *Basic materials chemistry* and *Food chemistry*. As in the period before, the firms of the 'Chemicals + Food Producers Cluster' have a diversified technology base and show a high propensity to patent.

Cluster 3 – Pharmaceuticals *(Specialised with focus on Pharmaceuticals and Organic fine chemistry)*:
The second pharmaceutical cluster consists mainly of pharmaceutical firms and has compared to Cluster 1 a more focused technology portfolio. On average this firms are active in seven technologies. The highest patent shares are achieved in the class *Pharmaceuticals*. About 70% of the clusters patent applications can be attributed to this technological class. Taking into account the diversification type exhibits furher that the technological portfolio is very balanced.

Table 18: Technology base characteristics of final clusters - 2001/05
Source: PATSTAT October 2007, own computations

Patent focus – Comparably high patent shares in ...	Cluster 1	Cluster 2	Cluster 3	Cluster 4	Cluster 5	Cluster 6
Medical technology				✔		✔
Organic fine chemistry	✔	✔	✔			
Biotechnology	✔				✔	
Pharmaceuticals	✔		✔	✔		
Food chemistry		✔				
Basic materials chemistry		✔				
Environmental technology						
Other special machines						

Technological diversification (average values)	Cluster 1	Cluster 2	Cluster 3	Cluster 4	Cluster 5	Cluster 6
Patents	562	252	95	61	*75*	*98*
Technologies	12	12	7	8	*6*	*10*
Total Diversification (TD)	0.543	0.663	0.358	0.514	0.401	0.345
Prevalent diversification type (DT)	0.695	0.593	0.484	0.485	0.686	0.483

Cluster characteristics

Cluster	Cluster 1	Cluster 2	Cluster 3	Cluster 4	Cluster 5	*Cluster 6*
Companies	17	32	29	3	19	*14*
Label	Pharma-ceuticals *(Diversified)*	Chemicals + Food Producers	Pharma-ceuticals *(Specialised with focus on Pharma-ceuticals and Organic fine chemistry)*	Pharma-ceuticals *(Specialised with focus on Pharma-ceuticals and Medical technology)*	Biotech-nology	Health Care Equipment & Services

Cluster 4 – Pharmaceuticals *(Specialised with focus on Pharmaceuticals and Medical technology)*:
The third pharmaceutical cluster comprises three companies, which have a clear focus on *Medical technology* and *Pharmaceuticals*. The average number of patent applications is comparably small.

Cluster 5 – Biotechnology:
This cluster comprises mainly Biotechnology companies and has a clear technological focus on *Biotechnology*. The technological activities are rooted towards related technological areas.

Cluster 6 – Health Care Equipment & Services:

Cluster 6 has its technological focus on *Medical technology* and consists exclusively of firms from the Health Care Equipment & Services sector. Firms within this cluster are characterised by comparably low levels of technological diversification.

The following sub-chapter summarises the results of the k-means clustering of the sample data set and draws the conclusions.

IV.4 Concluding remarks to Chapter IV

The empirical findings of this Chapter reveal the influence of sectoral innovation processes on the technological scope of life sciences companies. Table 19 summarises the observed sectoral clusters during the four periods of investigation.

Table 19: Sectoral clusters in the life sciences industry
Source: own compilation

Sectoral clusters		1986/90	1991/95	1996/00	2001/05
Biotechnology		×	×	×	×
Chemicals		×	×		
Food Producers		×	×		
Chemicals + Food Producers				×	×
Pharmaceuticals	*Diversified*	×	×	×	×
Pharmaceuticals	*Specialised*			×	×
Health Care Equipment & Services		×	×	×	×

During the whole period of investigation the chemical and food producing companies form clusters with large patent portfolios and diversified technology bases. Related diversification is prevalent and the patent focus is on *Organic fine chemistry* and *Basic materials chemistry* (Chemicals sector) or *Food chemistry* and *Other special machines* (Food Producers sector) respectively. Since the mid-1990s the Food Producers and Chemical companies are merged into one cluster with a large diversified knowledge base. Thus, the technological focus of these companies has become more similar during the period of investigation.

The developments in the Biotechnology and Health Care Equipment & Services cluster are rather stable over time. Companies from the Health Care Equipment & Services sector form a cluster with a comparably small and focused technology base. Their patent focus is on *Medical technology*. Also the

Biotechnology cluster is characterised by a comparably specialised technology portfolio. *Biotechnology* is the dominating technological class.

During the period of investigation numerous pharmaceutical clusters have evolved. This refers to the following facts: First, the pharmaceutical companies represent the largest sector in the sample. Second, the biotechnology revolution led to a structural change in the pharmaceutical industry (see also *Chapter II.6*). As a consequence, despite the established pharmaceutical companies new dedicated companies with a specialised competence base have been founded. The 'established' companies have a large, diversified technology base and technological focuses in *Organic fine chemistry, Pharmaceuticals* and *Biotechnology* and form the cluster of diversified pharmaceutical companies. Additionally, since the mid-1990s clusters of specialised pharmaceutical companies have evolved. They show a comparably focused technology base and competences in *Pharmaceuticals* and *Organic fine chemistry* or *Pharmaceuticals* and *Medical technology* dominate their technology portfolio.

This chapter has carried out an empirical investigation of the factors shaping the diversification patterns of firms. The results show that the national technological trajectories do not mainly influence the technological profiles of the sample companies. For all four time periods the k-means algorithm produced six clusters. Firms within the same clusters are more similar concerning their sector of main economic activity than their country of origin. Thus, it can be assumed that the technology profile of firms operating in the life sciences industry is mainly shaped by the sectoral innovation system. In Italy and the Netherlands a different development pattern can be observed. During the whole period of investigation about 50% of the Italian and Dutch firms were assigned to the same cluster (cf. *Chapter IV.3.2*). As a consequence, it can be assumed that the companies of these countries are affected by sectoral *and* national patterns as well.

The findings of the cluster analysis further confirm *Thesis 2a* and *Thesis 2b*. On the one hand it shows that the life sciences companies are shaped by their national environment (this is especially true with regard to the Italian and Dutch companies). On the other hand the empirical results reveal that the technological profiles of the life sciences companies are affected by sectoral innovation patterns.

Taking together the empirical findings of *Chapter II, Chapter III* and *Chapter IV*, all theses, which have been elaborated in *Chapter II* and *Chapter III,* are confirmed. Finally, *Chapter V* summarises the main results and draws the overall conclusions.

Chapter V Summary and conclusions

This doctoral dissertation explores the technological changes which have taken place in the European life sciences industry during the period 1986-2005. The main objective is to link the innovative processes at the technological, sectoral and national level with the technological scope decisions of companies. It is assumed that the technological portfolio of companies is shaped by the technological, sectoral and national environment. The life sciences industry represents a suitable research object because this industry is strongly science-based. Furthermore, the life sciences have faced remarkable changes during the last decades due to the evolution of modern biotechnology.

National technological trajectories

Chapter II has investigated the national technological trajectories in the life sciences industry. The empirical findings show that Germany, France, Italy, the Netherlands, Switzerland and the United Kingdom have developed distinct technological profiles.

Different knowledge base indicators were used in order to map the national technological trajectories. The analysis of the national knowledge bases reveals that each country has developed its specific technological competence profile. The core competences which have been generated in the 1980s are still present in the new millennium. Accordingly, the technological portfolios are rather persistent over time. The analysis of the technological co-occurrences shows that *Organic fine chemistry - Basic materials chemistry* as well as *Biotechnology - Pharmaceuticals* represent the core competences of the life sciences during the whole period of investigation. Thus, the technology bases of the sample nations are highly path dependent. Changes in the technological profiles are incremental and cumulative. However, during the period of investigation a shift from 'chemical' dominated technology bases to 'biological' oriented ones can be observed. Hence, there are also patterns of technological convergence. Competences in the technological classes *Biotechnology* and *Analysis of biological materials* are becoming more important, while technological co-occurrences in *Organic fine chemistry* and *Basic materials chemistry* are becoming less frequent since the mid-1990s. The dominating chemical paradigm is replaced by a biotechnology paradigm. In this context it has to be noted that the developments in the Netherlands are different to the ones in other countries.

Here, the technological competences in *Biotechnology* are of particular importance since the beginning of the 1990s.

The technological strengths of the sample countries were investigated using the indicator or Relative Technological Advantage (RTA). The analyses reveal that the sample companies have developed distinct patterns of technological advantage. Hence, the six European sample countries are characterised by country-specific technological trajectories. Furthermore, the stability of the technological specialisation patterns has been demonstrated. The path dependence in the evolution of the technological profiles was shown by the strength of the RTA_h-values during the period 1986-2005. For all countries a positive relationship between the technological specialisation patterns of subsequent periods can be observed. Thus, the distinctive technological strengths of the 1980s exercised an influence on the composition and depth of the technological profiles in subsequent periods.

Corporate technological diversification patterns

The technological diversification patterns of 114 European life sciences companies were investigated in *Chapter III*. The analyses distinguish between five different life sciences sectors and six European countries. At the aggregated industry level the analyses show that the technological diversification trend of the 1980s has come to a halt in the mid-1990s. Furthermore, at the beginning of the new millennium, there is a strong decrease in the technological diversification of the life sciences companies. Thus, the sample companies have begun to refocus their technological portfolios. With regard to the diversification type the prevalence of related technological diversification has been demonstrated.

The findings of *Chapter III* also exhibit that companies from different nations and sectors show varying rates and directions of technological diversification. Firms operating in the Chemicals and Food Producers sector are characterised by their over average degrees of technological diversification. Furthermore, in the Chemicals sector the propensity to patent is strongly above average. Focusing on the direction of technological diversification reveals that the technological activities of the Food Producers are rooted towards related technological areas. Nevertheless, these companies show the highest shares of new technology exploration. Firms from the Pharmaceutical sector are characterised by comparably large patent portfolios and moderate degrees of technological diversification. In contrast to this, the degree of technological diversification is under average in the sectors Health Care Equipment & Services and Biotechnology. The new technological opportunities of the Biotechnology sector arise mainly in the neighbourhood of the established technological competences.

Turning the analyses to the country level shows that companies from Germany, France and Switzerland are characterised by their over average degrees of technological diversification. On average these companies manage a technological portfolio comprising between ten and thirteen technologies. Differences can be observed regarding the diversification type. In France and Switzerland the related diversification is clearly prevalent. In contrast to this, Germany is characterised by high shares of unrelated diversification. Firms from the Netherlands and the United Kingdom show moderate levels of technological diversification. The accumulation of new technological knowledge takes place in the neighbourhood of the existing technological competences. The Italian firms are characterised by the lowest degrees in technological variety. Furthermore, the exploration of new technological areas is at very low level.

In general, the findings of *Chapter III* demonstrate the evolution of distinct technological profiles across the different life sciences sectors. The analysis of the technological specialisation profiles of the sample companies shows the path dependent evolution of the technological portfolios. Each sector has its specific technological core competences. Furthermore, the technological focuses which have been developed in the 1980s are still present in the specialisation profiles of the new millennium. However, the technological portfolios have also faced some incremental changes. These changes concern the development of technological capabilities in *Biotechnology*. This generic technological class pervades across the different life sciences sectors (expect Health Care Equipment & Services). Thus, the patterns of technological convergence which have already been observed at the national level are reflected in the corporate technological profiles.

Linking national technological trajectories and corporate technological diversification patterns

Drawing on the findings elaborated in *Chapter II* and *Chapter III* the factors shaping the technological profiles of companies have been investigated in *Chapter IV*. A cluster approach was used in order to specify the mechanisms underpinning technological decisions at the company level. By linking the national technological trajectories with the technological diversification patterns of the life sciences companies the main factors influencing the technology decisions of firms were determined.

A partitional cluster approach, the k-means algorithm, was chosen to group the life sciences companies based on their technological profiles. The technological profiles of the sample nations were used as initial cluster centers. By applying the cluster algorithm those companies which show homogenous characteristics – similar technological profiles – are assigned to the same cluster.

The empirical analyses are based on the following assumption: If the life sciences companies follow the national technological trajectories, it could be expected that the companies are arranged around the cluster centers which represent their home countries. In other words, the country of origin should be the common characteristic of those companies which are assigned to the same cluster (i.e. the companies sharing similar technological profiles).

For the sample data set of this dissertation the cluster analysis reveals that the technology decisions in the life sciences are not exclusively shaped by the national environment. Clustering the life sciences companies based on their technological profiles shows that firms within the different clusters are more similar concerning their sector of main economic activity than their country of origin. Thus, the companies which are assigned to the same cluster are frequently operating in the same industrial sector. During the period of investigation different sectoral clusters have evolved:

- The *Chemicals cluster* and the *Food Producers cluster* are characterised by large diversified technology bases and high shares of related technological diversification. Furthermore, in the mid-1990s the technological profiles of the companies from these sectors have become more similar. As a result, the food producing and chemical companies are merged into one cluster.
- The structural changes in the life sciences industry have brought forward different *Pharmaceutical clusters*. On the one hand established pharmaceutical companies form clusters with comparably diversified technology bases. On the other hand, in the mid-1990s clusters of specialised pharmaceutical companies with a more focused technological competence profile have evolved.
- The *Biotechnology cluster* and the *Health Care Equipment & Services cluster* are characterised by small and focused technological portfolios.

Technological similarities among companies from the same home country could mainly be observed in the case of the Italian and the Dutch companies. During the whole period of investigation about 50% of the Italian and Dutch companies are assigned to the same cluster based on their technological similarity. Hence, it can be assumed that the national technological environment has an impact on the technological profiles of these firms. These observations clearly show, that the sectoral and national perspective are intertwined and cannot be analysed in isolation.

Innovation systems of the life sciences from the viewpoint of an integrated framework

This thesis has investigated the links between the corporate technological diversification patterns and the technological, sectoral and national innovation patterns in the European life sciences industry. While previous research activities contended themselves with analysing sectoral or national patterns of technological diversification, this doctoral dissertation examined the impact of technological, sectoral and national innovation processes on the technological profiles of companies in their entirety. For this purpose, the quasi-static perspective of the 'traditional' systems of innovation approach is left.

The theoretical contributions of *Chapter II* stress that the technological profiles of firms are nowadays affected by different selection environments. Large R&D intensive companies are operating in numerous technologies and sectors. Furthermore, their activities are not limited to specific countries and often have a global dimension. Based on these observations, this dissertation argues that the technology decisions of companies are affected by different national, sectoral and technological innovation systems.

This thesis reveales that the European life sciences companies are embedded in different innovation systems. The six European sample countries have developed distinct national technological trajectories. Thus, it can be assumed, that the national innovation systems have an impact on the countries' technological profiles. Furthermore, the findings of *Chapter II* and *Chapter III* show the impact of the emerging biotechnology paradigm that shapes the national technological trajectories as well as the corporate technology decisions. Moreover, the cluster analysis of *Chapter IV* demonstrates that the technology profiles of European life sciences companies are affected by the sectoral environment (and in case of Italy and the Netherlands also by the national environment). Hence, there is a necessity to avoid one-way insights from one specific perspective. Consequently, the interactions between geographical, sectoral and technological systems have to be taken into account. Thus, the empirical findings of this thesis underline the need for an integrated framework which aims at bridging different aggregation levels. From the perspective of the innovation systems approach the findings show the impact of the national, sectoral and technological environment. Moreover, it has been demonstrated that the different levels of aggregation cannot be regarded in isolation. National, sectoral as well as technological factors shape the technological profiles of firms simultaneously. The results of the empirical analyses show the necessity of an integrated framework which detaches itself from the rigid borders of particular innovation systems. Thus, the perspective of the multi-level framework taking into account the transitions between the different aggregation levels is confirmed.

The approach of Markard/Truffer (2008) is suitable for mapping the interactions which take place between the different innovation systems. Furthermore, the concept offers the possibility to include further external factors which are not captured by the systems of innovation approach. In the context of this thesis, the integrated framework can be applied in order to map the innovation systems in the life sciences industry. Figure 62 provides a suggested interpretation of the innovation systems in the life sciences from the perspective of the integrated framework. It shows the dynamic interactions between the different conceptual elements and places particular emphasis on the mapping of the technological, sectoral and national environment within the framework of Markard/Truffer (2008).

Referring to the macro-level the impact of the national innovation system and further structural forces like the supra-national or global environment are discussed. At the meso-level the different sectors of the life sciences are linked to the regimes concept. The influence of the micro-level referring to the specific application contexts of technologies (niches) goes beyond the context of this thesis and is therefore not discussed in detail. The impact of the niches is subsumed under the technological innovation system (TIS) which encompasses the different niches.

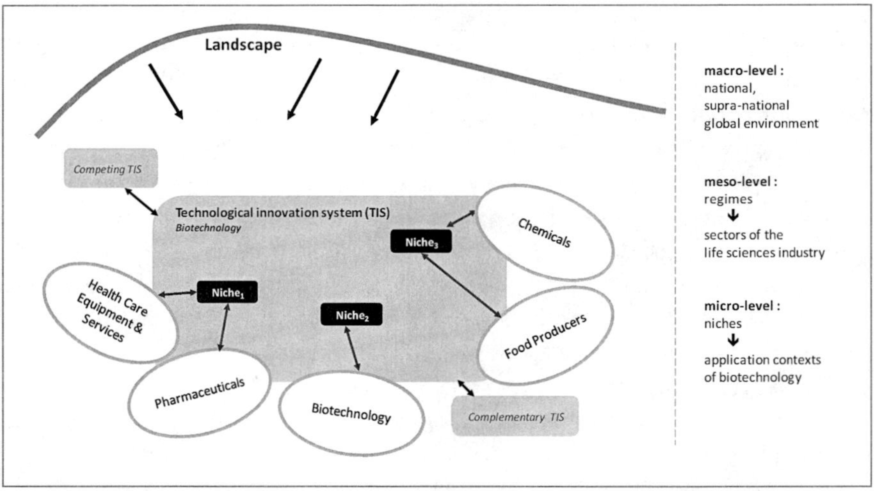

Figure 62: Multi-level dimension of the innovation systems in the life sciences industry

Source: cf. Markard/Truffer, 2008, p. 612, own illustration/extensions

The empirical findings of the cluster analysis clearly reveal that, at the macro-level, the national environment influences the technological portfolios of life sciences companies only to a certain degree. From the perspective of the integrated framework it is, therefore, argued that additional structural forces at the landscape level, which have not been investigated within the context of this thesis, may shape the technological profiles of life sciences companies. With regard to the international dimension of R&D activities it can be assumed that the technological developments in the life sciences industry are also affected by supra-national or global factors. Focusing on the European perspective of this thesis, it can be argued that supra-national factors like European funding activities shape the technological developments of the addressed countries. Especially in the life sciences industry, European cooperation networks like COST, which aim at coordinating national funded research activities, may act as additional macro-level forces.[43]

As a consequence, defining the landscape as an 'open' concept instead of simply replacing the landscape level by the national innovation systems offers the opportunity to take into account further macro-level factors. This seems to be of particular importance if the analysis of innovative activities is expanded to the European or global level.

Referring to the meso-level the empirical findings of this thesis seem to support the concept of the regime which acts as selection environment for the technological developments in the life sciences. However, Markard/Truffer (2008) argue that the systems delineation of the regime notation are not clear-cut. Thus, the concept can be used as synonym for sectors, sub-sectors or technologies. In the context of this thesis, the regime concept is defined at the level of the different life sciences sectors. The empirical findings clearly show the evolution of sector-specific technological profiles. Consequently, the regime concept seems to be more in line with the sub-industrial or sectoral level of the life sciences industry rather than the aggregated industry level. Hence, within the scope of this dissertation the integrated framework consists of five different regimes: The sectoral innovation systems of the 'Chemicals', 'Food Producers', 'Biotechnology', 'Health Care Equipment & Services' and 'Pharmaceuticals' industry. The rule-set of these regimes seems to guide the technological decisions of the firms into specific technological areas. As a consequence, firms within the same sectors show similar technological profiles. Additionally, the technological change within the life sciences sectors is also affected by the national technological trajectories which represent an essential part of the landscape. Moreover, the influence of additional macro-level factors is assumed.

43 Three out of the nine scientific domains of the COST program can be linked to the life sciences industry. This includes the domains 'Biomedicine and Molecular Biosciences (BMBS)', 'Food and Agriculture (FA)' as well as 'Chemistry and Molecular Sciences and Technologies (CMST)'. For further information see: COST (2011) and www.cost.eu.

The empirical findings of this thesis also show the platform characteristics of *Biotechnology*. The analyses of the technological specialisation patterns reveal comparative technological advantages in this technological class in nearly all life sciences sectors. Thus, in the context of the integrated framework, biotechnology represents the technological innovation system which interacts with the different regimes or life sciences sectors as well as with competing or complementary technological innovation systems. In this context, it has to be noted that the framework of Markard/Truffer (2008) lacks of clarity about the characteristics of these systems. Focusing on the life sciences industry, the question arises, how mature technological innovation systems can be integrated. Based on the empirical findings of this thesis a suggested interpretation is that the TIS of *Biotechnology* interacts with the competing technological innovation systems of *Medical technology*, *Food chemistry*, *Organic Fine Chemistry* and *Pharmaceuticals* as well as with the complementary technological innovation systems of *Environmental technology* or *Other special machines*.

Summarising it can be stated that the integrated framework of Markard/Truffer (2008) offers the possibility to exploit the strengths as well as the complementarities of the innovation systems approach and the multi-level framework. By taking into account the dynamic transistions between the different innovation systems, the concept allows to depart from the static perspective of the systems of innovation approach. The empirical analysis of this thesis clearly showed that the technological, sectoral and national environment cannot be detached from each other. The technological profiles of the life sciences companies are affected by technological, sectoral and national innovation patterns.

Furthermore, the integrated framework of Markard/Truffer (2008) detaches itself from the rigid borders of the innovation systems approach. The openness of the integrated framework seems to be of particular importance when innovative activities are considered from the perspective of the multi-national companies which invest in foreign R&D activities. These foreign technological activities enable the diffusion and production of technologies irrespective of national borders. Thus, by taking into account the international dimension of R&D activities, a concept which makes it possible to include further macro-level factors (like the supra-national environment) is needed.

This doctoral dissertation has empirically demonstrated the collective impact of technological, sectoral and national factors on firms' technological profiles. These results confirm the necessity of an integrated framework which takes into account the dynamic interactions between different aggregation levels and conceptual elements respectively.

Innovation policies which are limited to fixed geographical, sectoral or technological boundaries may not be appropriate for policy makers to address problems and developments in science-based industries like the life sciences. The international orientation of science-based industries, for instance, leads to transcend boundaries and increasing extents of foreign R&D activities. Hence, national innovation policies which are restricted to national boundaries cannot afford to support the dynamics in such industries. Modern innovation policies have to take into account not only the interactions between the actors of the respective innovation system itself (or the interaction with the national government), but also the interactions which take place between several innovation systems.

For instance, the national innovation system in biopharmaceuticals has been criticised for neglecting the coordination between those innovation policies addressing the beginning of the innovation chain and those focusing on their end. Thus, on the one hand policies were directed towards the stimulation of new innovative biopharmaceuticals, on the other hand health-care policies prevented their introduction into the market (OECD, 2006, p. 183). Ideally, the interaction of all policy instruments alongside the whole value chain of biopharmaceuticals should have been addressed.

This example makes clear that successful technology policies must take into account national, sectoral and technological factors in their entirety. From the sectoral perspective these policies must consider the whole value chain. Turning the focus on the technological level it can be argued that national instruments should be oriented on the specific nature of the different technologies. For instance, mature technologies need other support activities than emerging technologies. Moreover, policy makers have to bear in mind, that technology strategies which address one specific aggregation level can also affect the technological developments on higher and lower hierarchy levels.

By showing the necessity for a multi-dimensional and integrated perspective of innovative activities, the insights of this thesis help to lay the foundation for modern technology policies. Taking into consideration the multi-level dimension of innovative activities as well as the transitions which take place between the various aggregation levels offers a valuable support for policy makers to find the right strategies for defining future technology policies.

References

Andersen, B. (1998): *The evolution of technological trajectories 1890-1990*, Structural Change and Economic Dynamics, 9 (1), pp. 5-34

Andersen, B. (2001): *Technological change and the evolution of corporate innovation: The structure of patenting 1890-1990*, Cheltenham: Edward Elgar Publishing

Antonelli, C. (2006): *Path dependence, localized technological change and the quest for dynamic efficiency*, C. Antonelli, D. Foray, B.H. Hall, W.E. Steinmueller (ed.), New frontiers in the economics of innovation and new technology: essays in honour of Paul A. David, Cheltenham: Edward Elgar Publishing, pp. 51-69

Archibugi, D. (1992): *Patenting as an indicator of technological innovation: a review*, Science and Public Policy, 19 (6), pp. 357-368

Archibugi, D., Michie, J. (1997): *Technological globalisation or national systems of innovation?*, Futures, 29 (2), pp. 121-137

Archibugi, D., Howells, J., Michie, J. (1999): *Innovation Systems in a Global Economy*, Technology Analysis & Strategic Management, 11 (4), pp. 527-539

Argyres, N. (1996): *Capabilities, Technological Diversification and Divisionalization*, Strategic Management Journal, 17 (5), pp. 395-410

Arthur, W.B. (1989): *Competing Technologies, Increasing Returns, and Lock-In by Historical Events*, The Economic Journal, 99 (394), pp. 116-131

Arthur, W.B. (1990): *Positive Feedbacks in the Economy*, Scientific American, 262, pp. 92-99

Bachmann, A. (1998): *Profiles of corporate technological capabilities – a comparison of large British and German pharmaceutical companies*, Technovation, 18 (10), pp. 593-604

Backhaus, K., Erichson, B., Plinke, W., Weiber, R. (2006): *Multivariate Analysemethoden. Eine anwendungsorientierte Einführung*, Berlin: Springer

Basberg, B.L. (1987): *Patents and the measurement of technological change: A survey of the literature*, Research Policy, 16 (2-4), pp. 131-141

Becker, M.C. (2004): *Organizational routines: a review of the literature*, Industrial and Corporate Change, 13 (4), pp. 643-678

Becker, M.C., Lazaric, N., Nelson, R.R., Winter, S.G. (2005): *Applying organizational routines in understanding organizational change*, Industrial and Corporate Change, 14 (5), pp. 775-791

Bortz, J. (2005): *Statistik für Human- und Sozialwissenschaftler*, Heidelberg: Springer

Breschi, S., Malerba, F. (1997): *Sectoral Innovation Systems: Technological Regimes, Schumpeterian Dynamics, and Spatial Boundaries*, C. Edquist (ed.), Systems of Innovation: Technologies, Institutions and Organizations, London, Washington: Pinter, pp. 130-156

Breschi, S., Lissoni, F., Malerba, F. (1998): *Knowledge Proximity and Technological Diversification*, CESPRI Discussion Paper, Milan: Università L. Bocconi, http://www.druid.dk/uploads/tx_picturedb/ds1998-7.pdf [14/12/2011]

Breschi, S., Lissoni, F., Malerba, F. (2003): *Knowledge-relatedness in firm technological diversification*, Research Policy, 32 (1), pp. 69-87

Breschi, S., Lissoni, F., Malerba, F. (2004): *The empirical assessment of firm's technological "coherence": data and methodology*, J. Cantwell, A. Gambardella, O. Granstrand (ed.), The Economics and Management of Technological Diversification, London: Routledge, pp. 69-98

Bühl, A. (2006): *SPSS 14 – Einführung in die moderne Datenanalyse*, München: Pearson Studium

Cantwell, J. (2004): *A historical change in the nature of corporate technological diversification*, J. Cantwell, A. Gambardella, O. Granstrand (ed.), The Economics and Management of Technological Diversification, London: Routledge, pp. 265-296

Cantwell, J., Fai, F. (1999): *Firms as the source of innovation and growth: the evolution of technological competence*, Journal of Evolutionary Economics, 9 (3), pp. 331-366

Cantwell, J., Odile, J. (2000): *The Role of Multinational Corporations and National States in the Globalization of Innovatory Capacity: The European Perspective*, Technology Analysis & Strategic Management, 12 (2), pp. 243-262

Cantwell, J., Gambardella, A., Granstrand, O. (2004): *Technological and corporate diversification*, J. Cantwell, A. Gambardella, O. Granstrand (ed.), The Economics and Management of Technological Diversification, London: Routledge, pp. 1-17

Carlsson, B. (2006): *Internationalization of innovation systems: A survey of the literature*, Research Policy, 35 (1), pp. 56-67

Carlsson, B., Stankiewicz, R. (1991): *On the nature, function and composition of technological systems*, Journal of Evolutionary Economics, 1 (2), pp. 93-118

Carlsson, B., Jacobsson, S. (1994): *Technological systems and economic policy: the diffusion of factory automation in Sweden*, Research Policy, 23 (2), pp. 235-248

Carlsson, B., Jacobsson, S. (1997): *Diversity Creation and Technological Systems: A Technology Policy Perspective*, C. Edquist (ed.), Systems of Innovation: Technologies, Institutions and Organizations, London, Washington: Pinter, pp. 266-294

Castellacci, F. (2009): *The interactions between national systems and sectoral patterns of innovation: A cross-country analysis of Pavitt's taxonomy*, Journal of Evolutionary Economics, 19 (3), pp. 321-347

Cesaroni, F. (2004): *Technological diversification, technology strategies and licensing in the chemical processing industry*, J. Cantwell, A. Gambardella, O. Granstrand (ed.), The Economics and Management of Technological Diversification, London: Routledge, pp. 176-202

Chen, J.H., Jang, S.-L., Wen, S.H. (2010): *Measuring technological diversification: identifying the effects of patent scale and patent scope*, Scientometrics, 84 (1), pp. 265-275

Chiu, Y.-C., Lai, H.-C., Lee, T.-Y., Liaw, Y.-C. (2007): *Technological Diversification, Complementary Assets and Performance*, Technological Forecasting and Social Change, 75, pp. 875-892

Chiu, Y.-C., Lai, H.-C., Liaw, Y.-C., Lee, T.-Y. (2010): *Technological scope : diversified or specialized*, Scientometrics, 82 (1), pp. 37-58

Christ, J. (2007): *Varieties of Systems of Innovation: A survey of their Evolution in Growth Theory and Economic Geography*, Schriftenreihe des Promotionsschwerpunkts Globalisierung und Beschäftigung, 25, pp. 1-46

Cimoli, M., Dosi, G. (1995): *Technological paradigms, patterns of learning and development: An introductory roadmap*, Journal of Evolutionary Economics, 5 (3), pp. 243-268

Cockburn, I.M. (2004): *The Changing Structure Of The Pharmaceutical Industry*, Health Affairs, 23 (1), pp. 10-22

Coenen, L., Díaz López, F.J. (2010): *Comparing systems approaches to innovation and technological change for sustainable and competitive economies: an explorative study into conceptual commonalities, differences and complementarities*, Journal of Cleaner Production, 18 (12), pp. 1149-1160

Cohen, W.M., Levinthal, D.A. (1989): *Innovation and Learning: The Two Faces of R&D*, The Economic Journal, 99, pp. 569-596

Cohen, W.M., Levinthal, D.A. (1990): *Absorptive Capacity: A New Perspective on Learning and Innovation*, Administrative Science Quarterly, 35 (1), pp. 128-152

Comanor, W.S., Scherer, F.M. (1969): *Patent Statistics as a Measure of Technical Change*, Journal of Political Economy, 77 (3), pp. 392-398

Cooke, P. (2001): *Regional Innovation Systems, Clusters, and the Knowledge Economy*, Industrial and Corporate Change, 10 (4), pp. 945-974

COST (2011): *COST European Cooperation in Science and Technology 2011: About COST*, COST Office

David, P.A. (1985): *Clio and the Economics of QWERTY*, The American Economic Review, 75 (2), pp. 332-337

De Bresson, C. (1987): *The Evolutionary Paradigm and the Economics of Technological Change*, Journal of Economic Issues, 21 (2), pp. 751-762

De Looze, M.A., Ramani, S.V. (1999): *Biotechnology patent applications in Europe: A look at the differences between French, British and German patent application trends*, Nature Biotechnology, 17, pp. 83-85

Department for Business, Innovations and Skills (2010): *The 2009 R&D Scoreboard,* London: Department for Business, Innovations and Skills, UK government

Department for Innovation, Universities and Skills (2009): *The 2008 R&D Scoreboard,* London: Department for Innovation, Universities and Skills, UK government

Diday, E. (1971): *Une nouvelle méthode en classification automatique et reconnaissance des forms la méthode des nuées dynamiques*, Revue de statistique appliquée, 19 (2), pp. 19-33

Doloreux, D. (2002): *What we should know about regional systems of innovation*, Technology in Society, 24 (3), pp. 243-263

Dominguez Lacasa I. (2005): *Exploring technological change in the German pharmaceutical industry: A history friendly model of technological change and technology adoption in a science-based industry*, Dissertation, Universität Karlsruhe (TH), http://digbib.ubka.uni-karlsruhe.de/volltexte/1000004535 [12/14/2011]

Dosi, G. (1982): *Technological paradigms and technological trajectories: A suggested interpretation of the determinants and directions of technical change*, Research Policy, 11 (3), pp. 147-162

Dosi, G. (1988): *Sources, Procedures, and Microeconomic Effects of Innovation*, Journal of Economic Literature, 26, pp. 1120-1171

Dosi, G., Labini, M.S. (2007): *Technological paradigms and trajectories*, H. Hanusch, A. Pyka (ed.), Elgar Companion to Neo-Schumpeterian Economics, Cheltenham: Edward Elgar Publishing, pp. 331-343

Dosi, G., Grazzi, M. (2010): *On the nature of technologies: knowledge, procedures, artifacts and production inputs*, Cambridge Journal of Economics, 34 (1), pp. 173-184

Dreher, C., Frietsch, R., Hemer, J., Schmoch, U. (2006): *Die Beschleunigung von Innovationszyklen und die Rolle der Fraunhofer-Gesellschaft*, H.-J. Bullinger (ed.), Fokus Innovation: Kräfte bündeln – Prozesse beschleunigen, München: Carl Hanser, pp. 275-306

Enriquez, J., Goldberg, R.A. (2000): *Transforming Life, Transforming Business: The Life-Science Revolution*, Harvard Business Review, 78 (2), pp. 94-104

European Commission (2009): *Monitoring industrial research: the 2008 EU R&D Investment Scoreboard*, Luxembourg: Office for Official Publications of the European Communities

European Commission (2010): *Monitoring industrial research: the 2009 EU R&D Investment Scoreboard*, Luxembourg: Office for Official Publications of the European Communities

Fai, F.M. (2003): *Corporate technological competence and the evolution of technological diversification*, Cheltenham: Edward Elgar Publishing

Fai, F., von Tunzelmann, G.N. (2001): *Industry-specific competencies and converging technological systems: evidence from patents*, Structural Change and Economic Dynamics, 12 (2), pp. 141-170

Fischer, M.M. (2001): *Innovation, knowledge creation and systems of innovation*, The Annals of Regional Science, 35 (2), pp. 199-216

Fornahl, D., Stohr, J. (2008), *Technologische Diversifikation von Multi-Technologieunternehmen*, Wirtschaftswissenschaftliches Studium, 37 (12), pp. 630-636

Fromhold-Eisebith, M. (2007): *Bridging Scales in Innovation Policies: How to Link Regional, National and International Innovation Systems*, European Planning Studies, 15 (2), pp. 217-233

Freeman, C. (1995): *The 'National System of Innovation' in historical perspective*, Cambridge Journal of Economics, 19 (1), pp. 5-24

Freeman, C., Perez, C. (1988): *Structural Crises of Adjustment: Business Cycles and Investment Behaviour*, in G. Dosi, C. Freeman, R. Nelson, G. Silverberg. L. Soete (ed.), Technical Change and Economic Theory, London: Pinter Publishers, pp. 36-66

Frietsch, R. (2006): *Micro data for macro effects*, in P. Hingley, M. Nicolas (ed.), Forecasting Innovations: Methods for Predicting Numbers of Patent Filings, Heidelberg: Springer, pp. 159-189

Gambardella, A., Torrisi, S. (1998), *Does technological convergence imply Convergence in markets? Evidence from the electronics industry*, Research Policy, 27 (5), pp. 445-463

Garcia-Vega, M. (2006): *Does technological diversification promote innovation? An empirical analysis for European firms*, Research Policy, 35 (2), pp. 230-246

Geels, F.W. (2002): *Technological transitions as evolutionary reconfiguration processes: a multi-level perspective and a case study*, Research Policy, 31 (8-9), pp. 1257-1274

Geels, F.W. (2004): *From sectoral systems of innovation to socio-technical systems: Insights about dynamics and change from sociology and institutional theory*, Research Policy, 33 (6-7), pp. 897-920

Geels, F.W. (2006): *Multi-level perspective on System Innovation: Relevance for Industrial Transformation*, X. Olsthoorn, A.J. Wieczorek (ed.), Understanding Industrial Transformation: Views from Different Disciplines, Environment & Policy, 44, pp. 163-186

Genus, A., Coles, A.-M. (2008): *Rethinking the multi-level perspective of technological transitions*, Research Policy, 37 (9), pp. 1436-1445

Gerybadze, A., Stephan, M. (2002): *Determinants of Technological Diversification: An Analysis of Corporate Diversification Patterns*, Discussion Paper on International Management and Innovation (02-01), Stuttgart: University of Hohenheim, http://www.interman.uni-hohenheim.de/5_forschung/papers/DIMI0201.pdf [14/12/ 2011]

Grabowski, H., Vernon, J. (1994): *Innovation and Structural Change in Pharmaceuticals and Biotechnology*, Industrial and Corporate Change, 3 (2), pp. 435-449

Granstrand, O. (1998): *Towards a theory of the technology-based firm*, Research Policy, 27 (5), pp. 465-489

Granstrand, O., Oskarsson, C. (1994): *Technology Diversification in "MUL-TECH" Corporations*, IEEE Transactions on Engineering Management, 41 (4), pp. 355-364

Granstrand, O., Sjölander, S. (1990): *Managing innovation in multi-technology corporations*, Research Policy, 19, pp. 35-60

Granstrand, O., Patel, P., Pavitt, K. (1997): *Multi-technology corporations: why they have "distributed" rather than "distinctive core" competencies*, California Management Review, 39 (4), pp. 8-25

Griliches, Z. (1990): *Patent Statistics as Economic Indicators: A Survey*, Journal of Economic Literature, 28 (4), pp. 1661-1707

Grupp, H. (1994): *The measurement of technical performance of innovations by technometrics and its impact on established technology indicators*, Research Policy, 23 (2), pp. 175-193

Grupp, H. (1997): *Messung und Erklärung des Technischen Wandels: Grundzüge einer empirischen Innovationsökonomik*, Berlin, Heidelberg: Springer

Hekkert, M.P., Suurs, R.A.A., Negro, S.O., Kuhlmann, S., Smits, R.E.H.M. (2007): *Functions of innovation systems: A new approach for analysing technological change*, Technological Forecasting and Social Change, 74 (4), pp. 413-432

Hinze, S., Gaisser, S. (2003): *Nanotechnologie und Life Sciences*, Studie im Rahmen des TAB-Projekts "Nanotechnologie", Karlsruhe: Fraunhofer ISI

Hinze, S., Reiss, T., Schmoch, U. (1997): *Statistical Analysis on the Distance Between Fields of Technology,* Report for the research project "Innovation Systems and European Integration (ISI)" funded by the European Commission (DG XII). Sub-Project 3.2.5: Technological Entry: Diversification vs. New Innovators, Karlsruhe: Fraunhofer ISI

Hinze, S., Reiss, T., Dominguez-Lacasa, I., Wörner, S. (2001): *Einfluss der Biotechnologie auf das Innovationssystem der pharmazeutischen Industrie*, Bericht an das Bundesministerium für Bildung und Forschung, Referat Z25, Karlsruhe: Fraunhofer ISI

Howells, J. (1996): *Tacit Knowledge, Innovation and Technology Transfer*, Technology Analysis & Strategic Management, 8 (2), pp. 91-106

Hullmann, A. (2001): *Internationaler Wissenstransfer und technischer Wandel: Bedeutung, Einflussfaktoren und Ausblick auf technologiepolitische Implikationen am Beispiel der Nanotechnologie in Deutschland*, Heidelberg: Physica-Verlag

Jacobsson, S. (1997): *Systems Transformation: Technological and Institutional Change*, C. Edquist (ed.), Systems of Innovation: Technologies, Institutions and Organizations, London, Washington: Pinter, pp. 295-341

Jacobsson, S., Oskarsson, C. (1995): *Educational statistics as an indicator of technological activity*, Research Policy, 24 (1), pp. 127-136

Jacobsson, S., Oskarsson, C., Philipson, J. (1996): *Indicators of technological activities – comparing educational, patent and R&D statistics in the case of Sweden*, Research Policy, 25 (4), pp. 573-585

Jaffe, A.B. (1986): *Technological Opportunity and Spillovers of R&D: Evidence from Firms' Patents, Profits, and Market Value*, The American Economic Review, 76(5), pp. 984-1001

Jaquemin A.P. (1975): *Une mesure entropique de la diversification des entreprises*, Revue économique, 26 (5), pp. 834-838

Jaquemin, A.P., Berry, C.H. (1979): *Entropy Measure of Diversification and Corporate Growth,* The Journal of Industrial Economics, 27 (4), pp. 359-369

Kemp, R. (1994), *Technology and the transition to environmental sustainability: The problem of technical regime shifts*, Futures, 26 (10), pp. 1023-1046

Kemp, R., Schot, J., Hoogma, R. (1998): *Regime shifts to sustainability through processes of niche formation: The approach of strategic niche management*, Technology Analysis & Strategic Management, 10 (2), pp. 175-195

Kim, D.-J., Kogut, B. (1996): *Technological Platforms and Diversification*, Organization Science, 7 (3), pp. 283-301

Kodama, F. (1986): *Technological Diversification of Japanese Industry*, Science, 233 (4761), pp. 291-296

Kodama, F. (1992): *Technology Fusion and the New R&D*, Harvard Business Review, 10 (4), pp. 70-78

Kodama, F. (1995): *Emerging Patterns of Innovation: Sources of Japan's Technological Edge*, Boston: Harvard Business School Press

Kondratieff, N. (1926): *Die langen Wellen der Konjunktur*, Archiv für Sozialwissenschaft und Sozialpolitik, 56 (3), pp. 573-609

Koschatzky, K., Baier, E., Kroll, H., Stahlecker, T. (2009): *The spatial multidimensionality of sectoral innovation – the case of information and communication technologies*, Working Papers Firms and Region, No. R4/2009, Karlsruhe: Fraunhofer ISI

Krafft, J., Quatraro, F., Saviotti, P. (2009): *Evolution of the Knowledge Base in Knowledge Intensive Sectors*, Working Paper No. 06/2009, Torino: Università di Torino

Kuhn, T.S. (1962): *The Structure of Scientific Revolutions*, Chicago: University of Chicago Press

Lambooy, J.G., Boschma, R.A (2001): *Evolutionary economics and regional policy*, The Annals of Regional Science, 35 (1), pp. 113-131

Laursen, K. (1998): *Revealed Comparative Advantage and the Alternatives as Measures of International Specialisation*, DRUID Working Papers, 98-30, Copenhagen: Copenhagen Business School

Lester, R.K. (2005): *Universities, innovation, and the competitiveness of local economies: A Summary Report from the Local Innovation Systems Project – Phase I*, MIT Industrial Performance Center Working Paper, 05-010, Massachusetts Institute of Technology

Leten, B. (2008): *Technology scope decisions in large firms*, PhD thesis, Faculty of Business and Economics, KU Leuven, http://www.econ.kuleuven.be/msi/_docs/members/leten/phdthesis.pdf [11/10/2011]

Leten, B., Belderbos, R., van Looy, B. (2007): *Technological Diversification, Coherence and Performance of Firms*, Journal of Product Innovation Management, 24 (6), pp. 567-579

Leten, B., van Looy, B., Belderbos, R. (2008): *Direction and Success of Exploratory Technological Search: Technological Opportunities, Knowledge Relatedness and Technology Concentration*, Paper to be presented at the 25th Celebration Conference 2008, Copenhagen: Copenhagen Business School

Levin, C.R., Klevorick, A.K., Nelson, R.R., Winter, S.G., Gilbert, R., Griliches, Z. (1987): *Appropriating the Returns from Industrial Research and Development*, Brooking Papers on Economic Activity, 1987 (3), pp. 783-831

Liebowitz, S.J., Margolis, S.E. (1995): *Path dependence, Lock-In, and History*, Journal of Law, Economics and Organization, 11(1), pp. 205-226

Liebowitz, S.J., Margolis, S.E. (2000): *Path Dependence*, Encyclopaedia of Law and Economics, 0770, pp. 981-998

List, F. (1841): *The National System of Political Economy*, English Edition (1904), London: Longman

Lundvall, B.-A. (1992): *National Systems of Innovation. Towards a Theory of Innovation and Interactive Learning*, London: Pinter Publishers

Malerba, F. (1992): *Learning by Firms and Incremental Technical Change*, The Economic Journal, 102 (413), pp. 845-859

Malerba, F. (2002): *Sectoral systems of innovation and production*, Research Policy, 31 (2), pp. 247-264

Malerba, F. (2004): *Sectoral systems of innovation: basic concepts*, F. Malerba (ed.), Sectoral systems of innovation: Concepts, issues and analysis of six major sectors in Europe, Cambridge: Cambridge University Press, pp. 9-41

Malerba, F. (2005): *Sectoral systems of innovation: A framework for linking innovation to the knowledge base, structure and dynamics of sectors,* Economics of Innovation and New Technology, 14 (1-2), pp. 63-82

Malerba, F., Orsenigo, L. (1996): *The dynamics and evolution of industries*, Industrial and Corporate Change, 5 (1), pp. 51-87

Malerba, F., Orsenigo, L. (2002): *Innovation and market structure in the dynamics of the pharmaceutical industry and biotechnology: towards a history-friendly model*, Industrial and Corporate Change, 11 (4), pp. 667-703

Mandeville, T. (1998): *An information economics perspective on innovation*, International Journal of Social Economics, 25 (2/3/4), pp. 357-364

Mansfield, E. (1986): *Patents and Innovation: An Empirical Study*, Management Science, 32 (2), pp. 173-181

March, J.G. (1991): *Exploration and Exploitation in Organizational Learning*, Organization Science, 2 (1), pp. 71-87

Markard, J., Truffer, B. (2008): *Technological innovation systems and the multi-level perspective: Towards an integrated framework*, Research policy, 37 (4), pp. 596-615

Martin, R., Sunley, R. (2006): *Path dependence and regional economic evolution*, Journal of Economic Geography, 6 (4), pp. 395-437

McKelvey, M. (1997), *Using Evolutionary Theory to Define Systems of Innovation*, C. Edquist (ed.), Systems of Innovation: Technologies, Institutions and Organizations, London, Washington: Pinter, pp. 200-222

McKelvey, M., Orsenigo, L. (2001), *Pharmaceuticals as a Sectoral Innovation System*, Paper prepared for the ESSY Project (European Sectoral Systems of Innovation) and within the Epris Project, Milan: CESPRI, Bocconi University

McKelvey M., Orsenigo, L., Pammolli, F. (2004*): Pharmaceuticals analyzed through the lens of a sectoral innovation system*, F. Malerba (ed.), Sectoral Systems of Innovation: Concepts, issues and analyses of six major sectors in Europe, Cambridge: Cambridge University Press, pp. 73-120

Menrad, K. (2005): *Future employment in biotechnology in Germany*, Journal of Commercial Biotechnology, 12 (1), pp. 29-39

Metcalfe, J.S. (1995): *Technology systems and technology policy in an evolutionary framework*, Cambridge Journal of Economics, 19 (1), pp. 25-46

Meyer-Krahmer, F., Dreher, C. (2004): *Neuere Betrachtungen zu Technikzyklen und Implikationen für die Fraunhofer-Gesellschaft*, D. Spath (ed.), Forschungs- und Technologiemanagement: Potenziale nutzen – Zukunft gestalten, München: Hanser, pp. 27-35

Miller, D. J. (2006): *Technological diversity, related diversification, and firm performance*, Strategic Management Journal, 27 (7), pp. 601-619

Narin, F., Noma, E., Perry, R. (1987): *Patents as indicators of corporate technological strength*, Research Policy, 16 (2), pp. 143-155

Nelson, R. R. (1993): *National Systems of Innovation. A Comparative Analysis*, New York: Oxford University Press

Nelson R.R., Winter S.G. (1977): *In search of a useful theory of innovation*, Research Policy, 6 (1), pp. 36- 76

Nelson R.R., Winter S.G. (1982): *An evolutionary theory of economic change*, Cambridge, MA: Havard University Press

Nelson, R.R., Rosenberg, N. (1993): *Technological Innovation and National Systems*, R.R. Nelson (ed.), National Systems of Innovation. A Comparative Analysis, New York: Oxford University Press, pp. 3-21

Nesta, L., Saviotti, P.P. (2005): *Coherence of the Knowledge Base and the Firm's Innovative Performance: Evidence from the U.S. Pharmaceutical Industry*, The Journal of Industrial Economics, 53 (1), pp. 123-142

Nieto, M. (2004): *Basic propositions for the study of technological innovation process in the firm*, European Journal of Innovation Management, 7 (4), pp. 314-324

Niosi, J., Bellon, B. (1994): *The Global Interdependence of National Innovation Systems: Evidence, Limits and Implications*, Technology in Society, 16 (2), pp. 173-197

Nooteboom, B. (2000): *Learning and Innovation in Organizations and Economies*, Oxford, New York: Oxford University Press

Nooteboom, B., Van Haverbeke, W., Duysters, G., Gilsing, V., van den Oord., A. (2007): *Optimal cognitive distance and absorptive capacity*, Research Policy, 36 (7), pp. 1016-1034

OECD (1997): *National Innovation Systems*, Paris, OECD Publishing, http://www.oecd.org/dataoecd/35/56 /2101733.pdf [09/04/2009]

OECD (2006): *Innovation in Pharmaceutical Biotechnology: Comparing National Innovation Systems at the Sectoral Level*, Paris: OECD Publishing

Olsen O.E., Engen O. A. (2007): *Technological change as a trade-off between social construction and technological paradigms*, Technology in Society, 29, pp. 456-468

Palepu, K. (1985): *Diversification strategy, profit performance and the entropy measure*, Strategic Management Journal, 6 (3), pp. 239-255

Patel, P., Pavitt, K. (1994a): *National Innovation Systems: Why They Are Important, And How They Might Be Measured And Compared*, Economics of Innovation and New Technology, 3(1), pp. 77-95

Patel, P., Pavitt, K. (1994b): *The continuing, widespread (and neglected) importance of improvements in mechanical technologies*, Research Policy, 23 (5), pp. 533-545

Patel, P., Pavitt, K. (1997): *The technological competencies of the world's largest firms: Complex and path-dependent, but not much variety*, Research Policy, 26, pp. 141-156

Pavitt, K. (1982): *R&D, patenting and innovative activities: A statistical exploration*, Research Policy, 11 (1), pp. 33-51

Pavitt, K. (1985): *Patent Statistics as Indicators of Innovative Activities: Possibilities and Problems*, Scientometrics, 7 (1-2), pp. 77-99

Pavitt, K., Robson, M., Townsend, J. (1989): *Technological Accumulation, Diversification and Organisation in UK Companies, 1945-1983*, Management Science, 35 (1), pp. 81-99

Praest, M. (1998): *Processes of Technological Competence Accumulation: A Synthesis*, Paper prepared for the DRUID summer conference, Bornholm

Prahalad, C.K., Hamel, G. (1990): *The core competence of the corporation*, Harvard Business Review, 68 (3), pp. 79-91

Prencipe, A. (2004): *The changing boundaries of the firm: empirical evidence from the aircraft engine industry*, J. Cantwell, A. Gambardella, O. Granstrand (ed.), The Economics and Management of Technological Diversification, London: Routledge, pp. 234-261

Ramani, S.V., de Looze, M.-A. (2002): *Country-Specific Characteristics of Patent Applications in France, Germany and the UK in the Biotechnology Sectors*, Technology Analysis & Strategic Management, 14 (4), pp. 457-480

Rip, A., Kemp, R. (1998): *Technological change*, S. Rayner, E.L. Malone (ed.), Human Choice & Climate Change, 2, Columbos, Ohio: Battelle Press, pp. 327-399

Rosenberg, N. (1996): *Uncertainty and Technological change*, Conference Series [Proceedings], June, Boston: Federal Reserve Bank of Boston, pp. 91-125

Russel, A. (1999): *Biotechnology as a Technological Paradigm in the Global Knowledge Structure*, Technology Analysis & Strategic Management, 11 (2), pp. 235-254

Sahal, D. (1981): *Alternative concepts of technology,* Research Policy, 10 (1), pp. 2-24

Scherer, F.M. (1983): *The propensity to patent,* International Journal of Industrial Organization, 1 (1), pp. 107-128

Scherer, F.M. (2000): *The pharmaceutical industry*, Handbook of Health Economics, 1 (Part B), Chapter 25, pp. 1297-1336

Schmoch, U. (1990): *Wettbewerbsvorsprung durch Patentinformation: Handbuch für die Recherchenpraxis mit ausführlichem Online-Teil*, Köln: TÜV Rheinland GmbH,

Schmoch, U. (1999): *Impact of international patent applications on patent indicators*, Research Evaluation, 8 (2), pp. 119-131

Schmoch, U. (2007): *Double-boom cycles and the comeback of science-push and market-pull*, Research policy, 36 (7), pp. 1000-1015

Schmoch, U. (2008): *Concept of a Technology Classification for Country Comparisons*, Final Report to the World Intellectual Property Organisation (WIPO), Karlsruhe: Fraunhofer Institute for Systems and Innovation Research

Schmoch, U., Grupp, H., Mannsbart, W., Schwitalla, B. (1988): *Technikprognosen mit Patentindikatoren: Zur Einschätzung zukünftiger industrieller Entwicklungen bei Industrierobotern, Lasern, Solargeneratoren und immobilisierten Enzymen,* Köln: TÜV Rheinland GmbH

Schmoch, U., Laville, F., Patel, P., Frietsch, R. (2003*): Linking Technological Areas to Industrial Sectors,* Final Report to the European Commission, DG Research, Karlsruhe, Paris, Brighton

Schweizer, L. (2002): *The key drivers and success factors for M&A strategies in the biotechnological and pharmaceutical industry*, Pharmaceutical Policy and Law, 5, pp. 41-62

Shin, J. Jalajas, D.(2010): *Technological relatedness, boundary-spanning combination of knowledge and the impact of innovation: Evidence of an inverted-U relationship*, Journal of High Technology Management Research, 21 (2), pp. 87-96

Siegele, J. (2010): *Effizienzanalyse deutscher Wirtschaftsstandorte*, Karlsruher Beiträge zur wirtschaftspolitischen Forschung, Band 30, Baden-Baden: Nomos Verlagsgesellschaft, Zugl. Dissertation, Universität Karlsruhe (TH)

Smith, A. (1776): *The Wealth of Nations*, New York: Random House

Stephan, M. (2003): *Technologische Diversifikation von Unternehmen: Ressourcentheoretische Untersuchung der Determinanten*, Wiesbaden: Deutscher Universitätsverlag

Stephan, M. (2004): *Ein evolutionsökonomisches Modell der Unternehmensdiversifikation*, Marco Lehmann-Waffenschmidt, Alexander Ebner, Dirk Fornahl (ed.), Institutioneller Wandel, Marktprozesse und dynamische Wirtschaftspolitik: Perspektiven der Evolutorischen Ökonomik, Institutionelle und Evolutorische Ökonomik Band 24, Marburg: Metropolis-Verlag, pp. 219-258

Stephan, M. (2010): *Does Outsourcing Result in the Outsourcing of Technological Compentencies? An Empirical Analysis on the Effect of Vertical Specialization on the Technological Competence Base of Firms*, Management Revue, 21 (3), pp. 308-331

Stohr, J. (2007): *Technologischer Diversifikationsgrad der pharmazeutischen Industrie Deutschlands*, unveröffentlichte Diplomarbeit, Institut für Wirtschaftspolitik und Wirtschaftsforschung (IWW), Universität Karlsruhe (TH)

Suárez F.F., Utterback, J.M. (1995): *Dominant designs and the survival of firms*, Strategic Management Journal, 16 (6), pp 415-430

Teece, D.J. (1980): *Economies of Scope and the Scope of the Enterprise*, Journal of Economic Behavior & Organization, 1 (3), pp. 223-247

Teece, D.J. (1982): *Towards an economic theory of the multiproduct firm*, Journal of Economic Behavior & Organization, 3 (1), pp. 39-63

Teece, D.J. (1988): *Technological Change and the Nature of the Firm*, G. Dosi, C. Freeman, R. Nelson, G. Silverberg, L. Soete (ed.), Technical Change and Economic Theory, London: Pinter, pp. 256-281

Teece, D.J. (2008): *Dosi's technological paradigms and trajectories: insights for economics and management*, Industrial and Corporate Change, 17(3), pp. 507-512

Teece, D.J., Pisano, G., Shuen, A. (1997): *Dynamic Capabilities and Strategic Management*, Strategic Management Journal, 18 (7), pp. 509-533

Teece, D.J., Rumelt, R., Dosi, G., Winter, S. (1994): *Understanding corporate coherence: Theory and evidence*, Journal of Economic Behavior & Organization, 23 (1), pp. 1-30

Tidd, J., Bessant, J., Pavitt, K. (2005): *Managing Innovation: Integrating Technological, Market and Organizational Change,* Chichester: John Wiley & Sons

Torissi, S., Granstrand, O. (2004): *Technological and business diversification: a survey of theories and empirical evidence*, J. Cantwell, A. Gambardella, O. Granstrand (ed.), The Economics and Management of Technological Diversification, London: Routledge, pp. 21-68

Utterback, J.M., Suárez F.F. (1993): *Innovation, competition, and industry structure*, Research Policy, 22 (1), pp. 1-21

WIPO (2011): *Intellectual Property and Life Sciences*, http://www.wipo.int/patentscope/en/lifesciences/ [28/04/2011]

Zander, I. (1997): *Technological diversification in the multinational corporation – historical evolution and future prospects*, Research Policy, 26 (2), pp. 209-227

Annex

Annex I: WIPO IPC Technology Concordance Table

Source: cf. Schmoch (2008), own illustration

		Technology class	International Patent Classification (IPC) Symbols
I Electrical engineering	1	Electrical machinery, apparatus, energy	F21#, H01B, H01C, H01F, H01G, H01H, H01J, H01K, H01M, H01R, H01T, H02#, H05B, H05C, H05F, H99Z
	2	Audio-visual technology	G09F, G09G, G11B, H04N-003, H04N-005, H04N-009, H04N-013, H04N-015, H04N-017, H04R, H04S, H05K
	3	Telecommunications	G08C, H01P, H01Q, H04B, H04H, H04J, H04K, H04M, H04N-001, H04N-007, H04N-011, H04Q
	4	Digital communication	H04L
	5	Basic communication processes	H03#
	6	Computer technology	(G06# not G06Q), G11C, G10L
	7	IT methods for management	G06Q
	8	Semiconductors	H01L
II Instruments	9	Optics	G02#, G03B, G03C, G03D, G03F, G03G, G03H, H01S
	10	Measurement	G01B, G01C, G01D, G01F, G01G, G01H, G01J, G01K, G01L, G01M, (G01N not G01N-033), G01P, G01R, G01S; G01V, G01W, G04#, G12B, G99Z
	11	Analysis of biological materials	G01N-033
	12	Control	G05B, G05D, G05F, G07#, G08B, G08G, G09B, G09C, G09D
	13	Medical technology	A61B, A61C, A61D, A61F, A61G, A61H, A61J, A61L, A61M, A61N, H05G
III Chemistry	14	Organic fine chemistry	(C07B, C07C, C07D, C07F, C07H, C07J, C40B) not A61K, A61K-008, A61Q
	15	Biotechnology	(C07G, C07K, C12M, C12N, C12P, C12Q, C12R, C12S) not A61K
	16	Pharmaceuticals	A61K not A61K-008
	17	Macromolecular chemistry, polymers	C08B, C08C, C08F, C08G, C08H, C08K, C08L
	18	Food chemistry	A01H, A21D, A23B, A23C, A23D, A23F, A23G, A23J, A23K, A23L, C12C, C12F, C12G, C12H, C12J, C13D, C13F, C13J, C13K
	19	Basic materials chemistry	A01N, A01P, C05#, C06#, C09B, C09C, C09F, C09G, C09H, C09K, C09D, C09J, C10B, C10C, C10F, C10G, C10H, C10J, C10K, C10L, C10M, C10N, C11B, C11C, C11D, C99Z
	20	Materials, metallurgy	C01#, C03C, C04#, C21#, C22#, B22#
	21	Surface technology, coating	B05C, B05D, B32#, C23#, C25#, C30#

Annex I: WIPO IPC Technology Concordance Table (continued)

Source: cf. Schmoch (2008), own illustration

	Technology class	International Patent Classification (IPC) Symbols
III Chemistry	22 Micro-structural and nano-technology	B81#, B82#
	23 Chemical engineering	B01B, B01D-000#, B01D-01##, B01D-02##, B01D-03##, B01D-041, B01D-043, B01D-057, B01D-059, B01D-06##, B01D-07##, B01F, B01J, B01L, B02C, B03#, B04#, B05B, B06B, B07#, B08#, D06B, D06C, D06L, F25J, F26#, C14C, H05H
	24 Environmental technology	A62D, B01D-045, B01D-046, B01D-047, B01D-049, B01D-050, B01D-051, B01D-052, B01D-053, B09#, B65F, C02#, F01N, F23G, F23J, G01T, E01F-008, A62C
IV Mechanical engineering	25 Handling	B25J, B65B, B65C, B65D, B65G, B65H, B66#, B67#
	26 Machine tools	B21#, B23#, B24#, B26D, B26F, B27#, B30#, B25B, B25C, B25D, B25F, B25G, B25H, B26B
	27 Engines, pumps, turbines	F01B, F01C, F01D, F01K, F01L, F01M, F01P, F02#, F03#, F04#, F23R, G21#, F99Z
	28 Textile and paper machines	A41H, A43D, A46D, C14B, D01#, D02#, D03#, D04B, D04C, D04G, D04H, D05#, D06G, D06H, D06J, D06M, D06P, D06Q, D99Z, B31#, D21#, B41#
	29 Other special machines	A01B, A01C, A01D, A01F, A01G, A01J, A01K, A01L, A01M, A21B, A21C, A22#, A23N, A23P, B02B, C12L, C13C, C13G, C13H, B28#, B29#, C03B, C08J, B99Z, F41#, F42#
	30 Thermal processes and apparatus	F22#, F23B, F23C, F23D, F23H, F23K, F23L, F23M, F23N, F23Q, F24#, F25B, F25C, F27#, F28#
	31 Mechanical elements	F15#, F16#, F17#, G05G
	32 Transport	B60#, B61#, B62#, B63B, B63C, B63G, B63H, B63J, B64#
V Other fields	33 Furniture, games	A47#, A63#
	34 Other consumer goods	A24#, A41B, A41C, A41D, A41F, A41G, A42#, A43B, A43C, A44#, A45#, A46B, A62B, B42#, B43#, D04D, D07#, G10B, G10C, G10D, G10F, G10G, G10H, G10K, B44#, B68#, D06F, D06N, F25D, A99Z
	35 Civil engineering	E02#, E01B, E01C, E01D, E01F-001, E01F-003, E01F-005, E01F-007, E01F-009, E01F-01#, E01H, E03#, E04#, E05#, E06#, E21#, E99Z

Annex II: IPCs defining the life sciences

Source: cf. Hinze/Gaisser, 2003, own compilation

Technology class	IPCs
Medical technology	A61B, A61C, A61D, A61F, A61G, A61H, A61J, A61L, A61M, A61N, H05G
Biotechnology	C07G, C07K, C12M, C12N, C12P, C12Q, C12R, C12S
Pharmaceuticals	A61K not A61K-008, A61P
Food chemistry	A01H, A21D, A23B, A23C, A23D, A23F, A23G, A23J, A23K, A23L, C12C, C12F, C12G, C12H, C12J, C13D, C13F, C13J, C13K
Basic materials chemistry	A01N, A01P, C05#, C09F, C09H, C11B, C11C, C11D
Environmental technology	A62D, B01D-045, B01D-046, B01D-047, B01D-049, B01D-050, B01D-051, B01D-052, B01D-053, B09#, B65F, C02#, F01N, F23G, F23J, G01T, E01F-008, A62C
Other special machines	A01B, A01C, A01D, A01F, A01G, A01J, A01K, A01L, A01M, A21B, A21C, A22#, A23N, A23P, B02B, C12L, C13C, C13G, C13H, B28#

Note: *This list contains all IPCs which define the life sciences. Not relevant IPCs of the classes 'Basic materials chemistry' and 'Other special machines' are omitted. Additionally, the class 'Pharmaceuticals' is supplemented by the IPC code A61P, which was not listed in the revised concordance table.*

Annex III: Matrices of technology co-occurrences - CH

Source: PATSTAT October 2007, own computations

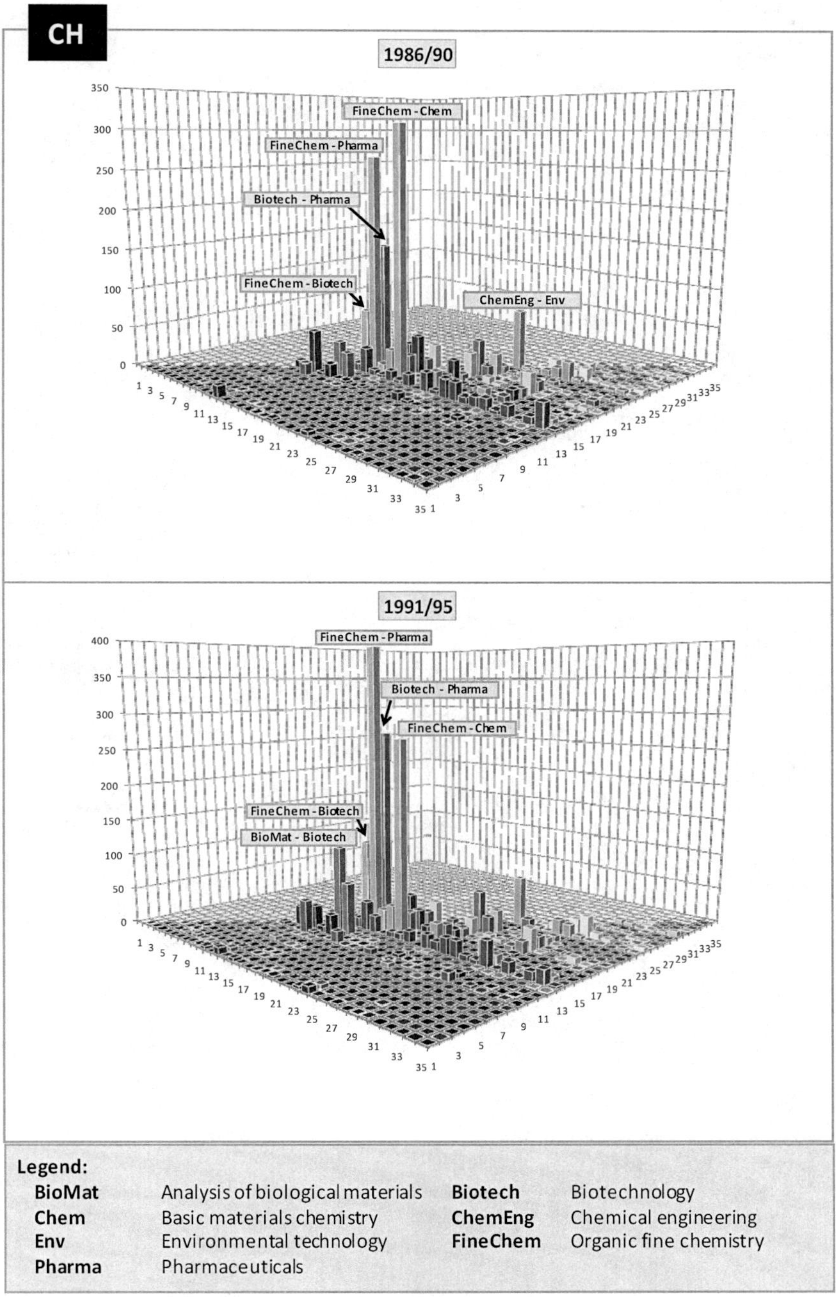

Legend:

BioMat	Analysis of biological materials	**Biotech**	Biotechnology
Chem	Basic materials chemistry	**ChemEng**	Chemical engineering
Env	Environmental technology	**FineChem**	Organic fine chemistry
Pharma	Pharmaceuticals		

Annex III: Matrices of technology co-occurrences - CH (continued)

Source: PATSTAT October 2007, own computations

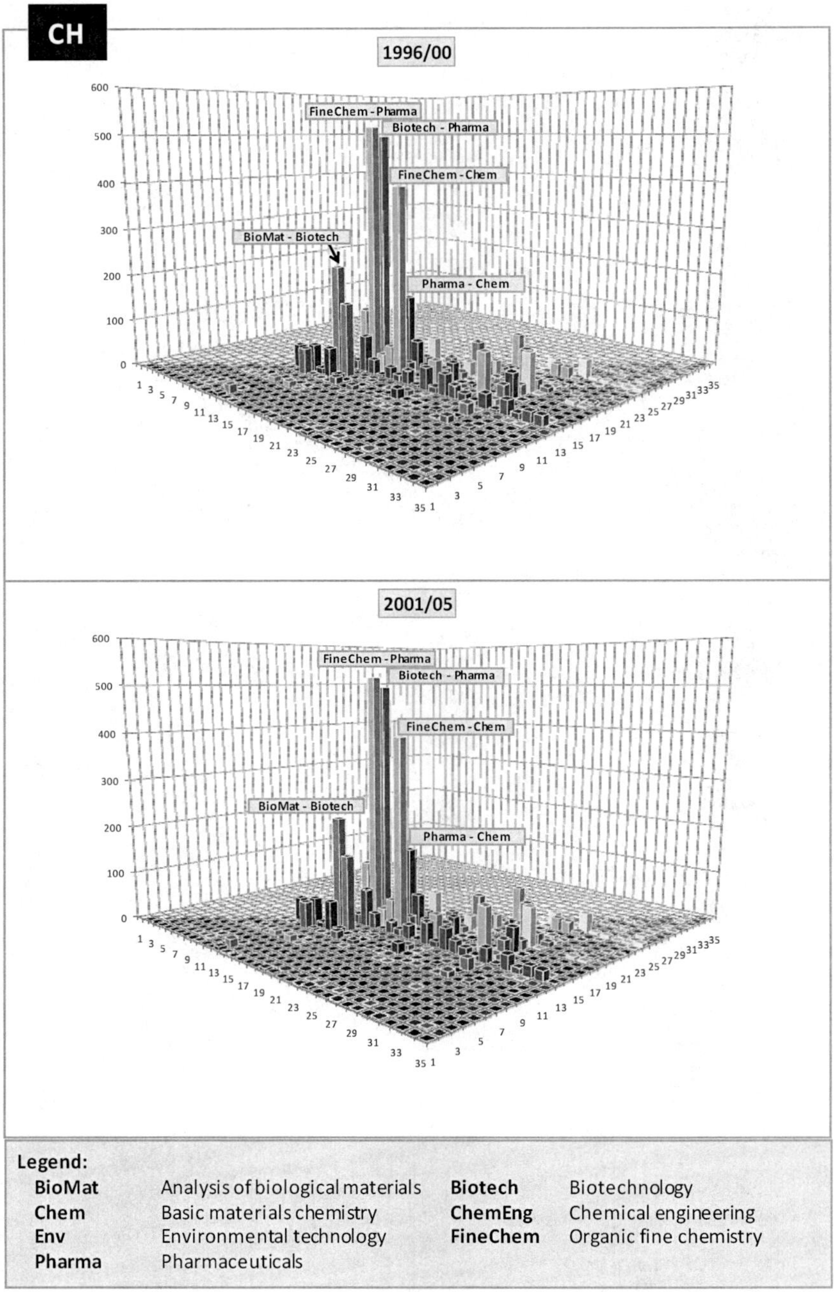

Legend:

BioMat	Analysis of biological materials	**Biotech**	Biotechnology
Chem	Basic materials chemistry	**ChemEng**	Chemical engineering
Env	Environmental technology	**FineChem**	Organic fine chemistry
Pharma	Pharmaceuticals		

Annex IV: Matrices of technology co-occurrences - DE

Source: PATSTAT October 2007, own computations

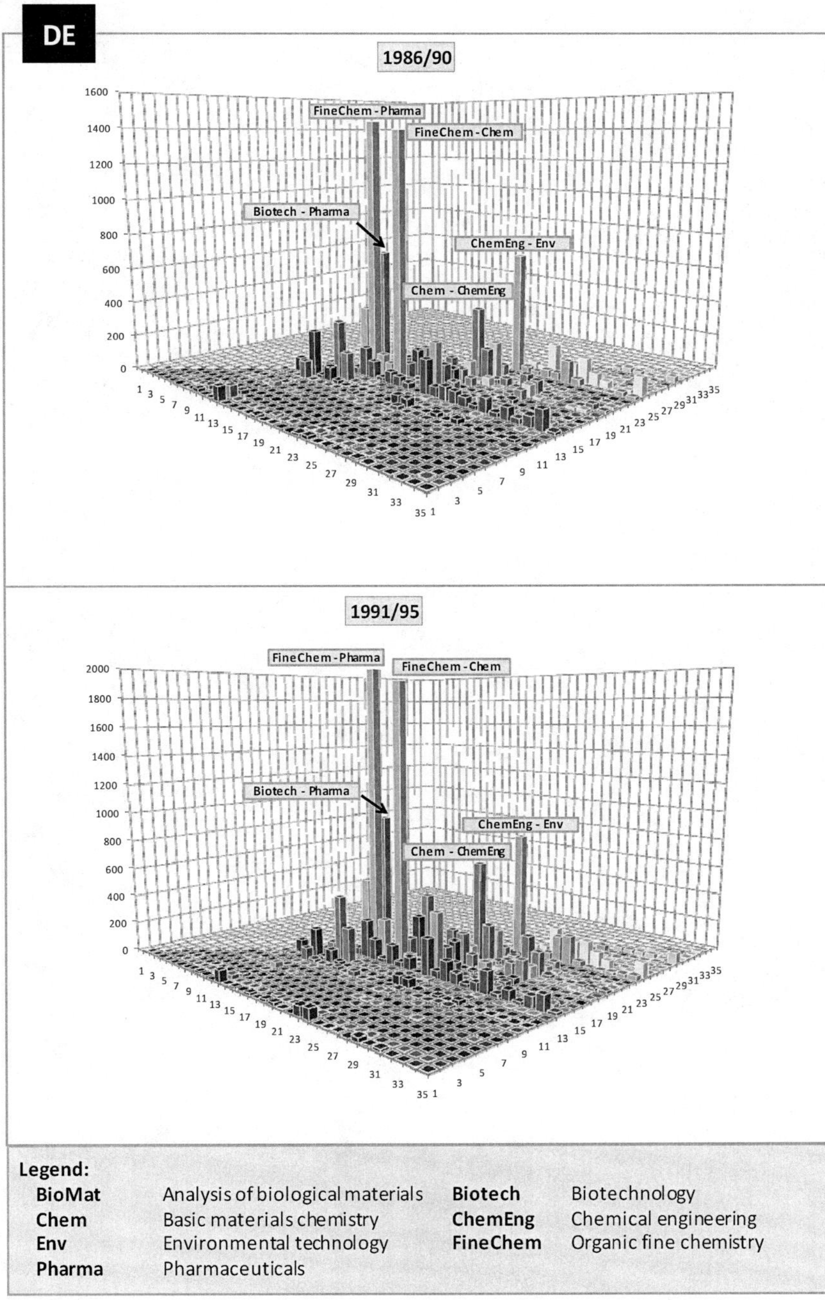

Legend:

BioMat	Analysis of biological materials	**Biotech**	Biotechnology
Chem	Basic materials chemistry	**ChemEng**	Chemical engineering
Env	Environmental technology	**FineChem**	Organic fine chemistry
Pharma	Pharmaceuticals		

Annex IV: Matrices of technology co-occurrences - DE (continued)

Source: PATSTAT October 2007, own computations

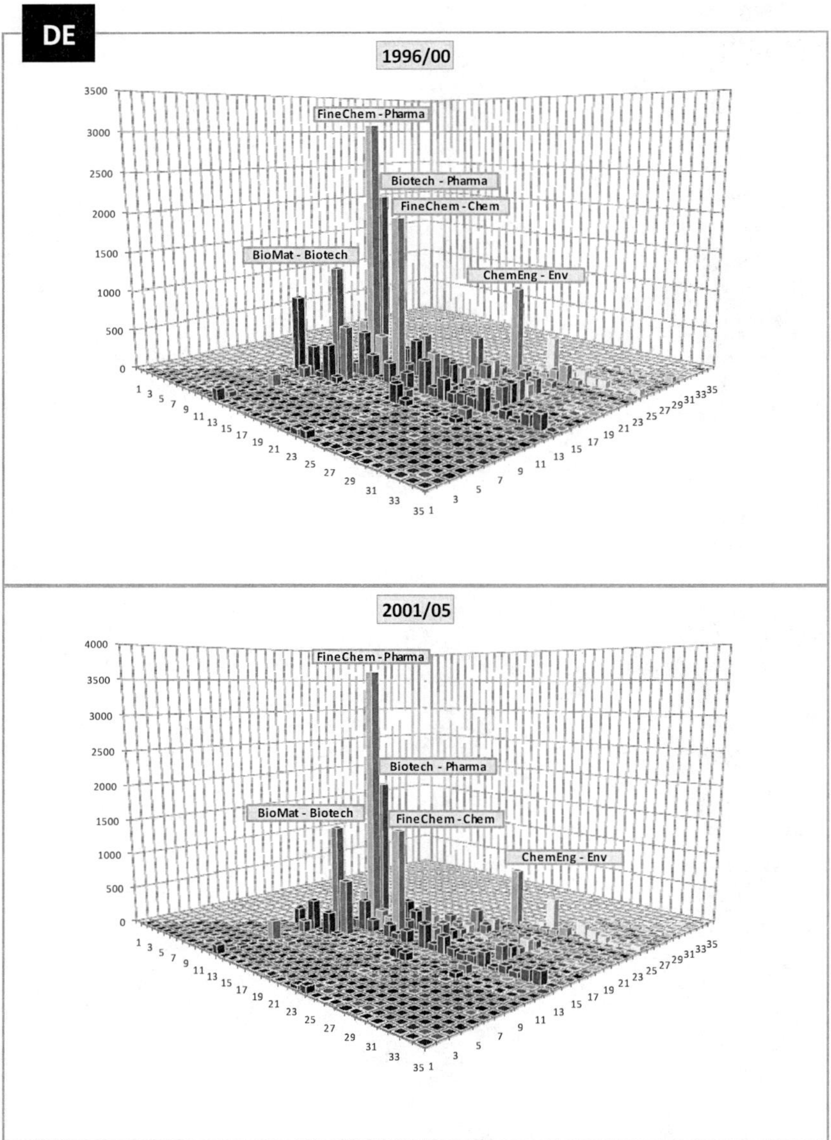

Legend:

BioMat	Analysis of biological materials	**Biotech**	Biotechnology
Chem	Basic materials chemistry	**ChemEng**	Chemical engineering
Env	Environmental technology	**FineChem**	Organic fine chemistry
Pharma	Pharmaceuticals		

Annex V: Matrices of technology co-occurrences - FR

Source: PATSTAT October 2007, own computations

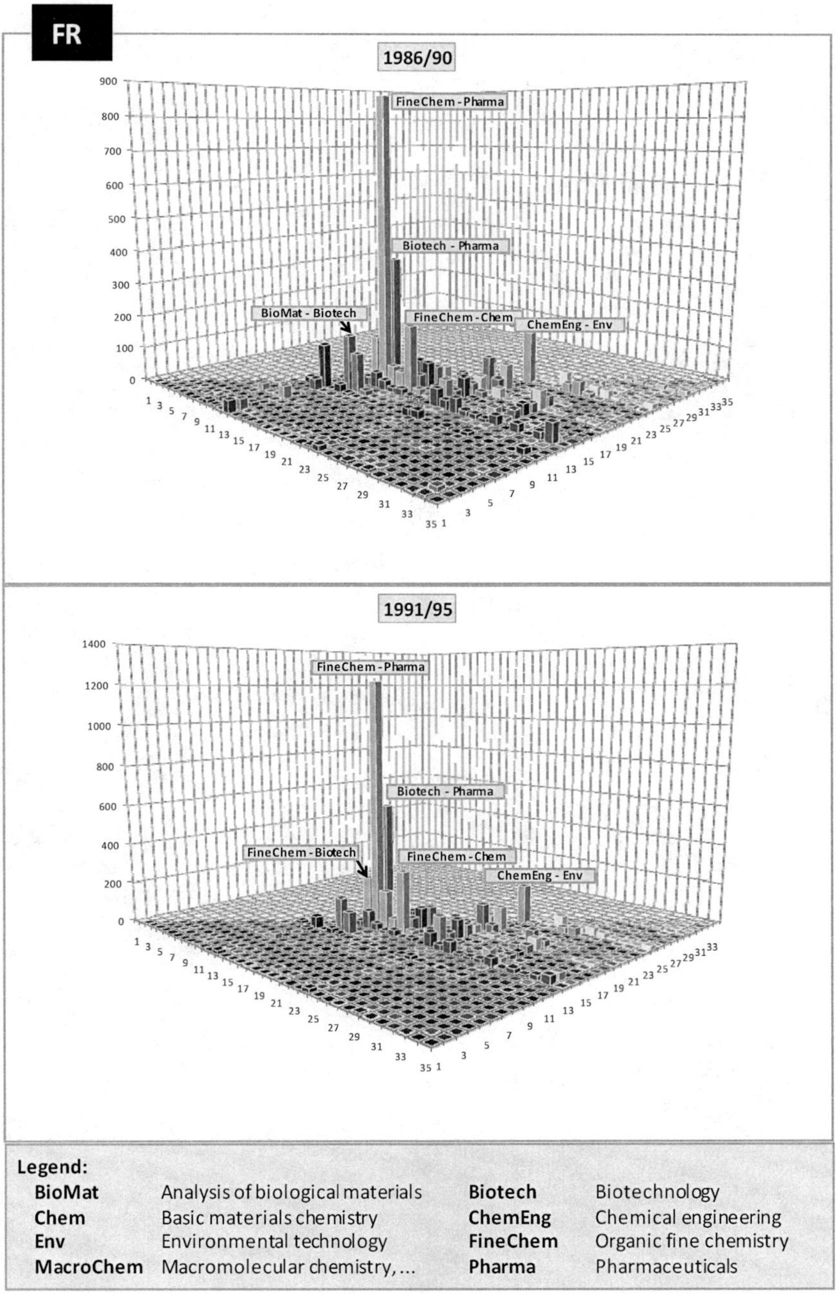

Legend:

BioMat	Analysis of biological materials	**Biotech**	Biotechnology
Chem	Basic materials chemistry	**ChemEng**	Chemical engineering
Env	Environmental technology	**FineChem**	Organic fine chemistry
MacroChem	Macromolecular chemistry, ...	**Pharma**	Pharmaceuticals

Annex V: Matrices of technology co-occurrences - FR (continued)

Source: PATSTAT October 2007, own computations

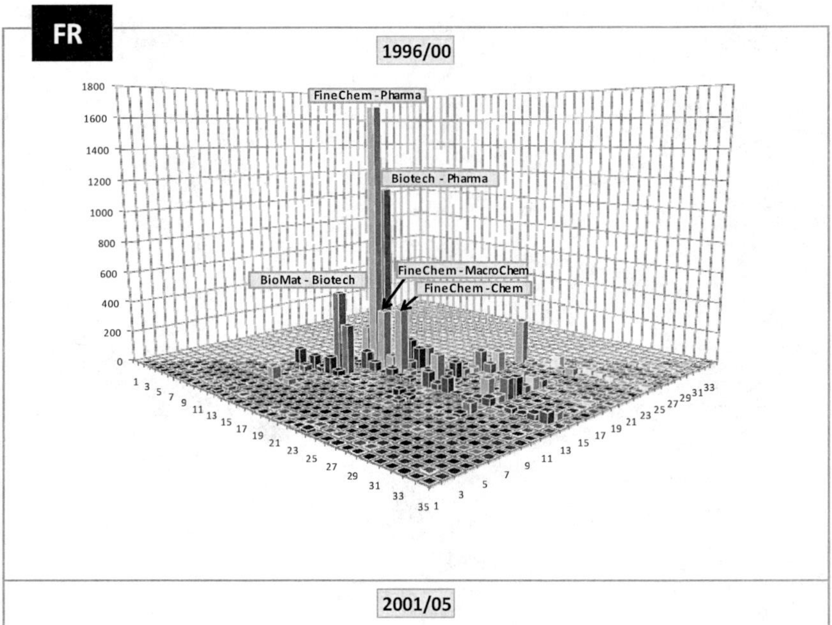

Legend:

BioMat	Analysis of biological materials	**Biotech**	Biotechnology
Chem	Basic materials chemistry	**ChemEng**	Chemical engineering
Env	Environmental technology	**FineChem**	Organic fine chemistry
MacroChem	Macromolecular chemistry, ...	**Pharma**	Pharmaceuticals

Annex VI: Matrices of technology co-occurrences - IT

Source: PATSTAT October 2007, own computations

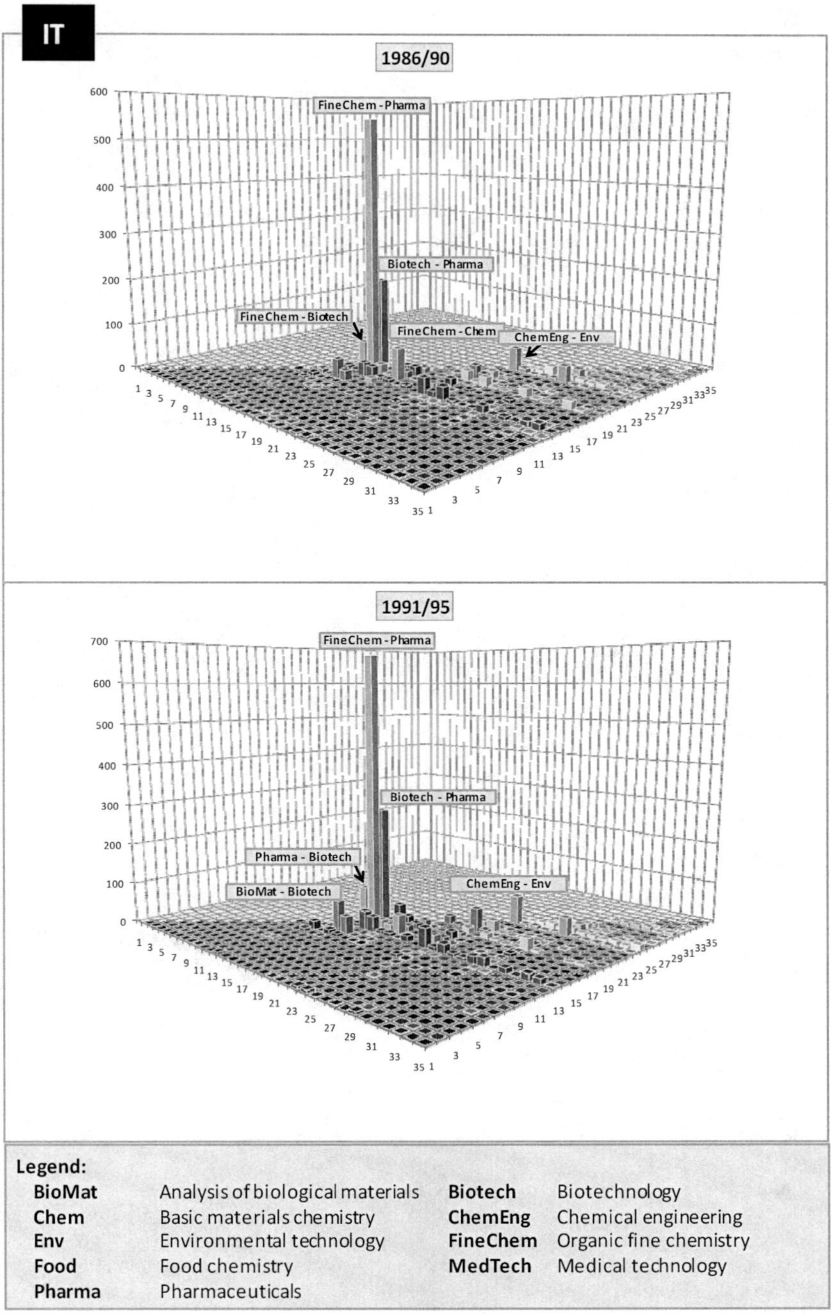

Legend:

BioMat	Analysis of biological materials	**Biotech**	Biotechnology
Chem	Basic materials chemistry	**ChemEng**	Chemical engineering
Env	Environmental technology	**FineChem**	Organic fine chemistry
Food	Food chemistry	**MedTech**	Medical technology
Pharma	Pharmaceuticals		

Annex VI: Matrices of technology co-occurrences - IT (continued)

Source: PATSTAT October 2007, own computations

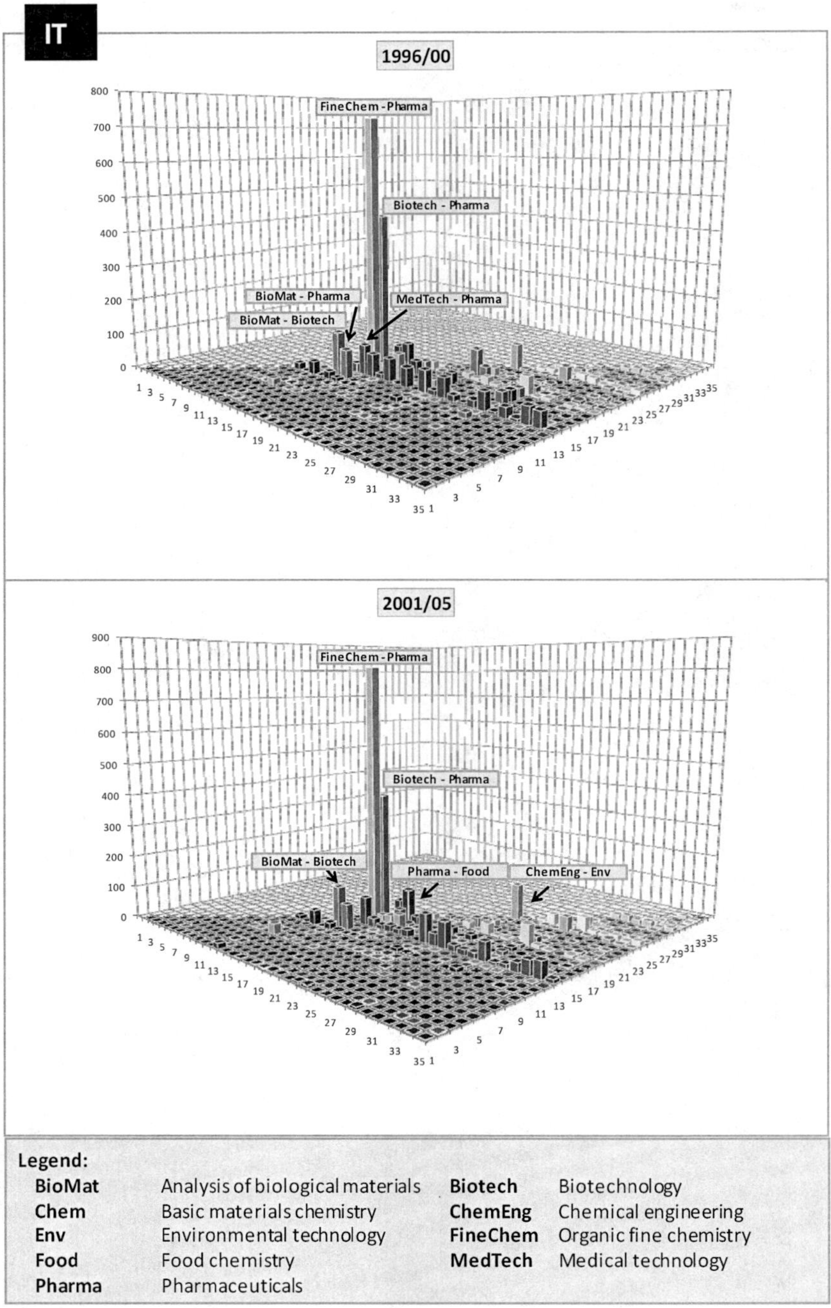

Legend:

BioMat	Analysis of biological materials	**Biotech**	Biotechnology
Chem	Basic materials chemistry	**ChemEng**	Chemical engineering
Env	Environmental technology	**FineChem**	Organic fine chemistry
Food	Food chemistry	**MedTech**	Medical technology
Pharma	Pharmaceuticals		

Annex VII: Matrices of technology co-occurrences - NL

Source: PATSTAT October 2007, own computations

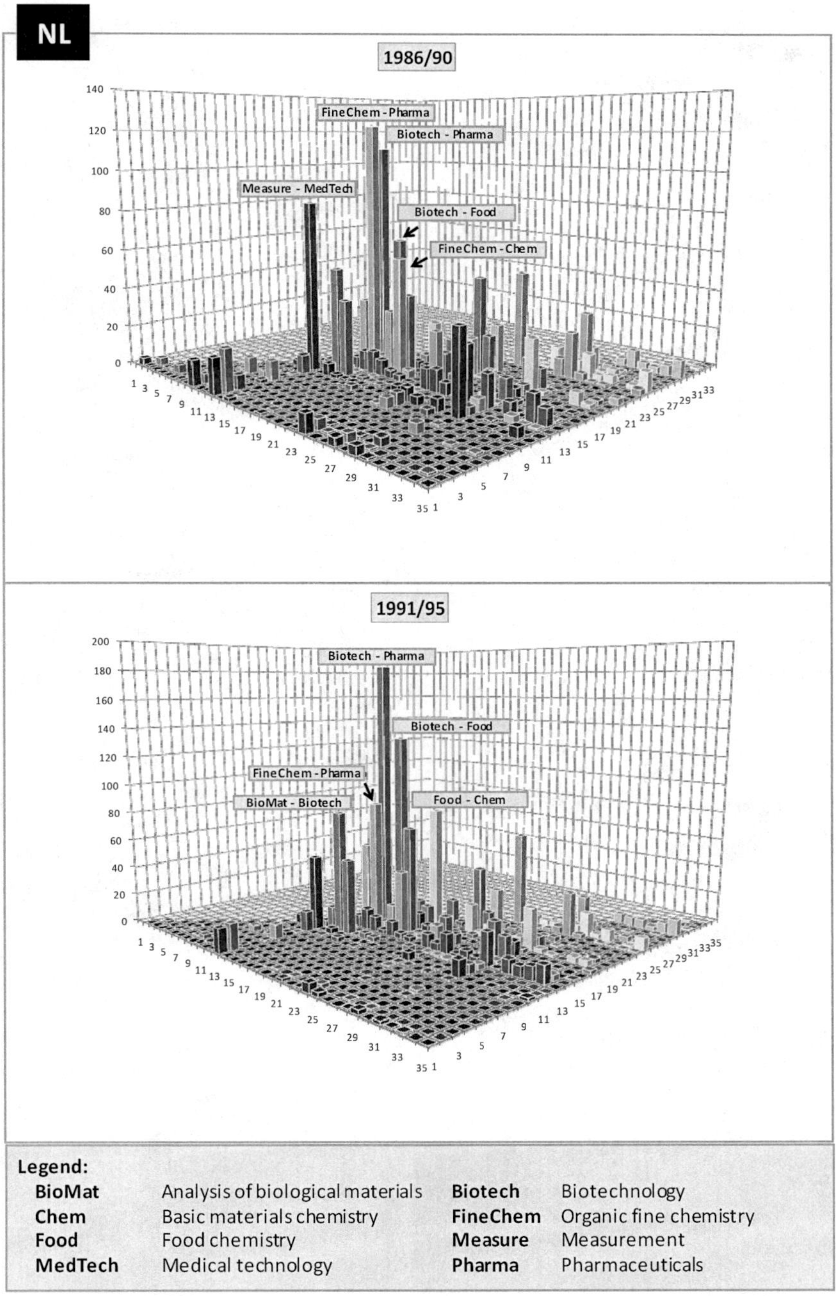

Legend:

BioMat	Analysis of biological materials	**Biotech**	Biotechnology
Chem	Basic materials chemistry	**FineChem**	Organic fine chemistry
Food	Food chemistry	**Measure**	Measurement
MedTech	Medical technology	**Pharma**	Pharmaceuticals

Annex VII: Matrices of technology co-occurrence - NL (continued)

Source: PATSTAT October 2007, own computations

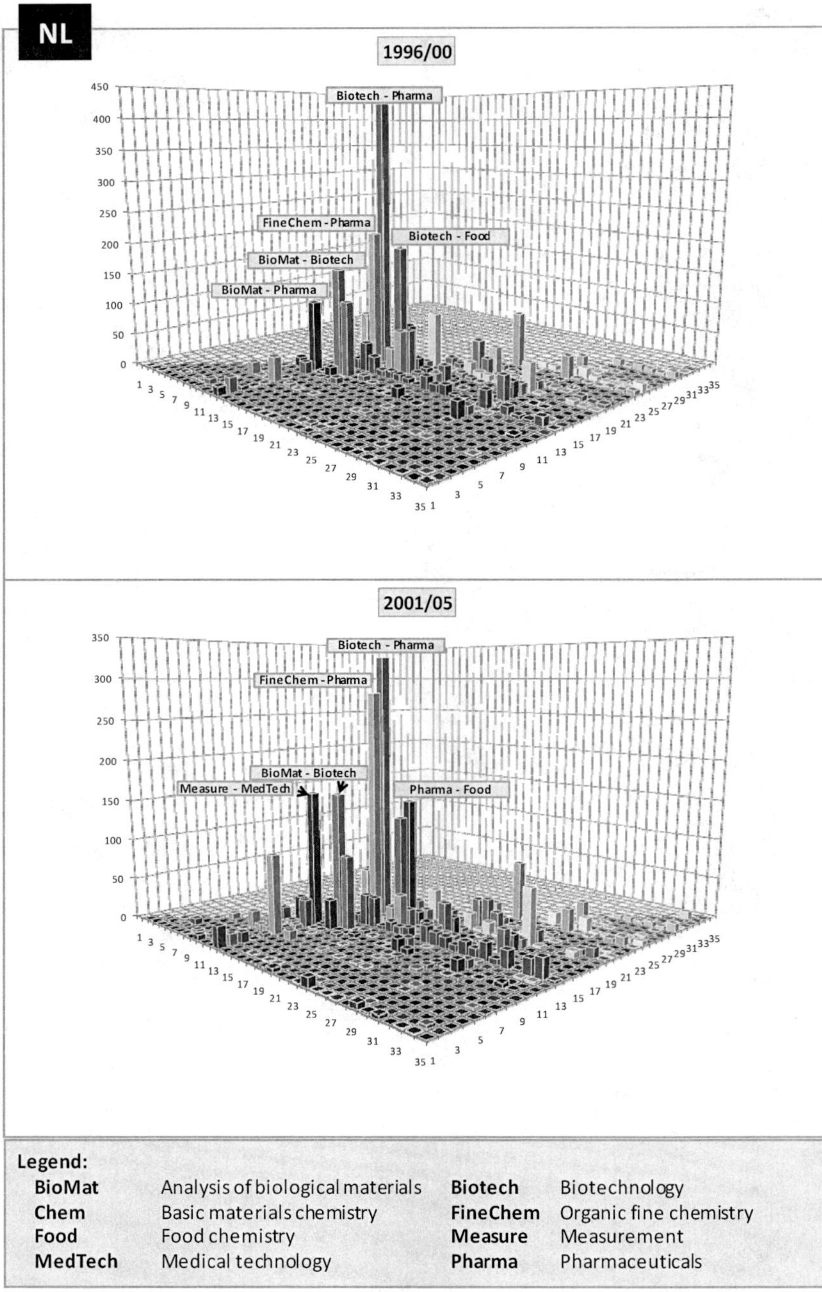

Legend:

BioMat	Analysis of biological materials	**Biotech**	Biotechnology
Chem	Basic materials chemistry	**FineChem**	Organic fine chemistry
Food	Food chemistry	**Measure**	Measurement
MedTech	Medical technology	**Pharma**	Pharmaceuticals

Annex VIII: Matrices of technology co-occurrences - UK

Source: PATSTAT October 2007, own computations

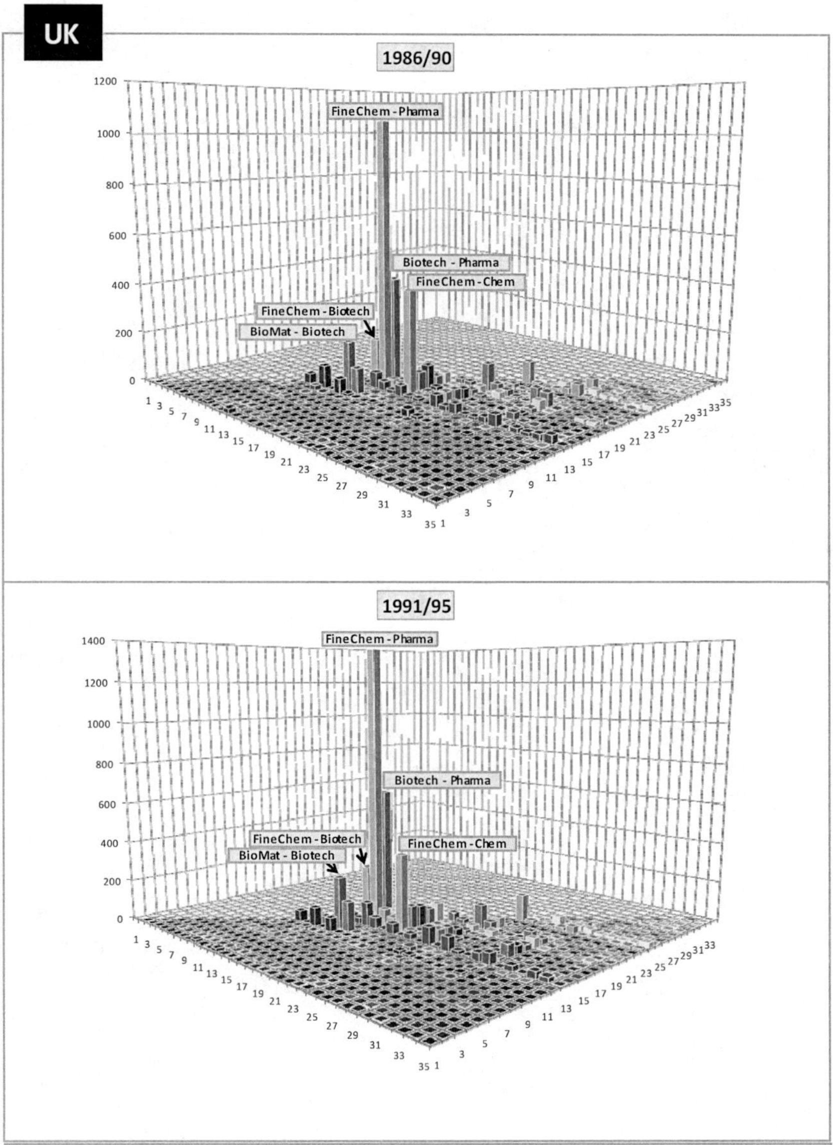

Legend:

BioMat	Analysis of biological materials	**Biotech**	Biotechnology
Chem	Basic materials chemistry	**FineChem**	Organic fine chemistry
Pharma	Pharmaceuticals		

Annex VIII: Matrices of technology co-occurrences - UK (continued)

Source: PATSTAT October 2007, own computations

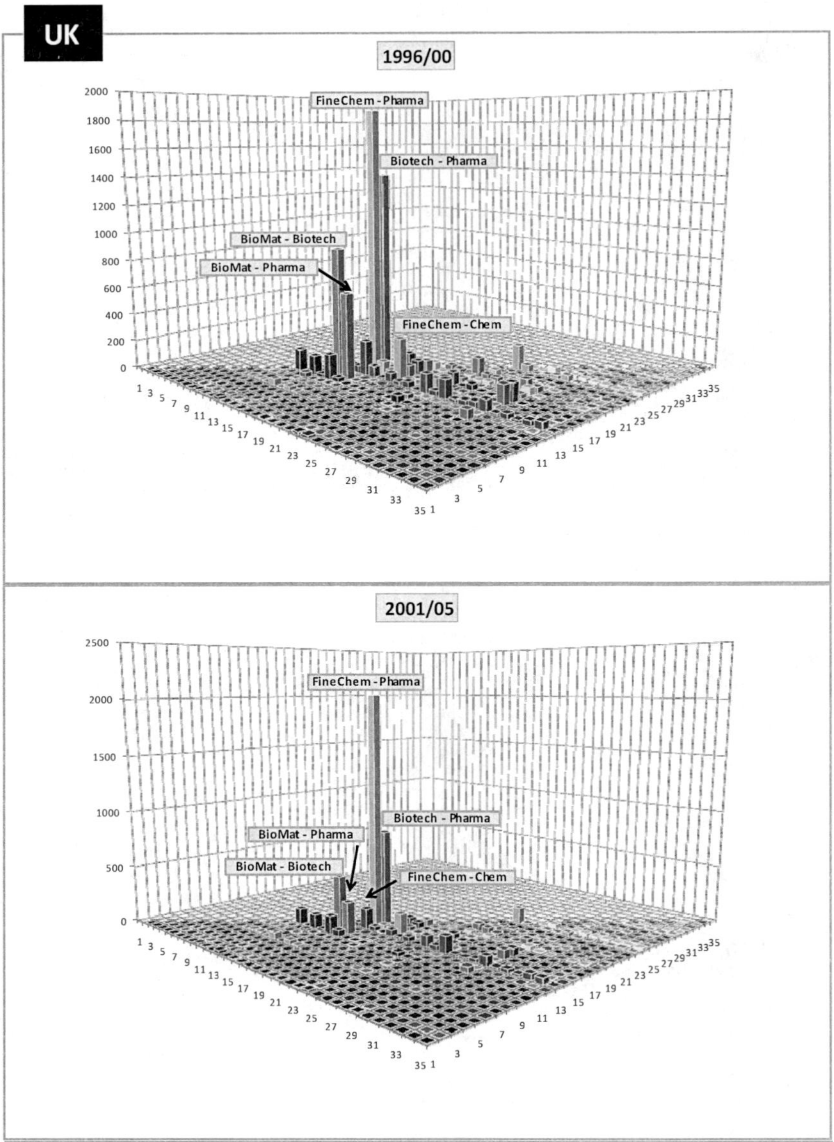

Legend:

BioMat	Analysis of biological materials	**Biotech**	Biotechnology
Chem	Basic materials chemistry	**FineChem**	Organic fine chemistry
Pharma	Pharmaceuticals		

Annex IX: Pairwise corrleation coefficients (RTA_h-values), at the 5% level

Source: PATSTAT October 2007, own computations

CH

	1986/90	1991/95	1996/00	2001/05
1986/90	1			
1991/95	0.5594 *0.1916*			
1996/00	0.5430 *0.2078*	0.6148 *0.1417*	1	
2001/05	0.2109 *0.6499*	0.0867 *0.8533*	0.7896* *0.0347*	1

IT

	1986/90	1991/95	1996/00	2001/05
1986/90	1			
1991/95	0.9546* *0.0008*	1		
1996/00		0.7342 *0.0602*	1	
2001/05	0.7145 *0.0712*	0.8769* *0.0095*	0.8239* *0.0227*	1

DE

	1986/90	1991/95	1996/00	2001/05
1986/90	1			
1991/95	0.9799* *0.0001*	1		
1996/00	0.9631* *0.0005*	0.9828* *0.0001*	1	
2001/05	0.8553* *0.0141*	0.9049* *0.0051*	0.9605* *0.0006*	1

NL

	1986/90	1991/95	1996/00	2001/05
1986/90	1			
1991/95	0.9466* *0.0012*	1		
1996/00	0.9326* *0.0022*	0.9851* *0.0001*	1	
2001/05	0.9506* *0.001*	0.9531* *0.0009*	0.9657* *0.0004*	1

FR

	1986/90	1991/95	1996/00	2001/05
1986/90	1			
1991/95	0.9336* *0.0021*	1		
1996/00	0.9331* *0.0021*	0.9612* *0.0006*	1	
2001/05	0.7215 *0.0672*	0.8400* *0.018*	0.8912* *0.0071*	1

UK

	1986/90	1991/95	1996/00	2001/05
1986/90	1			
1991/95	0.9655* *0.0004*	1		
1996/00	0.8996* *0.0058*	0.9611* *0.0006*	1	
2001/05	0.9691* *0.0003*	0.9856* *0*	0.9416* *0.0015*	1

Annex X: Preliminary company sample

Source: own compilation

	Scoreboard companies	Top applicants
CH	Actelion, Arpida, Basilea Pharmaceutica, Clariant, EMS-Chemie, Galenica, Lonza, Nestlé, Novartis, Roche, Siegfried, Sika, Sonova, Syngenta	Bühler, Cytos Biotechnology, Firmenich, Givaudan, Straumann Holding, Sulzer, Von Roll Umwelttechnik
DE	4SC, ALTANA, Analytik Jena, B Braun Melsungen, Balda, BASF, Bayer, Biolitec, Biotest, Boehringer Ingelheim , Carl Zeiss, Centrotec Sustainable, Drägerwerk, Epigenomics, Eppendorf, Evotec, Franz Haniel & Cie, Fresenius , Fuchs Petrolub, GPC Biotech , KWS SAAT, Lanxess, Linde, Medigene, Merck, Mologen, Morphosys, Nanogate, Paion, Paul Hartmann, Sartorius, Stada Arzneimittel, Stratec Biomedical System, Süd-Chemie, Südzucker, SYGNIS Pharma, Symrise, Uzin Utz, Wacker-Chemie, Wilex	Beiersdorf, Gruenenthal, Henkel, Karl Storz, LTS Lohmann Therapiesysteme
FR	Arkema, Bioalliance Pharma, BioMérieux, Boiron, Cerep, Danone, Dynaction, Essilor International, Evialis, ExonHit Therapeutics, Flamel Technologies, Hybrigenics, Innate Pharma, Laboratoire Francais de Fractionement et des Biotechnologies (LFB), L'Air Liquide, Medasys, METabolic Explorer, NicOx, Quantel, Rhodia, Sanofi-Aventis, SNPE, Unibel, Vetoquinol, Vivalis	Pierre Fabre Medicament, Roquette Frères
IT	Barilla, Chiesi Farmaceutici, DiaSorin, Gentium, Isagro, Newron Pharmaceuticals, Polynt, Recordati, Sorin	Bracco, Ferrero, Indena, Italfarmaco, Sigma-Tau, Zambon
NL	AKZO Nobel, Amsterdam Molecular Therapeutics, Crucell, CSM, DSM, Fornix Biosciences, Nutreco, OctoPlus, Pharming, Qiagen, Royal Cosun, Royal Friesland Foods	Keygene, Synthon
UK	Alizyme, Allergy Therapeutics , Amarin, Antisoma, Ardana, Ark Therapeutics, Astex Therapeutics, AstraZeneca, Avecia Holdings, Axis-Shield, Bernard Matthews , Biocompatibles International, BTG, Cadbury Schweppes (now Cadbury), Chroma Therapeutics, Consort Medical, Croda International, Dechra Pharmaceuticals, Devro, Dyson, Eco Animal Health, Elementis, GeneMedix, Genus, GlaxoSmithKline, GW Pharmaceuticals , Hikma Pharmaceuticals, Ineos , Intercytex, Johnson Matthey, Lectus Therapeutics , Lombard Medical Technologies, Meldex International, Minster Pharmaceuticals, Norbrook Laboratories , Northern Foods, Oxagen , Oxford Biomedica, Phytopharm, Plethora Solutions, Premier Foods, ProStrakan, Proteome Sciences, Randox Laboratories , ReNeuron , Renovo, Servier, Shire, Silence Therapeutics, SkyePharma, Smith & Nephew, Tate & Lyle, Unilever, Vectura, Vernalis, Victrex, Wittington Investments, Yule Catto	Owen Mumford

Annex XI: List of sample companies[44]

**Source: PATSTAT October 2007, own computations*

Company	Sector	Patents*	1986/90	1991/95	1996/00	2001/05
CH						
Arpida	Biotechnology	20		✔	✔	✔
Basilea Pharmaceutica	Biotechnology	40		✔	✔	✔
Cytos Biotechnology	Biotechnology	87		✔	✔	✔
Clariant	Chemicals	482	✔	✔	✔	✔
EMS-Chemie	**Chemicals**	**4**		✔	✔	✔
Firmenich	Chemicals	305	✔	✔	✔	✔
Givaudan	Chemicals	513	✔	✔	✔	✔
Lonza	Chemicals	233	✔	✔	✔	✔
Sika	**Chemicals**	**11**		✔		✔
Syngenta	Chemicals	1053	✔	✔	✔	✔
Nestlé	Food Producers	2788	✔	✔	✔	✔
Sonova	Health Care Equipment & Services	77		✔	✔	✔
Straumann Holding	Health Care Equipment & Services	90	✔	✔	✔	✔
Actelion	Pharmaceuticals	120			✔	✔
Galenica	Pharmaceuticals	26	✔	✔	✔	✔
Novartis	Pharmaceuticals	1242	✔	✔	✔	✔
Roche	Pharmaceuticals	4645	✔	✔	✔	✔
Siegfried	**Pharmaceuticals**	**12**	✔	✔	✔	✔
DE						
4SC	**Biotechnology**	**39**				✔
Analytik Jena	**Biotechnology**	**6**		✔	✔	✔
Epigenomics	Biotechnology	227			✔	✔
GPC Biotech	Biotechnology	46			✔	✔
Medigene	Biotechnology	88		✔	✔	✔
Mologen	**Biotechnology**	**16**		✔	✔	✔
Morphosys	Biotechnology	35		✔	✔	✔
Sartorius	Biotechnology	59	✔	✔	✔	✔
SYGNIS Pharma	Biotechnology	39			✔	✔
Wilex	Biotechnology	48			✔	✔
ALTANA	Chemicals	735	✔	✔	✔	✔
Balda	**Chemicals**	**---**				
BASF	Chemicals	7366	✔	✔	✔	✔
Bayer	Chemicals	7883	✔	✔	✔	✔
Centrotec Sustainable	**Chemicals**	**12**		✔	✔	✔
Henkel	Chemicals	4584	✔	✔	✔	✔

44 The companies which were not included in the final sample are highlighted.

Annex XI: List of sample companies (continued)

**Source: PATSTAT October 2007, own computations*

Company	Sector	Patents*	1986/90	1991/95	1996/00	2001/05
DE						
Fuchs Petrolub	**Chemicals**	**---**				
Lanxess	Chemicals	89		✔	✔	✔
Linde	Chemicals	232	✔	✔	✔	✔
Nanogate	**Chemicals**	**3**			✔	✔
Süd-Chemie	Chemicals	120	✔	✔	✔	✔
Symrise	Chemicals	356	✔	✔	✔	✔
Uzin Utz	**Chemicals**					
Wacker-Chemie	Chemicals	103	✔	✔	✔	✔
KWS SAAT	**Food Producers**	**14**		✔	✔	✔
Südzucker	Food Producers	191	✔	✔	✔	✔
B Braun Melsungen	Health Care Equipment & Services	805	✔	✔	✔	✔
Carl Zeiss	Health Care Equipment & Services	360	✔	✔	✔	✔
Drägerwerk	Health Care Equipment & Services	49	✔	✔	✔	✔
Eppendorf	Health Care Equipment & Services	81	✔	✔	✔	✔
Fresenius	Health Care Equipment & Services	562	✔	✔	✔	✔
Karl Storz	Health Care Equipment & Services	431	✔	✔	✔	✔
Paul Hartmann	Health Care Equipment & Services	207	✔	✔	✔	✔
Stratec Biomedical System	**Health Care Equipment & Services**	**1**				✔
Beiersdorf	Pharmaceuticals	1320	✔	✔	✔	✔
Biolitec	Pharmaceuticals	42		✔	✔	✔
Biotest	Pharmaceuticals	53	✔	✔	✔	✔
Boehringer Ingelheim	Pharmaceuticals	2087	✔	✔	✔	✔
Evotec	Pharmaceuticals	178		✔	✔	✔
Franz Haniel & Cie	**Pharmaceuticals**					
Gruenenthal	Pharmaceuticals	484	✔	✔	✔	✔
LTS Lohmann Therapiesysteme	Pharmaceuticals	555	✔	✔	✔	✔
Merck	Pharmaceuticals	2053	✔	✔	✔	✔
Paion	Pharmaceuticals	22	✔	✔	✔	✔
Stada Arzneimittel	Pharmaceuticals	42	✔	✔	✔	✔
FR						
ExonHit Therapeutics	Biotechnology	32			✔	✔
Flamel Technologies	Biotechnology	61		✔	✔	✔
Hybrigenics	Biotechnology	20			✔	✔
Innate Pharma	Biotechnology	35			✔	✔
Vetoquinol	**Biotechnology**	**12**	✔	✔	✔	✔
Vivalis	**Biotechnology**	**5**				✔
Arkema	Chemicals	99	✔	✔	✔	✔
Dynaction	**Chemicals**	**---**				
L'Air Liquide	Chemicals	699	✔	✔	✔	✔
METabolic Explorer	**Chemicals**	**11**			✔	✔

Annex XI: List of sample companies (continued)

**Source: PATSTAT October 2007, own computations*

Company	Sector	Patents*	1986/90	1991/95	1996/00	2001/05
FR						
Rhodia	Chemicals	490	✔	✔	✔	✔
SNPE	**Chemicals**	**8**	✔	✔	✔	✔
Danone	Food Producers	109	✔	✔	✔	✔
Evialis	**Food Producers**	**8**	✔	✔		✔
Roquette Frères	Food Producers	139	✔	✔	✔	✔
Unibel	**Food Producers**	**---**				
Bioalliance Pharma	**Health Care Equipment & Services**	**6**			✔	✔
BioMérieux	Health Care Equipment & Services	437	✔	✔	✔	✔
Essilor International	Health Care Equipment & Services	37	✔	✔	✔	✔
Medasys	**Health Care Equipment & Services**	**2**				✔
Quantel	**Health Care Equipment & Services**	**3**				✔
Boiron	**Pharmaceuticals**	**7**	✔	✔	✔	✔
Cerep	**Pharmaceuticals**	**9**			✔	✔
LFB[45]	**Pharmaceuticals**	**---**				
NicOx	Pharmaceuticals	113		✔	✔	✔
Pierre Fabre Medicament	Pharmaceuticals	236	✔	✔	✔	✔
Sanofi-Aventis	Pharmaceuticals	5417	✔	✔	✔	✔
IT						
DiaSorin	**Biotechnology**	**13**		✔	✔	✔
Gentium	**Biotechnology**	**14**		✔	✔	✔
Isagro	Chemicals	61	✔	✔	✔	✔
Polynt	**Chemicals**	**---**				
Barilla	Food Producers	82	✔	✔	✔	✔
Ferrero	Food Producers	63	✔	✔	✔	✔
Bracco	Health Care Equipment & Services	347	✔	✔	✔	✔
Sorin	Health Care Equipment & Services	275	✔	✔	✔	✔
Chiesi Farmaceutici	Pharmaceuticals	178	✔	✔	✔	✔
Indena	Pharmaceuticals	208	✔	✔	✔	✔
Italfarmaco	Pharmaceuticals	57	✔	✔	✔	✔
Newron Pharmaceuticals	Pharmaceuticals	49		✔	✔	✔
Recordati	Pharmaceuticals	81	✔	✔	✔	✔
Sigma-Tau	Pharmaceuticals	262	✔	✔	✔	✔
Zambon	Pharmaceuticals	137	✔	✔	✔	✔

45 Laboratoire Francais de Fractionement et des Biotechnologies

Annex XI: List of sample companies (continued)
**Source: PATSTAT October 2007, own computations*

Company	Sector	Patents*	1986/90	1991/95	1996/00	2001/05
NL						
Amsterdam Molecular Therapeutics	**Biotechnology**	**5**			✔	✔
Crucell	Biotechnology	178	✔	✔	✔	✔
Fornix Biosciences	**Biotechnology**	**10**			✔	✔
OctoPlus	**Biotechnology**	**17**		✔	✔	✔
Pharming	Biotechnology	27	✔	✔	✔	✔
Qiagen	Biotechnology	186	✔	✔	✔	✔
AKZO Nobel	Chemicals	1070	✔	✔	✔	✔
DSM	Chemicals	1172	✔	✔	✔	✔
CSM	Food Producers	90	✔	✔	✔	✔
Nutreco	Food Producers	21	✔	✔	✔	✔
Royal Cosun	**Food Producers**	**10**	✔	✔	✔	✔
Royal Friesland Foods	Food Producers	132	✔	✔	✔	✔
Unilever	Food Producers	5773	✔	✔	✔	✔
Keygene	Pharmaceuticals	43		✔	✔	✔
Synthon	Pharmaceuticals	56			✔	✔
UK						
Alizyme	**Biotechnology**	**10**			✔	✔
Amarin	**Biotechnology**	**11**			✔	✔
Antisoma	**Biotechnology**	**8**	✔	✔	✔	✔
Ark Therapeutics	Biotechnology	22			✔	✔
Astex Therapeutics	**Biotechnology**	**21**				✔
Avecia Holdings	Biotechnology	35	✔	✔	✔	✔
Axis-Shield	**Biotechnology**	**10**		✔	✔	✔
BTG	Biotechnology	455	✔	✔	✔	✔
Chroma Therapeutics	**Biotechnology**	**8**			✔	✔
GeneMedix	**Biotechnology**	**6**				✔
Genus	**Biotechnology**	**11**	✔	✔	✔	✔
Intercytex	**Biotechnology**	**10**		✔	✔	✔
Lectus Therapeutics	**Biotechnology**	**---**				
Oxagen	**Biotechnology**	**5**			✔	✔
Phytopharm	Biotechnology	20		✔	✔	✔
Randox Laboratories	**Biotechnology**	**14**			✔	✔
ReNeuron	**Biotechnology**	**7**		✔	✔	✔
Renovo	Biotechnology	20		✔	✔	✔
Servier	Biotechnology	227		✔	✔	✔
Silence Therapeutics	**Biotechnology**	**17**		✔	✔	✔
Vernalis	Biotechnology	81		✔	✔	✔
Croda International	Chemicals	73	✔	✔	✔	✔
Dyson	**Chemicals**	**8**			✔	✔
Elementis	**Chemicals**	**3**		✔	✔	✔

Annex XI: List of sample companies (continued)

**Source: PATSTAT October 2007, own computations*

Company	Sector	Patents*	1986/90	1991/95	1996/00	2001/05
UK						
Ineos	Chemicals	45	✔	✔	✔	✔
Johnson Matthey	Chemicals	130	✔	✔	✔	✔
Victrex	**Chemicals**	**1**				✔
Yule Catto	**Chemicals**	**1**		✔		
Bernard Matthews	**Food Producers**	**12**	✔	✔	✔	✔
Cadbury Schweppes (now Cadbury)	Food Producers	59	✔	✔	✔	✔
Devro	Food Producers	47	✔	✔	✔	✔
Northern Foods	**Food Producers**	**1**			✔	
Premier Foods	**Food Producers**	**5**		✔	✔	
Tate & Lyle	Food Producers	59	✔	✔	✔	✔
Unilever	Food Producers	5773	✔	✔	✔	✔
Wittington Investments	Food Producers	20	✔	✔	✔	✔
Biocompatibles International	Health Care Equipment & Services	50	✔	✔	✔	✔
Consort Medical	Health Care Equipment & Services	52	✔	✔	✔	✔
Lombard Medical Technologies	Health Care Equipment & Services	21	✔	✔	✔	✔
Owen Mumford	Health Care Equipment & Services	60	✔	✔	✔	✔
Smith & Nephew	Health Care Equipment & Services	476	✔	✔	✔	✔
Allergy Therapeutics	**Pharmaceuticals**	**4**		✔	✔	
Ardana	Pharmaceuticals	22		✔	✔	✔
AstraZeneca	Pharmaceuticals	1826	✔	✔	✔	✔
Eco Animal Health	**Pharmaceuticals**	**4**			✔	✔
GlaxoSmithKline	Pharmaceuticals	6177	✔	✔	✔	✔
GW Pharmaceuticals	**Pharmaceuticals**	**15**			✔	✔
Hikma Pharmaceuticals	**Pharmaceuticals**	**1**				✔
Meldex International	**Pharmaceuticals**	**17**		✔	✔	✔
Minster Pharmaceuticals	**Pharmaceuticals**	**1**		✔		
Norbrook Laboratories	**Pharmaceuticals**	**10**	✔	✔	✔	✔
Oxford Biomedica	Pharmaceuticals	79	✔	✔	✔	✔
Plethora Solutions	**Pharmaceuticals**	**4**		✔	✔	
ProStrakan	Pharmaceuticals	23		✔	✔	✔
Proteome Sciences	Pharmaceuticals	45		✔	✔	✔
Shire	Pharmaceuticals	95	✔	✔	✔	✔
SkyePharma	Pharmaceuticals	111	✔	✔	✔	✔
Vectura	Pharmaceuticals	140	✔	✔	✔	✔

Annex XII: Initial cluster centers

Source: PATSTAT October 2007, own computations

	1986/90 Cluster						1991/95 Cluster					
Technology class	1	2	3	4	5	6	1	2	3	4	5	6
1	0.004	0.003	0.006	0.003	0.006	0.004	0.004	0.004	0.002	0.003	0.005	0.003
2	0.002	0.001	0.003	0.001	0.005	0.001	0.001	0.001	0.001	0.000	0.004	0.002
3	0.000	0.000	0.000	0.000	0.000	0.000	0.001	0.000	0.001	0.000	0.000	0.000
4	0.000	0.000	0.000	0.000	0.000	0.000	0.000	0.000	0.000	0.000	0.000	0.000
5	0.000	0.000	0.001	0.000	0.000	0.000	0.000	0.000	0.000	0.000	0.000	0.000
6	0.001	0.002	0.004	0.001	0.003	0.001	0.001	0.003	0.002	0.001	0.002	0.001
7	0.000	0.000	0.000	0.000	0.000	0.000	0.000	0.000	0.000	0.000	0.000	0.000
8	0.000	0.001	0.001	0.000	0.001	0.000	0.001	0.001	0.001	0.000	0.000	0.001
9	0.004	0.003	0.004	0.001	0.002	0.004	0.003	0.002	0.001	0.002	0.002	0.006
10	0.013	0.014	0.016	0.003	0.031	0.016	0.010	0.008	0.011	0.005	0.013	0.011
11	0.008	0.011	0.009	0.007	0.007	0.004	0.008	0.007	0.011	0.005	0.009	0.008
12	0.002	0.002	0.002	0.004	0.002	0.001	0.002	0.001	0.002	0.003	0.002	0.002
13	0.176	0.147	0.176	0.187	0.139	0.232	0.164	0.175	0.145	0.191	0.160	0.211
14	0.137	0.162	0.133	0.136	0.052	0.148	0.144	0.176	0.150	0.112	0.031	0.136
15	0.079	0.114	0.099	0.091	0.110	0.072	0.077	0.101	0.119	0.081	0.155	0.103
16	0.119	0.200	0.157	0.252	0.083	0.138	0.137	0.185	0.234	0.272	0.078	0.157
17	0.013	0.011	0.014	0.011	0.005	0.007	0.020	0.015	0.012	0.011	0.007	0.008
18	0.034	0.050	0.060	0.048	0.101	0.051	0.027	0.041	0.041	0.050	0.124	0.067
19	0.103	0.104	0.043	0.039	0.097	0.086	0.127	0.051	0.104	0.044	0.084	0.067
20	0.011	0.005	0.009	0.005	0.007	0.006	0.009	0.010	0.006	0.006	0.008	0.006
21	0.004	0.004	0.003	0.002	0.000	0.005	0.004	0.004	0.003	0.002	0.001	0.001
22	0.000	0.000	0.000	0.000	0.000	0.000	0.000	0.000	0.000	0.000	0.000	0.000
23	0.047	0.023	0.031	0.029	0.032	0.037	0.047	0.029	0.025	0.032	0.030	0.024
24	0.103	0.041	0.063	0.051	0.055	0.054	0.095	0.067	0.042	0.056	0.061	0.048
25	0.009	0.010	0.010	0.012	0.011	0.010	0.008	0.009	0.009	0.008	0.009	0.007
26	0.006	0.003	0.005	0.005	0.004	0.008	0.006	0.003	0.002	0.005	0.002	0.006
27	0.008	0.004	0.005	0.004	0.006	0.005	0.007	0.005	0.004	0.005	0.003	0.002
28	0.004	0.007	0.005	0.001	0.003	0.008	0.007	0.004	0.007	0.005	0.003	0.004
29	0.083	0.058	0.114	0.083	0.214	0.076	0.066	0.074	0.049	0.078	0.183	0.097
30	0.006	0.003	0.004	0.003	0.004	0.005	0.006	0.004	0.002	0.004	0.005	0.005
31	0.006	0.003	0.006	0.004	0.004	0.005	0.006	0.004	0.003	0.004	0.004	0.005
32	0.003	0.003	0.002	0.003	0.002	0.001	0.003	0.003	0.002	0.002	0.005	0.002
33	0.003	0.004	0.004	0.007	0.005	0.005	0.004	0.004	0.003	0.005	0.003	0.003
34	0.006	0.005	0.006	0.006	0.003	0.008	0.004	0.006	0.003	0.004	0.004	0.005
35	0.006	0.003	0.004	0.002	0.004	0.002	0.005	0.003	0.003	0.003	0.004	0.003

Legend: 1 Electrical machinery, apparatus, energy, 2 Audio-visual technology, 3 Telecommunications, 4 Digital communication, 5 Basic communication processes, 6 Computer technology, 7 IT methods for management, 8 Semiconductors, 9 Optics, 10 Measurement, 11 Analysis of biological materials, 12 Control, 13 Medical technology, 14 Organic fine chemistry, 15 Biotechnology, 16 Pharmaceuticals, 17 Macromolecular chemistry, polymers, 18 Food chemistry, 19 Basic materials chemistry, 20 Materials, metallurgy, 21 Surface technology, coating, 22 Micro-structural and nano-technology, 23 Chemical engineering, 24 Environmental technology, 25 Handling, 26 Machine tools, 27 Engines, pumps, turbines, 28 Textile and paper machines, 29 Other special machines, 30 Thermal processes and apparatus, 31 Mechanical elements, 32 Transport, 33 Furniture, games, 34 Other consumer goods, 35 Civil engineering

Annex XII: Initial cluster centers (continued)

Source: PATSTAT October 2007, own computations

	1996/00 Cluster						2001/05 Cluster					
Technology class	1	2	3	4	5	6	1	2	3	4	5	6
1	0.004	0.002	0.002	0.001	0.002	0.001	0.001	0.003	0.002	0.002	0.004	0.002
2	0.001	0.002	0.001	0.001	0.003	0.002	0.001	0.001	0.001	0.000	0.001	0.001
3	0.001	0.001	0.001	0.000	0.001	0.000	0.000	0.001	0.000	0.000	0.001	0.001
4	0.000	0.000	0.000	0.000	0.000	0.000	0.000	0.000	0.000	0.000	0.000	0.000
5	0.000	0.000	0.000	0.000	0.000	0.000	0.000	0.000	0.000	0.000	0.000	0.000
6	0.003	0.005	0.003	0.001	0.006	0.002	0.005	0.005	0.004	0.003	0.012	0.003
7	0.000	0.000	0.000	0.000	0.000	0.000	0.000	0.000	0.000	0.000	0.000	0.000
8	0.001	0.001	0.001	0.000	0.000	0.000	0.001	0.001	0.001	0.000	0.001	0.001
9	0.003	0.003	0.002	0.001	0.002	0.005	0.002	0.003	0.001	0.001	0.003	0.005
10	0.012	0.008	0.012	0.005	0.019	0.010	0.006	0.011	0.011	0.006	0.022	0.010
11	0.012	0.011	0.019	0.006	0.011	0.009	0.012	0.017	0.015	0.007	0.010	0.012
12	0.001	0.001	0.001	0.002	0.000	0.001	0.001	0.001	0.001	0.001	0.002	0.001
13	0.176	0.161	0.159	0.232	0.154	0.248	0.158	0.196	0.187	0.239	0.182	0.282
14	0.127	0.182	0.120	0.085	0.038	0.116	0.213	0.124	0.146	0.076	0.033	0.135
15	0.121	0.125	0.149	0.078	0.184	0.115	0.133	0.137	0.121	0.081	0.159	0.115
16	0.166	0.196	0.273	0.257	0.132	0.178	0.214	0.187	0.267	0.254	0.156	0.218
17	0.016	0.018	0.008	0.008	0.007	0.008	0.011	0.009	0.007	0.007	0.008	0.006
18	0.027	0.044	0.035	0.051	0.101	0.091	0.038	0.027	0.038	0.062	0.131	0.061
19	0.100	0.040	0.081	0.073	0.068	0.070	0.037	0.077	0.062	0.036	0.063	0.050
20	0.006	0.008	0.004	0.003	0.006	0.005	0.004	0.005	0.002	0.003	0.003	0.002
21	0.004	0.002	0.003	0.005	0.002	0.003	0.002	0.004	0.002	0.003	0.002	0.003
22	0.000	0.000	0.000	0.000	0.000	0.000	0.000	0.000	0.000	0.000	0.000	0.000
23	0.035	0.028	0.019	0.022	0.023	0.018	0.016	0.024	0.016	0.021	0.019	0.015
24	0.075	0.058	0.037	0.043	0.048	0.034	0.054	0.066	0.035	0.058	0.039	0.022
25	0.007	0.007	0.009	0.009	0.008	0.008	0.006	0.006	0.011	0.010	0.009	0.005
26	0.004	0.002	0.001	0.004	0.003	0.004	0.002	0.004	0.003	0.004	0.001	0.004
27	0.011	0.005	0.003	0.002	0.002	0.005	0.005	0.008	0.003	0.004	0.003	0.004
28	0.006	0.006	0.005	0.003	0.002	0.007	0.004	0.004	0.004	0.002	0.001	0.003
29	0.061	0.066	0.040	0.084	0.160	0.042	0.059	0.061	0.042	0.089	0.115	0.024
30	0.003	0.003	0.002	0.003	0.004	0.004	0.003	0.004	0.002	0.007	0.003	0.002
31	0.004	0.004	0.003	0.006	0.003	0.004	0.003	0.004	0.003	0.004	0.003	0.003
32	0.003	0.002	0.002	0.003	0.002	0.002	0.002	0.003	0.003	0.003	0.001	0.002
33	0.004	0.003	0.003	0.007	0.003	0.004	0.002	0.003	0.004	0.007	0.004	0.004
34	0.004	0.005	0.003	0.004	0.002	0.003	0.004	0.004	0.004	0.006	0.004	0.003
35	0.003	0.002	0.002	0.002	0.003	0.002	0.002	0.002	0.002	0.003	0.002	0.001

Legend: 1 Electrical machinery, apparatus, energy, 2 Audio-visual technology, 3 Telecommunications, 4 Digital communication, 5 Basic communication processes, 6 Computer technology, 7 IT methods for management, 8 Semiconductors, 9 Optics, 10 Measurement, 11 Analysis of biological materials, 12 Control, 13 Medical technology, 14 Organic fine chemistry, 15 Biotechnology, 16 Pharmaceuticals, 17 Macromolecular chemistry, polymers, 18 Food chemistry, 19 Basic materials chemistry, 20 Materials, metallurgy, 21 Surface technology, coating, 22 Micro-structural and nano-technology, 23 Chemical engineering, 24 Environmental technology, 25 Handling, 26 Machine tools, 27 Engines, pumps, turbines, 28 Textile and paper machines, 29 Other special machines, 30 Thermal processes and apparatus, 31 Mechanical elements, 32 Transport, 33 Furniture, games, 34 Other consumer goods, 35 Civil engineering

Annex XIII: Final cluster centers

Source: PATSTAT October 2007, own computations

Technology class	1986/90 Cluster 1	1986/90 Cluster 2	1986/90 Cluster 3	1986/90 Cluster 4	1986/90 Cluster 5	1986/90 Cluster 6	1991/95 Cluster 1	1991/95 Cluster 2	1991/95 Cluster 3	1991/95 Cluster 4	1991/95 Cluster 5	1991/95 Cluster 6
1	0.000	0.000	0.001	0.007	0.006	0.006	0.001	0.020	0.000	0.000	0.000	0.009
2	0.000	0.000	0.000	0.001	0.000	0.002	0.000	0.000	0.000	0.000	0.002	0.016
3	0.000	0.000	0.000	0.000	0.000	0.000	0.000	0.000	0.000	0.000	0.000	0.001
4	0.000	0.000	0.000	0.000	0.000	0.000	0.000	0.000	0.000	0.000	0.000	0.000
5	0.000	0.000	0.001	0.000	0.000	0.001	0.000	0.000	0.000	0.000	0.000	0.000
6	0.000	0.000	0.000	0.009	0.000	0.001	0.001	0.000	0.000	0.000	0.000	0.004
7	0.000	0.000	0.000	0.000	0.000	0.000	0.000	0.000	0.000	0.000	0.000	0.000
8	0.001	0.000	0.000	0.000	0.000	0.000	0.002	0.000	0.000	0.000	0.000	0.000
9	0.000	0.000	0.008	0.000	0.000	0.040	0.028	0.001	0.000	0.000	0.001	0.019
10	0.002	0.006	0.002	0.005	0.000	0.016	0.003	0.002	0.015	0.003	0.002	0.010
11	0.002	0.016	0.001	0.008	0.000	0.005	0.002	0.005	0.018	0.006	0.004	0.001
12	0.000	0.000	0.002	0.000	0.000	0.001	0.000	0.000	0.000	0.000	0.000	0.005
13	0.031	0.003	0.053	0.063	0.006	**0.634**	0.045	0.030	0.028	0.046	0.020	**0.759**
14	**0.168**	0.032	0.051	**0.203**	0.025	0.028	**0.144**	**0.376**	0.048	**0.184**	0.037	0.003
15	0.067	**0.747**	0.020	**0.156**	0.047	0.021	0.072	0.097	**0.591**	0.061	0.041	0.007
16	0.097	0.069	0.089	**0.499**	0.055	0.067	0.080	**0.356**	**0.174**	**0.638**	0.088	0.035
17	0.023	0.001	0.003	0.008	0.024	0.013	0.052	0.023	0.004	0.012	0.012	0.003
18	0.071	0.061	**0.254**	0.004	**0.707**	0.002	0.066	0.006	0.040	0.007	**0.537**	0.004
19	**0.240**	0.011	0.026	0.013	0.028	0.007	**0.258**	0.054	0.021	0.012	0.030	0.012
20	0.026	0.001	0.000	0.001	0.001	0.006	0.035	0.003	0.002	0.002	0.002	0.004
21	0.009	0.000	0.013	0.001	0.000	0.012	0.003	0.001	0.000	0.001	0.003	0.002
22	0.000	0.000	0.000	0.000	0.000	0.000	0.000	0.000	0.000	0.000	0.000	0.000
23	0.087	0.010	0.010	0.010	0.027	0.036	0.073	0.013	0.043	0.013	0.049	0.031
24	**0.114**	0.008	0.001	0.001	0.001	0.003	0.080	0.004	0.004	0.010	0.014	0.009
25	0.008	0.001	0.091	0.002	0.023	0.025	0.002	0.001	0.000	0.002	0.037	0.016
26	0.001	0.000	0.003	0.000	0.013	0.008	0.010	0.000	0.001	0.000	0.002	0.008
27	0.004	0.000	0.000	0.001	0.000	0.010	0.006	0.000	0.000	0.000	0.000	0.011
28	0.018	0.001	0.001	0.001	0.000	0.010	0.011	0.005	0.001	0.000	0.001	0.002
29	0.019	0.033	**0.359**	0.006	0.036	0.022	0.017	0.003	0.009	0.002	**0.115**	0.007
30	0.003	0.000	0.000	0.000	0.000	0.001	0.003	0.000	0.000	0.000	0.000	0.001
31	0.004	0.000	0.000	0.000	0.000	0.008	0.000	0.000	0.000	0.000	0.001	0.013
32	0.001	0.000	0.000	0.000	0.000	0.000	0.000	0.000	0.000	0.000	0.000	0.000
33	0.000	0.000	0.008	0.000	0.000	0.000	0.000	0.000	0.000	0.000	0.004	0.000
34	0.004	0.000	0.001	0.000	0.000	0.016	0.003	0.000	0.000	0.001	0.000	0.008
35	0.001	0.000	0.001	0.000	0.001	0.000	0.000	0.000	0.000	0.000	0.000	0.000

Legend: 1 Electrical machinery, apparatus, energy, 2 Audio-visual technology, 3 Telecommunications, 4 Digital communication, 5 Basic communication processes, 6 Computer technology, 7 IT methods for management, 8 Semiconductors, 9 Optics, 10 Measurement, 11 Analysis of biological materials, 12 Control, 13 Medical technology, 14 Organic fine chemistry, 15 Biotechnology, 16 Pharmaceuticals, 17 Macromolecular chemistry, polymers, 18 Food chemistry, 19 Basic materials chemistry, 20 Materials, metallurgy, 21 Surface technology, coating, 22 Micro-structural and nano-technology, 23 Chemical engineering, 24 Environmental technology, 25 Handling, 26 Machine tools, 27 Engines, pumps, turbines, 28 Textile and paper machines, 29 Other special machines, 30 Thermal processes and apparatus, 31 Mechanical elements, 32 Transport, 33 Furniture, games, 34 Other consumer goods, 35 Civil engineering

Annex XIII: Final cluster centers (continued)

Source: PATSTAT October 2007, own computations

	1996/00 Cluster						2001/05 Cluster					
Technology class	1	2	3	4	5	6	1	2	3	4	5	6
1	0.001	0.000	0.006	0.000	0.000	0.021	0.019	0.001	0.000	0.000	0.000	0.002
2	0.000	0.000	0.000	0.000	0.000	0.013	0.000	0.001	0.000	0.000	0.000	0.011
3	0.000	0.000	0.000	0.000	0.000	0.000	0.000	0.000	0.000	0.000	0.000	0.001
4	0.000	0.000	0.000	0.000	0.000	0.001	0.000	0.000	0.000	0.000	0.000	0.000
5	0.000	0.000	0.000	0.000	0.000	0.001	0.000	0.000	0.000	0.000	0.000	0.000
6	0.000	0.003	0.000	0.000	0.007	0.004	0.001	0.000	0.001	0.018	0.002	0.006
7	0.000	0.000	0.000	0.000	0.000	0.000	0.000	0.000	0.000	0.000	0.000	0.000
8	0.001	0.000	0.000	0.000	0.000	0.000	0.000	0.000	0.000	0.000	0.000	0.001
9	0.001	0.001	0.000	0.006	0.000	0.035	0.000	0.000	0.000	0.000	0.001	0.041
10	0.003	0.008	0.001	0.003	0.023	0.009	0.004	0.002	0.002	0.008	0.012	0.013
11	0.002	0.015	0.004	0.000	0.050	0.004	0.009	0.002	0.006	0.001	0.044	0.000
12	0.000	0.000	0.000	0.000	0.001	0.001	0.000	0.000	0.002	0.004	0.000	0.000
13	0.028	0.060	0.032	**0.496**	0.005	**0.696**	0.036	0.022	0.034	**0.435**	0.008	**0.747**
14	**0.120**	**0.234**	**0.180**	0.023	0.033	0.008	**0.308**	**0.095**	**0.127**	0.053	0.052	0.004
15	0.082	**0.162**	0.049	0.030	**0.623**	0.008	**0.109**	0.082	0.072	0.013	**0.649**	0.005
16	0.085	**0.415**	**0.679**	**0.419**	0.196	0.034	**0.443**	0.103	**0.712**	**0.422**	0.188	0.032
17	0.030	0.013	0.017	0.013	0.003	0.019	0.015	0.023	0.008	0.003	0.001	0.007
18	**0.233**	0.006	0.006	0.000	0.015	0.001	0.004	**0.243**	0.021	0.000	0.011	0.000
19	**0.171**	0.048	0.010	0.002	0.015	0.026	0.027	**0.201**	0.003	0.009	0.014	0.011
20	0.015	0.003	0.000	0.000	0.000	0.005	0.001	0.011	0.001	0.000	0.000	0.005
21	0.003	0.002	0.001	0.003	0.001	0.010	0.001	0.006	0.000	0.000	0.001	0.007
22	0.000	0.000	0.000	0.000	0.001	0.000	0.000	0.000	0.000	0.000	0.000	0.000
23	0.064	0.013	0.004	0.003	0.016	0.019	0.011	0.042	0.003	0.000	0.010	0.012
24	0.063	0.003	0.004	0.000	0.001	0.000	0.003	0.064	0.000	0.007	0.001	0.000
25	0.014	0.005	0.003	0.001	0.001	0.015	0.001	0.009	0.006	0.015	0.000	0.006
26	0.001	0.000	0.000	0.000	0.002	0.003	0.000	0.002	0.000	0.000	0.000	0.007
27	0.002	0.000	0.000	0.000	0.000	0.042	0.000	0.004	0.000	0.000	0.000	0.001
28	0.007	0.003	0.000	0.000	0.001	0.004	0.001	0.007	0.000	0.000	0.000	0.009
29	0.064	0.005	0.002	0.000	0.007	0.007	0.006	0.062	0.002	0.000	0.006	0.009
30	0.003	0.000	0.000	0.000	0.000	0.000	0.000	0.003	0.000	0.000	0.000	0.000
31	0.001	0.000	0.000	0.000	0.000	0.004	0.000	0.002	0.000	0.003	0.000	0.003
32	0.000	0.000	0.000	0.000	0.000	0.000	0.000	0.001	0.000	0.000	0.000	0.000
33	0.001	0.000	0.000	0.000	0.000	0.002	0.000	0.004	0.001	0.000	0.000	0.001
34	0.004	0.000	0.000	0.000	0.000	0.005	0.001	0.007	0.000	0.008	0.000	0.056
35	0.000	0.000	0.000	0.000	0.000	0.000	0.000	0.000	0.000	0.000	0.000	0.000

Legend: 1 Electrical machinery, apparatus, energy, 2 Audio-visual technology, 3 Telecommunications, 4 Digital communication, 5 Basic communication processes, 6 Computer technology, 7 IT methods for management, 8 Semiconductors, 9 Optics, 10 Measurement, 11 Analysis of biological materials, 12 Control, 13 Medical technology, 14 Organic fine chemistry, 15 Biotechnology, 16 Pharmaceuticals, 17 Macromolecular chemistry, polymers, 18 Food chemistry, 19 Basic materials chemistry, 20 Materials, metallurgy, 21 Surface technology, coating, 22 Micro-structural and nano-technology, 23 Chemical engineering, 24 Environmental technology, 25 Handling, 26 Machine tools, 27 Engines, pumps, turbines, 28 Textile and paper machines, 29 Other special machines, 30 Thermal processes and apparatus, 31 Mechanical elements, 32 Transport, 33 Furniture, games, 34 Other consumer goods, 35 Civil engineering